PRAISE
and *The*

'I have always admired Manne for his unfashionable virtue of determined reasonableness and his ravishingly cool analyses. His performance here increases my admiration... *The Culture of Forgetting* is written in the language of the heart: informed, reasoned, immaculately argued, profoundly impassioned... we need books precisely like the one that Robert Manne has written.'   Inga Clendinnen, *Australian Book Review*

'*The Culture of Forgetting* is living proof that there is no evil but good comes thereof... clear, passionate, informed... there is divine comedy in Manne's slow burn, in the drama of an eminent academic thinker struggling with his credulity, as the full extent of the intellectual incompetence of his literary colleagues across the corridor dawns on him.'
Howard Jacobson, *Times Literary Supplement*

'It has always been a pleasure to read Robert Manne as a commentator on culture and politics. His clear undecorated prose seems equally adaptable to broad moral themes and to the nuances of week-to-week political debate... something of the quality of Orwell or John Berger.'
Austin Gough, *Adelaide Review*

'*The Culture of Forgetting* in my view is a superb book. I cannot imagine how anyone could fail to be moved and enlightened by the quiet yet sustained intensity of feeling in it. This is a book written out of pain... a book of surpassing quality.'   Michael Gawenda, *Age*

Robert Manne is
associate professor of
politics at La Trobe
University, a newspaper
columnist and a regular
commentator on ABC
radio. In 1990 he was
appointed editor of
Quadrant. His resignation
from the magazine
sparked a significant
public controversy.

Other books by the author
The Petrov Affair
The Shadow of 1917
The Culture of Forgetting

The New Conservatism in Australia (ed.)
Shutdown (co-ed.)

ROBERT MANNE
THE WAY WE LIVE NOW
THE CONTROVERSIES OF THE NINETIES

TEXT PUBLISHING
MELBOURNE AUSTRALIA

The Text Publishing Company
171 La Trobe Street
Melbourne Victoria 3000
Australia

Copyright © Robert Manne 1998

All rights reserved. Without limiting the rights under copyright above, no part of this publication shall be reproduced, stored in or introduced into a retrieval system, or transmitted in any form or by any means (electronic, mechanical, photocopying, recording or otherwise), without the prior permission of both the copyright owner and the publisher of this book.

First published 1998, reprinted 1998 (twice)

Printed and bound by Griffin Press
Designed by Chong WengHo
Typeset in 12/15.5 Bembo by Midland Typesetters

National Library of Australia
Cataloguing-in-Publication data:

Manne, Robert.
The way we live now: the controversies of the nineties.
ISBN 1 875847 70 7.

1. Australia - Social conditions - 1990- . 2. Australia - Politics and government - 1990- . I. Title.
306.0994

'The Stolen Generations' is the text of the Stephen Murray-Smith Memorial Lecture, delivered at the Victorian State Library on 27 November 1997.

CONTENTS

Introduction 1

PART ONE
WHISPERINGS OF THE HEART

Whisperings of the Heart 7
The Coalition and the Aborigines 11
The Stolen Generations 15

PART TWO
PARTY GAMES

The Aborted Revolution 45
Dr Hewson and Middle Australia 50
Labor (Still) in Power 56
A Voyage of Rediscovery 62
The Keating Collapse 67
The Strange Personality of Jeffrey Kennett 73
Lying in Politics 77
Trivial Pursuits 80

PART THREE
THE NEW POLITICS OF RACE

Our First Anti-Politician 87
Hanson and the Populist Right 91
Pauline Hanson's Truth 95
The Counter-Revolution in Sensibility 100

PART FOUR
POLITICAL CULTURE

Thoughts on Australia 107
The Young Menzies 113

Why I Am Not a Republican 124
On the Manning Clark Affair 127
The Whitlam Whirlwind 133
The Kerr Conundrum 141
Why I Am No Longer Not a Republican 148
The Manning Clark Affair II 155
Bob Santamaria 168
The Republic's Unanswered Question 174

PART FIVE
ECHOES OF THE HOLOCAUST

The Road to Auschwitz 181
David Irving 188
The Case of Konrad Kalejs 193
Reflections on the Demidenko Affair 197
The Problem of *Schindler's List* 206

PART SIX
THE WAY WE LIVE NOW

Innocence 213
Suffer the Feral Children 216
Childcare 222
A Case for Censorship 227
The First Stone 238
The Second Stone 243
The President and Paula Jones 247
Life and Death on the Slippery Slope 252
The University Question 258
Gang Warfare 262
Short Cuts 267
Raimond, My Friend 272
Why I Have Resigned 277

Introduction

THE articles collected in *The Way We Live Now* were written in the past few years, while I was editor of *Quadrant* and a regular commentator in newspapers and on the ABC. These years have been for me a time of passionate public engagement, fierce dispute, intense self-scrutiny and inner political change.

As the child of Jewish refugees from Hitler's Europe my earliest political thoughts circled around one of the darkest chapters in modern history, the Holocaust. As a young Australian born in the early postwar years my earliest political experiences were of life in one of the most materially comfortable, politically stable and humanly decent societies on earth. The moral distance between past and present created a strange dichotomy in my political identity of which I was, I think, even then, dimly aware.

Because of the Holocaust I became, while an undergraduate at the University of Melbourne, an anticommunist. The teachers who influenced me most deeply—Frank Knopfelmacher and Vincent Buckley—and the political writers they encouraged me to read—

George Orwell, Hannah Arendt, Aleksandr Solzhenitsyn—convinced me that Nazism and communism were not so much ideological alternatives as morally equivalent political evils, which had, between them, inflicted unimaginable suffering on the peoples who had the misfortune of living under them. Becoming an anticommunist opened me to a conservative undertow in my thought that might otherwise have been silent. It did not make me a right-winger, in the Australian sense of the term. I was, at the university, a social democrat. In my instincts I remain so today. There was, however, one curious aspect of my anticommunism. Throughout the years of the Cold War I was more deeply interested in the political affairs of the Soviet Union and Eastern Europe, of China and Indochina, than of those in my own country.

As I see it now, but did not then, my involvement in the struggles for the Cold War was not without personal cost. I was intensely aware of the fundamental contradiction of the left—which had involved itself in politics because of a concern with justice but which had associated itself, directly or indirectly, with one of the most extensive systems of injustice history had ever seen. I was less clear-sighted about the contradiction at the heart of the anticommunist camp—which opposed communism in the name of justice but which, by a series of blind spots and intellectual evasions, managed to avert its gaze from the injustices in its own society and those of its Third World allies.

The end of the Cold War created problems for the intellectuals of both camps. The left was obliged to explain to itself why, on the communist question, it had been for so long deluded and, with the sudden collapse of the twentieth century's dominant idea of socialism, what being on the left now meant. Anticommunists, despite their vindication on the central issue of the Cold War, were faced with the loss of the common enemy; with the disappearance of the issue which, despite all their differences, had allowed conservatives, economic liberals and social democrats to unite; and, most importantly of all, with the need to respond intelligently and freshly to many of the issues—feminism, environmentalism, multiculturalism, anti-racism—which, during the Cold War, the left had placed at the centre of the political agenda. As I see it, the articles collected in this volume represent my personal journey from the Cold War.

In the early 1990s, I experienced both the exhilaration of a new freedom, but also a kind of vertigo. As I looked down upon an unfamiliar landscape I became aware that I was now required to live in a world without certainties and signposts, where some old political allies would become enemies and some old enemies friends, where there was now no alternative but to think about fundamental questions, one by one, and by oneself, and where one had to learn to listen more attentively and to converse more openly. When I finally planted my feet firmly on the soil of the post-Cold War world, I made some interesting discoveries. I found that my interest in the history, politics and culture of my own country had become much keener. I also found that long-buried disagreements with some former Cold War political friends had become much more intense.

I did not, as it happened, start out upon my exploration of the post-Cold War landscape unencumbered. On the day the Berlin Wall fell I was appointed editor of Australia's most influential anti-communist magazine. Some of the *Quadrant* old guard hoped the magazine would became the standard-bearer of the New Right, devoted to the politics of Margaret Thatcher and the philosophy of Adam Smith. Some hoped that *Quadrant* would become the magazine of pugnacious anti-leftism, the enemy of feminism, environmentalism, sexual liberation, anti-racism, multiculturalism. As readers of this book will see neither of these post-Cold War trajectories attracted me.

The different pieces collected in this volume do not add up to a comprehensive whole. They are by their nature occasional pieces, attempts to come to terms with events of the day—an election, a new book, a troubling social issue, a major public scandal, a divisive cultural affair. Nor do they represent a fixed point of view. Since the end of the Cold War on many issues my thoughts have changed. On other issues they have not. Where I have changed I hope I have not disguised the fact and have explained why. I hope, too, that despite the changes, readers will still find here consistency of vision and some sustained attempt to contribute, through reflection and argument, to the building in Australia of a more humane world.

This book records, I suppose, my breaking of ranks with the right. It does not record my embrace of the left. It is my firm conviction that with the end of the sterile certainties of the Cold War, we have moved to a world beyond left and right. In my opinion, at least, it is in such a world that, for better or worse, we all live now.

The pieces collected here appeared first in the *Age*, the *Australian*, the *Sydney Morning Herald*, *Quadrant*, the *Australian's Review of Books*, *Australian Book Review* and the *Times Literary Supplement*. Some have been slightly shortened, to avoid repetition. None have been edited in such a way as to change their meaning. I owe the title of this book to Anthony Trollope. Before me, Polly Toynbee, Bernard Levin and Richard Hoggart were similarly indebted. For a certain kind of social critic, as a title it seems irresistible. In preparing this book I am again indebted to the splendid small team at Text Publishing and especially to Michael Heyward.

Four people—my friends Raimond Gaita, Martin Krygier and John Spooner and my wife, Anne—have been my constant companions during my journey of the past years. Without Rai's friendship and generosity this book would not have been possible. I owe to Anne more than I can express. The book is devoted to her and to our daughters, Kate and Lucy, with hope and love.

PART ONE

WHISPERINGS OF THE HEART

Whisperings of the Heart

THE remarkable television series about the dispossession of the Australian Aborigines, *Frontier*, shown recently on the ABC, began with the haunting words of a colonist: 'Consideration of the rights of the Aborigines to the enjoyment of their lands and customs, to the soil of the country, to its wild animals, is closed, settled, the chain of reasoning complete... How is it that our minds are not satisfied? What means this whispering in the bottom of our hearts?'

The whispering concerned, of course, the sense that in the dispossession of the Aborigines a terrible wrong had been done. Although there have been long periods of Australian history when the whisper could scarcely be heard, it would never be altogether silenced. Indeed, it was one of the great virtues of *Frontier* that it showed how a deep sense of the injustice that had been done to the Aborigines remained vividly alive, in certain individuals, even during the era of the most violent conflicts between settlers and Aborigines, of vile atrocities on both sides.

Whispering eventually ceased. From the early 1970s the question of Aboriginal dispossession and reparation became a central issue in Australian politics. In 1992 with the *Mabo* judgment of the High Court—one of the turning points in our history—the legal basis of the dispossession, *terra nullius*, was overturned. What was of the greatest importance about *Mabo* was not the precise legal reasoning of the judgment, which most citizens found difficult to follow, but the moral premise on which it was based. Time and again, since *Mabo*, I have noticed how both admirers and opponents have begun their serious arguments by turning to the sombre remarks of Justices Deane and Gaudron that the dispossession of the Aborigines has left 'a national legacy of unutterable shame'.

Political division over these words goes deep. Admirers of *Mabo* see in them plain and undeniable truth. Opponents—even among those who grudgingly accept that, for political reasons, the *Mabo* judgment cannot be undone—see in them little but historical distortion and moral humbug. They are completely resistant to the idea of *Mabo* as a central event in our history, as both a legal recognition of, and moral reparation for, the wrongs done to the Aborigines in the settlement of Australia. They see in the more recent majority judgment of the High Court on *Wik*—that native title and pastoral leases can co-exist—not so much a legal error as economic vandalism and judicial activism gone mad. Views on these matters have surrounded the High Court with a climate of hostility and contempt the like of which, in all my observation of Australian politics, I have never before seen.

The suspicion of farmers, graziers and their political representatives regarding the High Court after *Mabo* and *Wik* is not difficult to understand. The hostility of the conservative intelligentsia is more puzzling. Conservatives are normally the defenders of a society's fundamental institutions. On this occasion they form the radical advance guard. Why?

One explanation may be tied up with the deadening force of political habit. During the long period of the Cold War the most important question dividing the left-wing and the conservative intelligentsias was the assessment of communism. At the end of the Cold War, concerning this question, the left emerged deeply compromised. The judgment of the anticommunists was vindicated. Perhaps, however, the anticommunists also paid a price for this vindication, for their failure during the Cold War to distinguish those parts of the left agenda which were foolish or foul from those parts which were founded on a genuine understanding of injustice. It was, undoubtedly, the left in Australia—including a part of the communist left—which was first alert to questions of Aboriginal injustice, which first pressed for Aboriginal land rights. It sometimes seems to me that current conservative resistance to the idea of the injustice done to the Aborigines is rooted in nothing deeper than a kind of reflex anti-leftism, which those who were right about communism have been unable or unwilling or too lazy to shrug off.

Yet I am sure there is more to the question than this. As the Cold War was drawing to a close, and as anticommunism was becoming increasingly irrelevant, a new ideological breeze blew up as a more or less unifying force within the conservative intelligentsia—economic rationalism. It seems to me that economic rationalism has had two main consequences for conservatives in Australia. Firstly, under its influence, almost all political questions came to be examined primarily from the economic point of view. Secondly, a far more rationalistic spirit than had previously been seen began to pervade Australian conservatism. In this mood, Australian conservatism became increasingly blind to the force of any idea which was driven by moral rather than economic considerations, as *Mabo* obviously was, and especially hostile to the possibility that for moral reasons some economic sacrifices might have to be borne. In its rationalistic mood, Australian conservatism became not only radically dissociated from mainstream Christian thought—which provided one of the main sources of support for *Mabo* and Aboriginal reconciliation—but also, strangely enough, prone to the kind of feeling of contempt for Aboriginal religion and forms of spirituality which was once found on the Marxist left.

And yet there is something deeper to be fathomed about conservative resistance to the moral significance of *Mabo* than this. It seems to me that at least some of the left-wing identification with the injustice done to the Aborigines is founded on a certain kind of rancour in regard to their own society, on taking pleasure at its denigration, on a systematic exaggeration of its shortcomings and underestimation of its virtues. Many conservatives, particularly of the older generation, suspect this kind of leftism. They cannot distinguish John Pilger from Henry Reynolds. They are aware of the great institutional and political strengths of their country and proud of those who endured hardships in building it.

It seems to me precisely because of the depth of their patriotism that this kind of conservative is pained by the thought that the dispossession of the Aborigines has left an ineradicable stain on their country's past. Such a view is considered an offence to proportion and commonsense, or as an unhealthy dwelling on the past. The conservatives I have in mind are genuinely concerned with Aboriginal health, education, employment. They cannot or will not see what *Mabo* is about. What is finest about their attachment to their country paradoxically, then, leads such conservatives to avert their gaze from the terrible story of Aboriginal dispossession, from their country's legacy of shame. It is here that they and I part company.

1997

The Coalition and the Aborigines

I did not anticipate, when I voted for the Coalition in the 1996 federal election, how swiftly its relationship with the Aboriginal leadership in Australia would deteriorate. At the heart of this deterioration, or so it seems to me, is a curious kind of ambivalence within the Coalition in regard to that great sea change in relations between Aboriginal and non-Aboriginal Australians that has taken place in recent years.

The sea change has centred on the High Court's *Mabo* judgment, which generated the political process known as reconciliation. The greatest political champion of *Mabo* and reconciliation was, of course, the former prime minister, Paul Keating. The embracing of *Mabo*, the understanding of what it might mean for his country, seems to me to have been Keating's most important contribution as prime minister. Unfortunately, as the election of Pauline Hanson revealed, Keating was not particularly successful, over *Mabo* and reconciliation, in carrying opinion in Australia with him. It is a telling criticism of him that he never seemed to grasp how difficult it would be to bring the nation along with him. And it is an even more telling criticism that he never seemed willing to try.

In coming to power there was no doubt that the Coalition leadership accepted, as a kind of irrevocable fact, the High Court's *Mabo* judgment, and, within the limits of 'workability' amendments, the Keating government's *Mabo* legislation. What in my view it did not, and still does not, accept is the moral basis of *Mabo* and of reconciliation; the acceptance of shame. There are very few senior Coalition politicians who would not baulk to some extent at the Gaudron–Deane suggestion that the treatment of the indigenous population during the British settlement of Australia cast a shadow across our history. There are few who would disagree with Professor Geoffrey Blainey that such a view represents the typically self-lacerating, left-wing, 'black-armband' version of history.

Certainly this seems to be the view of the prime minister. According to Lois O'Donoghue, John Howard explained in a recent conversation that while non-Aboriginal Australians are more than willing to do their bit in bringing about reconciliation, they do not want to dwell on the past and are simply unwilling to take upon themselves the burden of previous generations' supposed wrongdoings. These words take us to the heart of the breakdown in relations between the Coalition and the Aboriginal leadership and reveal the fundamental confusion at present bedevilling Coalition thinking on the question of Aboriginal reconciliation.

As the philosopher Raimond Gaita pointed out in two very important columns published in *Quadrant* in 1993, the confusion here stems from the failure among Australian conservatives to distinguish between the ideas of collective guilt and historical shame. Because guilt for wrongs done is always a matter of individual responsibility, the idea of collective guilt genuinely makes no sense. An individual cannot be charged with the crimes of others. He or she cannot experience remorse on someone else's behalf. Those who claim to bear guilt for the actions of others, including historical forebears, are either pretending to feelings and responsibilities they do not have, or misdescribing genuine feelings and responsibilities they do. Talk of sharing in a collective guilt over the dispossession of the Aborigines is one thing; talk, however, of sharing in a legacy of historical shame is altogether another. This distinction is most easily explained by analogy.

Conservatives like John Howard or Tim Fischer would have no difficulty in feeling admiration and a kind of pride in, let us say, the resourcefulness shown by the pioneers or the courage shown by the soldiers at Gallipoli. I am sure, too, that they would hope that other Australians would share in their admiration and their pride. Yet if it is possible and just to feel pride in the achievements of forebears it surely cannot be regarded as impossible or unjust to feel shame about past wrongs. The case I am making can be put simply. To be an Australian is to be embedded or implicated in this country's history in a way outsiders or visitors cannot be. To be implicated in this history opens—as conservatives easily acknowledge—the possibility of reasonable pride. But to be open to the possibility of pride in achievement is also, necessarily, to be open to the possibility of shame in wrongdoing. Neither the idea of pride or of shame involved here is, of course, connected to questions of individual moral responsibility or worth. Gallipoli does not make me courageous. Aboriginal dispossession does not cover me with guilt. And yet, because Australia is my country, both may matter to me deeply.

When John Howard informed Lois O'Donoghue that non-Aboriginal Australians cannot take upon themselves a collective guilt for the harm inflicted by the settlers on the indigenous population, he was right. But when he told her that Australians are simply not interested in dwelling on the past and cannot be asked to take seriously the burden of what Justices Gaudron and Deane called our legacy of shame in regard to the dispossession of the Aborigines, he was profoundly and dispiritingly wrong.

The prime minister's words express here more than he realises. With them he is turning his back on the moral foundation of both *Mabo* and of the reconciliation process he claims to support. In my opinion the Aboriginal leadership has intuited correctly the meaning of this repudiation. A deterioration of relations has been the result.

1996

The Stolen Generations

I

FROM the late nineteenth century to the late 1960s—even the dates are somewhat uncertain, so little do we know—Australian governments, as a practice and as a policy, removed part-Aboriginal children from their mothers, parents, families and communities, often by force. Some of these children were taken at birth, some at two years of age, some in their childhood years. The babies and children were sent either to special-purpose institutions or, in later years especially, to foster homes. In some cases mothers or families knew where their children had been taken and were able to maintain some continuing connection with them. In other cases they had no idea of the whereabouts of the babies or children who had been taken from them. In some cases within the institutions and the foster homes the children were treated well, although even here, it would appear, frequently with a kind of benign contempt. In other cases physical mistreatment, sexual exploitation and more extreme forms of humiliation were common.

In the period before, roughly speaking, 1940, the part-Aboriginal children were taken from their mothers and families under separate legislation which gave unlimited guardianship to the Aboriginal protectors in their state of origin, frequently without even giving to the parents the right of appeal to a court of law. Increasingly after 1940 these part-Aboriginal children were taken from their mothers and families under the general child welfare legislation which was, in their cases, interpreted in such a way that the practices of child removal seem to have continued much as before. Only very gradually did the custom of separating part-Aboriginal babies or children from their mothers merge with general non-Aboriginal practices concerning child abuse and neglect. This time came, probably, as late as the early 1970s. No one knows exactly how many babies and children were, between the late nineteenth century and the late 1960s, removed. The degree of uncertainty is captured in the figures of the 1997 Human Rights and Equal Opportunity Commission report, *Bringing Them Home*. It suggests that somewhere between one in three and one in ten Aboriginal children were separated from their mothers during these years. A figure of one in ten is startling enough. But the difference between one in ten and one in three is very great indeed. All that one can say for certain is that in the seventy or so years in question tens of thousands of babies and children were removed. Yet there is an even more extraordinary fact than this. Until the last year or so most non-Aboriginal Australians either did not know or were at best dimly aware that for some seventy years Australian governments had been involved in a more or less routine practice of part-Aboriginal child removal. This was something almost every Aborigine understood.

The words you are reading now about all this are at once belated and premature. Belated in the sense that, like many non-indigenous Australians, I have come to a serious interest in the question of the maltreatment of the Aborigines far too late. Premature in the sense that I am only now beginning to make up for lost time by trying to discover as much as I can about the particular issue of the stolen children. As I came to write about this topic I was only too aware of how much more I wished I understood about it and almost paralysed by an awareness of how much I still did not understand. But the report on the stolen children and the nature of the government's response to that report seem to me to be the most important public issue of our time. I would ask readers to regard everything I say as tentative and provisional, and to bear in mind that, because in so far as I have any detailed knowledge of the topic it centres on developments in Western Australia and the Northern Territory before World War II, what I say is fundamentally concerned with those territories and those times. It will take years of work for me to begin to resolve in my mind several of the issues I intend to raise in this essay.

II

I want to begin by quoting two passages, one lengthy and one short.

The lengthy passage comes from Margaret Tucker's autobiography, published in 1977, *If Everyone Cared*. The second from a letter written by Senator John Herron, on behalf of the prime minister, John Howard, to Father Frank Brennan in October 1997.

Here first is the passage from Margaret Tucker:

> One day when we were at school I was thrilled because an older boy and I were the only ones to get the answer to a difficult sum. Mrs Hill praised us and as I am not brainy it really meant a lot to me. Between morning school and lunch break, we heard the unmistakable sound of a motor car... I cannot remember everything that went on, but the next thing I do remember was that the policeman and Mr Hill came into the school. Mrs Hill seemed to be in a heated argument with her husband. She was very distressed.

The children were all standing (we always stood up when visitors came and the police were no exception). My sister May and another little girl, an orphan, started to cry. Then others. They may have heard the conversation. I was puzzled to know what they were crying for, until Mr Hill told all the children to leave the school, except myself and May and Myrtle Taylor, who was the same age as May (eleven years). Myrtle was an orphan reared by Mrs Maggie Briggs. She was very fair-skinned and pretty.

I had forgotten about Brungle and the gang of men representing the Aborigines Protection Board who had visited when we were staying there. But then it came to me in a rush! But I didn't believe for a moment that my mother would let us go. She would put a stop to it! All the children who had been dismissed must have run home and told their parents what was happening at school. When I looked out that schoolroom door, every Moonahculla Aboriginal mother—some with babies in arms—and a sprinkling of elderly men were standing in groups... Suddenly that little group were all talking at once, some in the language, some in English, but all with a hopelessness, knowing they would not have the last say. Some looked very angry, others had tears running down their cheeks. Then Mr Hill demanded that we three girls leave immediately with the police. The Aboriginal women were very angry.

Mr Hill was in a situation he had never experienced before. He did not take into account that Aboriginal hearts could break down with despair and helplessness, the same as any other human hearts. Mrs Hill, the tears running down her cheeks, made a valiant attempt to prolong our stay... We started to cry again and most of our school mates and the mothers too, when our mother, like an angel, came through the schoolroom door. Little Myrtle's auntie rushed in too. I thought: 'Everything will be right now. Mum won't let us go.'

Myrtle was grabbed up by her auntie. We had our arms round our mother, and refused to let go. She still had her apron on, and must have run the whole one and a half miles. She arrived just in time, due to the kindness of Mrs Hill.

As we hung onto our mother she said fiercely, 'They are my children and they are not going away with you.'

The policeman, who no doubt was doing his duty, patted his handcuffs, which were in a leather case on his belt, and which May and I thought was a revolver. 'Mrs Clements,' he said, 'I'll have to use this if you do not let us take these children now.' Thinking that policeman would shoot Mother, because she was trying to stop him, we screamed, 'We'll go with him Mum, we'll go.' I cannot forget any detail of that moment, it stands out as though it were yesterday. I cannot even see kittens taken from their mother cat without remembering that scene. It is just on sixty years ago.

However, the policeman must have had a heart, because he allowed my mother to come in the car with us as far as Deniliquin. She had no money, and took nothing with her, only the clothes she had on. Then the policeman sprang another shock. He said he had to go to the hospital to pick up Geraldine, who was to be taken as well. The horror on my mother's face and her heartbroken cry! I tried to reason why all this was happening to us, and tried not to think. All my mother could say was, 'Oh, no, not my Baby, please let me have her. I will look after her.'

As that policeman walked up the hospital path to get my little sister, May and Myrtle and I sobbed quietly.

Mother got out of the car and stood waiting with a hopeless look. Her tears had run dry I guess. I thought to myself, I will gladly go, if they will only leave Geraldine with Mother.

'Mrs Clements, you can have your little girl. She left the hospital this morning,' said the policeman. Mother simply took that policeman's hand and kissed it and said, 'Thank you, thank you.'

Then we were taken to the police station, where the policeman no doubt had to report. Mother followed him, thinking she could beg once more for us, only to rush out when she heard the car start up. My last memory of her for many years was her waving pathetically, as we waved back and called out goodbye to her, but we were too far away for her to hear us.

I heard years later how after watching us go out of her life, she wandered away from the police station three miles along the road leading out of the town to Moonahculla. She was worn out, with no food or money, her apron still on. She wandered off the road to rest in the long grass under a tree. That is where old Uncle and Aunt found her the next day. They had arrived back with Geraldine from the Deniliquin hospital and they were at once surrounded by our people at Moonahculla, who told them the whole story. Someone immediately offered the loan of a fresh horse to go back and find Mother. They found our mother still moaning and crying. They heard the sounds and thought it was an animal in pain. Uncle stopped the horse and got out of the buggy to investigate. Auntie heard him talking in the language. She got down and rushed to old Uncle's side. Mother was half demented and ill. They gave her water and tried to feed her, but she couldn't eat. She was not interested in anything for weeks, and wouldn't let Geraldine out of her sight. She slowly got better, but I believe for months after, at the sight of a policeman's white helmet coming round the bend of the river, she would grab her little girl and escape into the bush, as did all the Aboriginal people who had children.

Here, then, is a passage from the letter of Senator Herron to Father Brennan:

> The Prime Minister acknowledges and thanks you for your support for his personal apology to indigenous people affected by past practices of separating indigenous children from their families. However, the government does not support an official national apology. Such an apology could imply that present generations are in some way responsible and accountable for the actions of earlier generations, actions that were sanctioned by the laws of the time, and that were believed to be in the best interests of the children concerned.

The extract from Margaret Tucker's autobiography represents, of course, a very singular experience. But it may remind us that there were tens of thousands of individual experiences in this century of a similar kind. It is concerning these kind of experiences that Senator Herron, on behalf of the prime minister and the Australian government, refuses to offer an apology. He does so on two grounds.

He tells us, firstly, that the act of removing Margaret Tucker and tens of thousands of others like her was legal. And he tells us, secondly, that however unfortunate we may now find such removals, they were grounded in the good intentions of Australian policy-makers and people in previous generations.

One half of this justification is trivial and need not unduly detain us. It may be true that acts like that inflicted on Margaret Tucker were authorised under the laws which gave the state protectors of Aborigines sole guardian rights over Aboriginal children under sixteen or under twenty-one. But it is clearly not the legality of these acts but their morality which is in question. In the United

States, at the same time as Australian states removed part-Aboriginal children from their families, thirty states passed laws for the sterilisation of those suffering mental or hereditary illness of various kinds. These governments were democratically elected. The sterilisation statutes were according to law. Both facts do not remove from the legislators or governments the responsibility for what they did. The same is true *a fortiori* for the governments, parliaments and public servants who sought or gave the state the legal capacity to remove part-Aboriginal children from their mothers.

The good-intentions defence is more serious than the legality defence. Yet it rests on two different kinds of misunderstanding. The first is pretty straightforward. It involves the belief that a policy may be justified on the grounds of its good intentions so long as the policy-maker assures us—as no doubt the architects of the stolen children policy would—that their intentions were good. Such an argument can be disposed of quickly. When the Nazis, to take an extreme example, decided to rid the earth of the Jews, the chief executors of such a policy argued the goodness of their intentions. The Jews befouled the world. Their extermination would free humanity from their corrupting presence. For a policy to be defended on the grounds of its good intentions such a defence must rest not on the policy-makers' professions of their good intentions, but on their intentions being recognisable to us as, in some sense or another, good. We would never regard the Nazi policy of Jewish annihilation or the American colonists' policy of slavery as mistaken but well intentioned. The question, then, that arises in regard to the policy of the separation of part-Aboriginal children from their mothers and families is whether there exists any construal of that policy as well intentioned which we could now find plausible.

Many Australians, including it seems John Howard and Senator Herron, clearly believe that in regard to the stolen children such a plausible good-intentions defence exists. What they seem to believe is that part-Aboriginal babies and children were separated from their families for what might be called social welfare reasons, because the particular children so removed were assessed by those in authority at the time of being in the future in danger of physical or moral harm. According to this social welfarist-good intentions line of defence, part-Aboriginal children were removed essentially for the same kind of reason that a contemporary child welfare department might decide to remove a child from a mother or from parents who were deemed likely to inflict upon it future harm.

This line of defence lies, I believe, at the centre of the present confusion in Australia concerning the policy of Aboriginal child removal—a confusion found even in the recent report by Elliott Johnston into Aboriginal deaths in custody. Yet to persist with the social welfarist-good intentions defence in the light of the *Bringing Them Home* report seems to me astonishing. For while it must of course in fact have been true that some of the part-Aboriginal children separated from their families were in danger of harm, it is absolutely false to claim that the motives of those who made or executed the separation policy were of a social-welfare kind. They were driven by altogether different motives. It is to such motives that I will now turn.

The policy and practice of Aboriginal child removal was, at its very heart, the response of Australian governments to a problem that stirred parliaments, public opinion and Aboriginal administrators alike in the first half of our century—the problem of the so-called 'half-caste'. In the late nineteenth and early twentieth century educated opinion in Australia seems, generally, to have been of the view that the full-blood tribal Aborigine represented a dying race, doomed in the fullness of time to extinction. It would be quite wrong, of course, to think that this belief about impending Aboriginal extinction was not, in general, held with regret, as a kind of settled scientific fact. Lesser cultures, it was believed, could not survive contact with higher civilisations. Eventually, in the 1920s and 1930s, some Australians came to think that the extinction of full-blood Aborigines might not be inevitable.

In the first decades of the twentieth century a new development, a kind of by-product of human relations on the fringes of European settlement, became apparent. This was the emergence of mixed-descent children or of what Australians at that time called 'half-castes', that is to say of those children born to Aboriginal mothers after sexual encounters—sometimes fleeting, sometimes exploitative, occasionally more permanent or even matrimonial—with European and sometimes Chinese or Pacific Islander males. Almost invariably the Australian settlers in the first half of the twentieth century thought of these mixed-descent children, and of the descendants of these children, whom they labelled, almost zoologically, as half-castes or crossbreeds, as quadroons and octoroons, as a growing, fearful social problem. Late nineteenth and early twentieth-century thought in Australia, as elsewhere in the European cultural sphere, had been deeply corrupted by a racially based Darwinian social science.

Australians, like others, generally thought that the races of mankind could be fitted neatly into a civilisational hierarchy overlain by some idea of moral worth and of fitness to survive. North Europeans were on the highest rung of this civilisational ladder, Aborigines on the lowest. Australians also, in general, looked upon the progeny of sexual unions between Europeans and Aborigines with undisguised distaste and fear. For such unions the ugly term, miscegenation, was deployed.

In regard to full-blood Aborigines there existed a certain ambivalence. They were regarded with sentimental, albeit almost invariably condescending sympathy sometimes as 'noble savages' or as members of a 'child-race'. Concerning the half-castes there was, in general, little but cultural contempt and social alarm. The Perth *Sunday Times* in 1927 put it thus: 'Central Australia's half-caste problem…must be tackled boldly and immediately. The greatest danger, experts agree, is that three races will develop in Australia—white, black and the pathetic sinister third race which is neither.'

Concerning the 'problem' of the half-caste in the first forty years of this century panicky statistical calculations were frequently made, purporting to show that while the full-blood Aborigine was, according to one point of view, slowly dying out and, according to another, maintaining its numbers as a 'slow breeder', the numbers of half-castes, negligible at century's beginning, were increasing at an alarming rate. These statistical predictions claimed that, unless something was done, in fifty or one hundred years Australia would be threatened by a population of several hundred thousand Aboriginal–European hybrids.

It is commonly believed that the White Australia Policy was more or less exclusively concerned with restrictive immigration policies. The White Australia Policy also played its part, however, in poisoning the well in regard to the mixed-descent population. What good was a restrictive immigration policy, it was argued, if the growth of half-castes was, in the next fifty or hundred years, to present Australia with an indigenous colour problem of its own?

To perceive of a group of human beings as a 'problem' is, of course, to hanker after a 'solution'. In the first half of the twentieth century many solutions were posed in regard to the problem of the half-caste. One kind of solution focused on geographic or legal separation, attempts to prevent as far as possible and by one means or another, physical contact between blacks and whites and in particular between young European males and young Aboriginal women.

The most important solution of the policy-makers and legislators to the problem of the 'half-caste' was, however, child removal. In all states and territories, in one way or another, legislation was passed in the early years of the twentieth century which gave Aboriginal protectors guardianship rights over Aborigines up to the age of sixteen or twenty-one. In all states and territories, policemen or other agents of the states began to locate and transfer babies and children of mixed descent, like Margaret Tucker, from their mothers or families or communities into institutions. In these Australian states and territories half-caste institutions—government or missionary—were established in the early decades of the twentieth century for the reception of these separated children. If these children were separated permanently from family, if they were taught to despise their Aboriginal inheritance, if they were even brought up without the knowledge of that inheritance, if they were sent to work as domestic servants or station hands in the hope that they would eventually merge into European society and marry out, if they were sent to foster homes where knowledge of their Aboriginality was denied, all this was done, in my view, *not* as a social welfare measure, but as an attempt to break the cultural connection between the children of mixed descent and their Aboriginal families and cultures, to drag the children out of the world of the native settlements and camps and prepare them for a place in the lower strata of European society. Because the policy-makers and agents of state viewed these children and the worlds from which they had come through racist spectacles—seeing nothing but racial degeneration and social squalor—they genuinely believed that in taking the children from their family and culture they were acting in the long-term best interest of the children, whatever temporary grief or pain they caused. Because they thought of half-castes as a social problem which had to be solved, and through their alarmist statistical analyses as a threatening demographic trend of the kind which had confronted the United States with a stubborn colour problem, they also wished, in part through the child removal policy, to help keep White Australia pure.

III

I come now to an even more troubling dimension of the interwar child separation policy. The 1920s and 1930s were years when the science of eugenics—the science that taught that one of the responsibilities of the contemporary state was to improve a nation's racial stock by breeding programs—was, throughout the western world, extremely influential. Eugenics had a negative and a positive face. The negative part of the program suggested that people with mental illness or genetically transmitted disease or even subnormal intelligence, might be sterilised. Such a policy was implemented most radically in Nazi Germany, of course, but it was also implemented widely in, for example, progressive Scandinavian countries and in thirty states of the USA. The positive part of the program focused on breeding programs that would refine the nation's racial-biological stock. A minor subcategory of positive eugenics was what one study of this movement in Latin America calls 'constructive miscegenation', that is to say, government-initiated inter-racial breeding programs. In the late 1920s and early 1930s in Australia small circles of anthropologists, medical scientists and publicists began to advocate—as their solution to the problem of the half-caste—a policy of what was called at the time the breeding out of colour and what has subsequently come to be called the policy of biological assimilation or absorption.

The policy they advocated combined anthropological speculation and Mendelian biology. The anthropological speculation was the claim that the Australian Aborigines belonged to the Caucasian or Aryan race, that is to say that they were related through their blood to the peoples of contemporary Europe and Britain. One proponent of this view, the anthropologist Herbert Basedow, put it thus: 'The Australian Aboriginal stands somewhere near the bottom rung of the great evolutionary ladder we have ascended—he the bud, we the glorified flower of human culture.' The biological base of the policy was the claim that, given the remote racial affinity between the Aborigine and the European, a program of controlled breeding out of half-castes, quadroons and octoroons had every prospect, in a matter of three or four or five generations, and without the danger of what was called 'atavism' or biological 'throwback', of turning part-Aborigines into whites. An author, 'Physicus', put forth the case for biological assimilation of part-Aborigines in the *West Australian* of 22 July 1933 thus:

A century ago the Abbé Mendel discovered that hybrids follow a distinct law of their own in regard to breeding... Human hybrids follow the same rule... It is strange, in these days when eugenics and a craving after the methodical application of scientific discoveries and deductions are so much talked about, that no publicist has arisen to sound the tocsin for a movement to guide the half-caste and the person of mixed blood along the road he (and she) should take for happiness, not only of themselves but of their descendants... The application of Mendelianism is the only solution, and that urges the mating of the half-caste with the quadroon and the octoroon, so that the confirmed infiltration of white blood will finally stamp out the black colour which, when all is said and done, is what we really object to.

The eugenics program of constructive miscegenation, of breeding out the colour of the half-castes, might have represented a mere footnote in the history of Australian ideas were it not for the fact that in the late 1920s and early 1930s two of the three most important administrators of Aboriginal affairs, the protectors in the Northern Territory and Western Australia, Dr Cecil Cook and A. O. Neville, were enthusiastic converts to this cause, and that both devoted a part of their energies to the creation of a blueprint for the implementation of a policy for the breeding out of the mixed-descent population under their control.

Both Cook and Neville were progressivist bureaucrats whose plans in this regard were not so much embraced as unresisted by the ministers with whom they served. The evidence concerning their conversion to the policy of breeding out is not controversial. Those who are interested should consult, in regard to Dr Cook, Russell McGregor's *Imagined Destinies* and Tony Austin's *Never Trust a Government Man* and, in regard to A. O. Neville, Pat Jacobs' *Mister Neville* and Anna Haebich's *For Their Own Good*.

Dr Cook seems to have been a thoroughgoing eugenicist. He was of the view that if, as seemed to be the case, forced sterilisations or legalised abortions would never be countenanced in Australia, the most positive policy was to encourage actively the marriage of part-Aboriginal women and white males. During the 1930s, somewhat modestly, he brokered sixty or so arranged marriages between inmates of the Darwin half-caste home and European men. On one occasion Cook expressed his point of view thus: 'Generally by the fifth and invariably by the sixth generation, all native characteristics of the Australian Aborigine are eradicated. The problem of our half-castes will quickly be eliminated by the complete disappearance of the black race, and the swift submergence of their progeny in the white.'

A. O. Neville's views on the question of breeding out colour were the same as Cook's. His administrative blueprint, however, was more ambitious. In 1936 he managed to convince his minister and the Western Australian parliament to pass legislation which allowed him to attempt to implement his breeding-out policy. This legislation made uncontrolled sexual relations between Europeans and Aborigines a punishable offence. It required Aborigines to seek the permission of the native commissioner to marry. It more or less forbade marriages between half-castes and full-bloods. It prohibited the association of quadroons with those deemed to be 'native' under the act. Most importantly of all it gave the commissioner guardianship rights over all Aborigines up to the age of twenty-one, allowing him to remove all children, whether legitimate or not, from their families.

In April 1937 the key administrators of Aboriginal affairs gathered in Canberra. It was the first such meeting in Australia's history. It was at this meeting that the link between half-caste policies and child removal was most clearly revealed. Neville was the intellectually dominant figure in the Canberra discussions. He began his formal address with the following words: 'The problem of the native race, including the half-castes, should be dealt with on a long-range plan. We should ask ourselves what will be the position, say, fifty years hence.' His state, he informed the gathering, had developed precisely such a plan. It was for the total 'absorption' of the detribalised Aboriginal population into the white. Neville believed the prospects for absorption were bright. His optimism was founded on the view that the Aborigines sprang from 'Caucasian' rather than 'Negroid' stock and that there was not, in the process of racial outbreeding of Aborigines, any tendency towards 'atavism'.

What, then, did Neville propose to do? He spoke first of what he called 'half-castes'. If they were effectively to be absorbed it was imperative, he believed, to get hold of the babies or infants before the age of six. By puberty it was too late. Under Western Australian law, he pointed out, he had the power to seize by force, and to institutionalise, any native under the age of twenty-one. It mattered not at all that the child was with its parents or that these parents were legally married. The question of neglect was not even raised.

Neville readily admitted the difficulty of his scheme was that 'it is well known that coloured races all over the world detest institutionalism' and that they have 'a tremendous affection for their children'. What of it? He had handled this difficulty by establishing 'native settlements divided into two parts'. The infants were sent to compounds, the mothers and fathers to nearby camps. For a few months the parents of the seized children were shown the conditions in the compounds. Most, he claimed, eventually lost interest. Some, however, continued to try 'to entice' their children back to the camps. 'That difficulty,' he told the conference, 'is now being overcome.'

Once inside his institutions, the native infants were to be given basic education and to be kept in good health. At adolescence they were to be sent out to work At the conference some scepticism rose at this point. Would the native girls not fall pregnant to white males? Neville was unconcerned. 'If a girl comes back pregnant our rule is to keep her for two years. The child is taken away from the mother and sometimes never sees her again. It really does not matter if she has half a dozen children.' What did matter was to prevent half-castes marrying full-bloods. Such marriages were now, he pointed out, more or less prohibited in his state. The encouragement of racial outbreeding was at the core of Neville's radical plan for the solution of the Aboriginal 'problem'. Child removal was an essential means.

For him the problem could be summarised thus: 'Are we going to have a population of 1,000,000 blacks in the Commonwealth, or are we going to merge them into our white community and eventually forget that there were any Aborigines in Australia?'

To Neville the fate of the full-bloods was a non-problem. Their breeding rates were far lower than those of the half-castes. 'The problem,' he told the conference, 'is one which will eventually solve itself. There are a great many full-blooded Aborigines in Western Australia living their own natural lives. They are not, for the most part, getting enough food, and they are, in fact, being decimated by their own tribal practices. In my opinion, no matter what we do, they will die out.' At the Canberra conference the question of whether or not a handful of tribal natives might survive was left open.

The key resolution of the conference was called 'the destiny of the race' and it was unanimously endorsed. It called for the total absorption into the white community of all non-full-blood natives. Removing part-Aboriginal children from their mothers and families was, of course, a vital part of the scheme for the realisation of this ambition.

If there exists a more terrible moment in the history of the twentieth-century Australian state than the Canberra conference of April 1937 I for one do not know where it is to be discovered.

IV

Let me turn to some questions about the policy and practice I have been analysing. The first question—although not the answer to it—is simple. How can the cruelty of the child separations be explained?

Here I believe a number of important considerations are involved. The first is the habit of mind of the key policy-makers—the protectors. In our century the marriage between bureaucratic rationality and the scientific point of view has been at the heart of many political tragedies. In inter-war Australia, in both the Northern Territory and Western Australia, Aboriginal policy was determined by energetic, reform-minded, progressivist bureaucrats with an interest in eugenics, racial demographics, anthropology and social Darwinism. The human style of Dr Cook was described by a critic thus:

> Dr Cook has always been courteous and polite to me, but he is one of those scientifically inhuman automata, to whom you are not a living personality, but merely Class…Genera…Record…File…and so on… He is, I think, far too removed from genuine human feeling, too much of the scientist, and too little of the real man to be a good Chief Protector.

For his part, Neville was an amateur but enthusiastic anthropologist and a particularly authoritarian bureaucrat who exercised detailed control over the lives of the Aborigines under his care; who thought of himself, according to Paul Hasluck, as 'the virtual sole proprietor of Aborigines in Western Australia'; and who, in 1934, informed a Royal Commission that Aborigines of mixed descent had 'to be protected against themselves whether they like it or not'. The style of scientific, bureaucratic rationality served to shield the key policy-makers from the extreme acts of cruelty their policy prescriptions inflicted on thousands of human beings.

Not everyone involved in the policy of child removal could

be thus shielded from reality. There is in policy such as this always a chain of command where decisions taken in administrative offices and voted on the floors of parliaments are implemented on the ground by police officers, welfare workers and schoolteachers. At the beginning of this lecture I read a passage which outlined the cruelty of child removal from the point of view of a victim. But for at least some of the executors of the policy on the ground the cruelty was also obvious. Earlier this year a remarkable letter appeared in the *Age*, written by Lang Dean.

> My father was a Victorian policeman from 1922 until 1946. He spent a long spell of duty at Echuca and he was there when the Deniliquin and Balranald railway spurs were constructed.
>
> The rail workers came to Echuca to spend their earnings and let off steam. My father made 343 arrests on average in those years. He was a good and conscientious policeman. During 1937–38, when I was seven or eight years old, he would sometimes come off duty and, as was his custom, sit on a stool outside our kitchen and take his helmet off. On occasions he would be crying and sobbing like a child, I would be upset to see such a strong man cry and I asked him why. He said he would not tell me as I was too young to understand but he would tell me when I grew up. What he did say then was: 'Son, don't ever be a policeman, it's a dirty job.'
>
> After he left the force, when I was about sixteen years old, he and I were camping on a fishing trip and we were sitting around the campfire. I had often thought about how Dad cried years ago so I asked him would he tell me the reason. He told me that when he went on duty those mornings his sergeant would order him to accompany two welfare officers to Cumragunga, a mission station, to give them bodily protection when they

entered nice clean simple homes of half-caste people and bodily removed nine, ten, eleven and twelve-year-old children from loving mothers and fathers into commandeered taxis. They were then taken to the Echuca railway station and sent to the far reaches of NSW and Queensland. They were farmed out to service to wealthy businessmen and graziers. No doubt a few were treated well but the rest would be thrown on the human scrap-heap when finished with.

So that was the reason my father cried on those days.

One of the elements that strikes me as interesting, although not at all surprising in this letter, is what it reveals about the willingness of good-hearted individuals to carry out, in the course of their duties, terrible actions which they know to be utterly wrong. Partly it is because of their dependence on a job, partly because of the habit of deference towards an authority which is assumed to know best or to have deeper reasons which simple folk cannot fathom. An even more striking instance of the dangers of deference is found in the biography of Neville. In the 1930s Neville worked closely with Kate Clutterbuck, Sister Kate, to establish an institution for light-skinned part-Aborigines in a suburb of Perth. By all accounts, Sister Kate was a fine and charitable woman. On one occasion she wrote the following letter to Neville: 'We should of course like to have the most poorest and neglected children, not those who have mothers who love and care for them, but those who are most unwanted to the State. But we must leave that to you.'

The sting of this letter is in the tail. Kate Clutterbuck has imagined that there might well be children taken by the state from mothers who love and care for them. She would prefer not to have these delivered to her home. But if authority in its wisdom decides to send her such infants she will not object. The dangers of deference could scarcely be more clearly seen. The virtues of rebelliousness with regard to authority were displayed by another charitable woman, Mary Bennett. We will have reason to speak of her soon.

Not all of those who were implicated in the practice of child removal were, of course, as humane in their instincts as the father of Lang Dean. No doubt many local protectors, policemen and welfare officers routinely carried out actions of a similar kind without a care. To explain how this was almost certainly so takes us to what Raimond Gaita has argued lies at the very heart of racism: the blindness to the reality that other people, seen through the prism of racism as lesser, simpler, more primitive, can experience, with the same intensity and depth as we do, love and attachment, bereavement and grief.

It is impossible to read the stories of the separation of Aboriginal children without stumbling, time and again, upon non-Aboriginal Australians for whom this incapacity to grasp the depth of suffering of Aborigines lies at the heart of the harm they inflict. In the passage I quoted at the beginning, Margaret Tucker was aware that her schoolteacher, although not his wife, faced with a situation not faced before, was incapable, as she puts it, of taking into account that 'Aboriginal hearts could break down with despair and helplessness, the same as any other human hearts'. I have referred to the article by 'Physicus' in the *West Australian* in defence of the policy of biological assimilation. His advocacy of state-arranged marriages went thus: 'Love as we know it did not animate the breasts of the blacks of Australia.' Earlier in the century the local Western Australian protector, James Isdall, explained his involvement in the forcible removal of part-Aboriginal babies from their mothers in the following way: 'I would not hesitate for one moment to separate any half-caste from its Aboriginal mother, no matter how frantic her momentary grief might be at that time. They soon forget their offspring.' The wrong that he did was done because he thought of Aborigines as incapable of feeling with the intensity or fixity of Europeans, in short because he did not think of Aborigines as fully human.

One of the most important aspects of *Bringing Them Home* is precisely to place on record the permanence of the grief and the guilt many Aboriginal mothers experienced, after being separated from their children, for the rest of their lives. We learn in its pages of a woman so ashamed of having surrendered her children that she carried on her person, throughout her life, letters testifying to her good character. We learn of a family which, every sunrise and sunset, for thirty-two years, ritually mourned the loss of their daughter.

V

Many Australians now accept that the practice of child removal was wrong. Many, however, also think it wrong to condemn earlier generations for their role in this policy. Like Senator Herron in his letter to Frank Brennan they think of this policy as misguided but well intentioned. Is it not all too easy to judge simply and harshly with the wisdom of hindsight?

It is true that a certain kind of callow judgment, which condescends to the past from the standpoint of contemporary conventional wisdom, is the enemy of historical understanding. Nonetheless, I have never been able to understand how we think it is either possible or preferable to contemplate the past with moral faculties disengaged. Far from leading us into complacent self-satisfaction, a moral engagement with the past and an alertness to the injustices of other times ought, if anything, to remind us of the precariousness of our judgments about ourselves and of the need for searching self-questioning and self-criticism.

It seems to me important to remember also that not all Australians, in regard to child removal and biological assimilation, were morally blind. Among such Australians no one was more impressive than Neville's most unrelenting enemy, the maternal feminist and supporter of Aboriginal women's rights, Mary Bennett. At the Royal Commission in 1934 she condemned the practice of child removal thus: 'Many of these poor children are parted from their mothers...but first for years they suffer from the misery of hunted animals, always running away from the police... always in fear that at any moment they may be torn away... They are captured at all ages, as infants in arms, perhaps, and until they are grown up. They are not safe until they are dead...'

For her the solution to the problem of the half-caste child was very far indeed from the kind of solutions preferred by her age. 'Institutionalism seems to destroy all sentiment in the character,' she quoted, and then went on. 'The only remedy is for them to be given back what they have lost—human ties. They need fellowship, and they will get it only among the mother's people... They need *their* homes, *their* families, and not to be interfered with.'

To Mary Bennett the policy of breeding out the colour spoke as plainly as it does to us. Cook's 'real policy', she wrote, was 'still the extermination of the unhappy native race, and the leaving of the most unfortunate native women at the disposal of lustful white men—this policy is euphemistically described by Australian officialdom as the absorption of the native race and the breeding out of colour!!! We shall be better able to evaluate this policy when another race applies it to ourselves as the absorption of the white race and the breeding out of white people!!!'

Mary Bennett's was an exceptional voice. It is also one worth remembering and cherishing.

VI

This brings me to my final question. Does the systematic and protracted removal of children of mixed descent from their mothers and families amount to a policy of genocide? This is a large and terrible question. In my mind many of the issues surrounding it are still unsettled. I will say here only a few words.

There are two ways of approaching the matter. One is legal; to appraise the policies and practices of Australian governments against international law, most importantly against the United Nations Convention on the Prevention and Punishment of

Genocide. This is what is done in *Bringing Them Home*. There a case is mounted to show that, from a legal point of view, genocide is committed when governments forcibly transfer children from a racial, ethnic or national group with the purpose of destroying that group. According to this legal argument genocide may occur even where no killing is involved, even where the destruction is of a sizeable part of the group, not the whole, and even where the intentions of those implementing the policy, are, in part, to benefit the members of the group. *Bringing Them Home* quotes from a delegate to the general assembly of the UN who summarised the position of those who succeeded in having child removal included in the UN convention on genocide:

> The forced transfer of children to a group where they would be given an education different from that of their own group, and would have new customs, a new religion and probably a new language, was in practice tantamount to the destruction of their group, whose future depended on that generation of children. Such transfer might be made from a group with a low standard of civilisation… to a highly civilised group…yet if the intent of the transfer were the destruction of the group, a crime of genocide would undoubtedly have been committed.

This summary in general fits the facts of the Australian case, with, however, one important caveat. So far as I know the policy of child removal was concerned not with full-blood Aborigines but with Aborigines of mixed descent. For the purposes of the argument about genocide this is not a minor caveat. I am not sure whether the legal argument is sound. I am surprised, however, that those who flatly and almost superciliously deny the charge of genocide have not felt compelled to show where the weaknesses of the legal arguments in *Bringing Them Home* lie.

My own approach to the question of genocide is not so much legal as historical and conceptual. In my thinking on the question of genocide as a general concept certain comments of Hannah Arendt in *Eichmann in Jerusalem* have been central. Arendt here wrote of the crime of genocide as driven by the desire to make a distinct people 'disappear from the earth'. She saw such a desire as an attack on the idea of 'human diversity' which she took to be at the core of the very idea of 'mankind' or 'humanity'. For her the crime of genocide is committed when one group decides that another group is unfit to inhabit the earth and takes action to eliminate them. Because the Nazi attack upon the Jews was the subject of her book—and because that attack involved mass murder on an almost unimaginable scale—she did not consider the question of whether genocide could be committed without the use of murderous means.

It is with the bearing of Arendt's argument on the question of Aboriginal child removal that I have been wrestling this year. The argument is too complicated to be pursued in detail now. Let me conclude by outlining the present state of my thinking on the questions raised.

Firstly, I am persuaded, both legally and conceptually, that the crime of genocide in the Arendtian sense can be committed, as Raimond Gaita has argued, without the use of murderous means. The sterilisation of an entire ethnic or racial group would seem to me, quite uncontroversially, to constitute genocide. The fact that violence against Aborigines was not only not used but was genuinely unthinkable to those who designed child-removal policies is not a knockdown argument against the accusation of genocide as some deriders of *Bringing Them Home* seem to believe.

Secondly, in regard to the question of the Aborigines it seems to me also uncontroversial that in the 1930s, in Western Australia and the Northern Territory, the key administrators in Aboriginal matters planned and, to a very limited extent, tried to implement policies aiming at the elimination of Aboriginal people of mixed descent. It seems to me important to acknowledge that these policies were not driven by an idea that the Aborigines were, as a people, unfit to inhabit the earth, but rather by the idea that the elimination of 'half-castes' would constitute an unambiguous good. This terrible thought was shared by a large part of public opinion in the inter-war period. It was even shared, as Ron Brunton has argued, by two Aboriginal activists of mixed descent. That these two thought the solution to the problem they posed was to breed out their own Aboriginal blood bears some resemblance to one of the most abject Jewish responses to European anti-Semitism—Jewish self-hatred.

Thirdly, it seems to me significant that while practices of child removal, similar to those of Western Australia and the Northern Territory in the 1930s, occurred throughout Australia both before and after the thirties, those practices did not necessarily rely on any attempt to eliminate the mixed descent population by biological assimilation. Especially after World War II, the motive driving child-removal policies shifted everywhere from biological to socio-cultural assimilation. Unlike the legal case mounted in *Bringing Them Home*, socio-cultural assimilation does not seem to me to be describable as genocide. To say this is, of course, not the same as saying the policy was well intentioned (in my sense of that term) let alone benign.

Fourthly, it seems to me important to acknowledge that the administrators in Western Australia and the Northern Territory who were implicated in the policies of biological assimilation did not plan or hope for the elimination of full-blood Aborigines as a distinct people. But it also seems to me important to recognise that their desire for the elimination of Aborigines of mixed descent was in no way moderated by their conviction that, in the fullness of time, the full-blood Aborigines of Australia were certain, or at least highly likely, to be extinct. Let it be remembered that in 1937 A. O. Neville could look forward to the time when even the existence of an Aboriginal people in Australia would no longer be remembered. Not one of his colleagues was shocked by his words.

My position on the question of genocide comes, then, to this. If a case is to be made that genocide was committed it can only be made with regard to a particular policy plan, biological assimilation; at a particular time, the 1930s; and in particular places, the Northern Territory and Western Australia. And even here the case would have to concede, in my opinion, that the policy was more one of intentions than effective actions, and that, after 1940, it was, everywhere in Australia, abandoned in both thought and deed.

Let me, then, finally say this. Even if the charge of genocide remains contentious between people of good will, as I suspect it might, that does nothing to change the fact that the policy of child removal constitutes one of the most shameful, if not *the* most shameful episode in twentieth-century Australian history. That our government refuses to apologise to the victims of that policy, now that the facts are known has deepened that shame.

1997

PART TWO

PARTY GAMES

The Aborted Revolution

IN July 1992 John Hewson promised an audience of Western Australian Liberals 'the most significant revolution that this country has seen in decades'. In March 1993 this revolution was aborted. The Liberal Party now confronts its deepest crisis since its foundation.

All revolutions have intellectual origins. Dr Hewson's revolution was rooted in the remarkable 1970s revival, throughout the English-speaking world and beyond, of pure free-market economics—most importantly of the Austrian school of Friedrich Hayek and the Chicago school of Milton Friedman.

All revolutions also have political foundations. Dr Hewson's revolution originated in 1980 in a series of secret meetings with Liberal Party politicians (John Hyde, Jim Carlton), prominent Fraser government staffers (David Kemp, Cliff Walsh), politically minded academic economists (Richard Blandy, Michael Porter) and activist businessmen (Hugh Morgan, John Elliott). The group called itself Crossroads. It was, as Paul Kelly points out, the beginnings of a Liberal counter-establishment. At this time John Hewson was on its fringe.

A set of fixed politico-ideological objectives, for the transformation of the Australian economy along free-market lines, emerged from this group: financial deregulation; the rapid removal of all protection for manufacturing and rural industries; dismantling of all aspects of the centralised system of wage fixation; the privatisation of public sector business; small government via the partial withering away of the welfare state; micro-economic reform of transport and communications.

In part, the Liberal counter-establishment had the Whitlam government in its sights. It was blamed for the ruinous growth of wages, bureaucracy and public expenditure. More deeply these Liberals aimed their fire at the two great pillars of the Deakinite edifice: arbitration and protectionism. A special anger, however, was reserved for Malcolm Fraser. Fraser was portrayed as the failed leader, the prophet who might have delivered his people to the promised land of deregulation, but who lacked the wisdom or courage so to do. The Seven Wasted Years of Fraser was one of the foundation myths of the Hewson revolution.

During the 1980s the free-market party developed a formidable momentum: partly as a result of the excitement generated in the early years of the Thatcher and Reagan governments; partly because of the work of a number of associated think-tanks (IPA, CIS, AIPP, the Sydney Institute, the Tasman Institute); partly because of the near-universal support given these ideas by the finance and political journalists of the quality press; partly because it had the support of almost the entire corps of academic and public-service economists. The ideas of the Liberal counter-establishment passed rapidly from the margins to the centre of the Australian political culture, having of course an enormous impact on the policy of the Hawke and Keating Labor governments.

Under this pressure the Old Liberal-National Party collapsed. In 1983 and 1984 the last conservative Deakinites—Malcolm

Fraser and Doug Anthony—withdrew from party politics. Opposition to the radical free-market cause, restricted now to the Liberal Party left wing (Macphee, Puplick), was short-lived and feeble. As early as the Liberal Party program of 1984, the opposition had embraced the free-market agenda, at least in principle, more or less *tout court*.

For the post-Fraser Liberal Party the problem was not the definition of ideology but the attainment of power. For seven years the Liberal Party (to paraphrase Paul Kelly) was crippled by an unresolvable conflict between one leader, Andrew Peacock, with style but no substance, and another, John Howard, with substance but no style. Howard sought to fashion a marriage between social conservatism and economic radicalism. Peacock simply sought to become prime minister—wet, dry or damp.

Howard was the most ill-used of the conservative politicians of the eighties. He was, in reality, the only Liberal Party leader in the post-Fraser years with social touch, with a real understanding of the hopes and fears of ordinary Australians. However, despite his intelligence, he never gained the respect of the media. More importantly, despite his 'ideological soundness', he never gained the confidence of the party's powerbrokers. When a strange alliance of entrepreneurial rednecks and free-market ideologues joined the bizarre Joh-for-Canberra push in 1987 Howard was doomed. The powerbrokers restored Peacock for the 1990 election, but once again without result.

In the post-election vacuum, Dr Hewson was handed the Liberal Party leadership without so much as a struggle and after a mere three years in parliament. The counter-establishment was now poised for power.

Unlike Peacock, Hewson was no ideological sceptic. Indeed he was drier than the Nullarbor. Unlike Howard, he had little personal interest in or feel for the conservative social agenda. He was, in reality, interested in only one thing—the transformation of the Australian economy (and society) along radical, free-market lines.

For Hewson, politics was merely a means to this end. He was the anti-political politician. Moreover, he equated pragmatism and moderation with timidity and caution. He was the anti-conservative conservative.

By November 1991, Dr Hewson and his inner circle (drawn largely from the Liberal counter-establishment) had produced a detailed and radical plan—*Fightback!* The pace of the Hawke government's anti-protectionist, privatising and micro-economic reform programs was to be accelerated. The centralised wage-fixing system was, effectively, to be dismantled. The size of government was substantially to be reduced. Most importantly, Dr Hewson produced a massive and complex taxation reform. Its economic heart was the reduction of taxation on business. The part which interested the general public most deeply, however, was the creation of a vast new consumption tax, the GST, which was to pay for the cuts in business, petrol and income taxes. Astonishingly enough, the Coalition accepted the entirety of this radical program without even a serious discussion. Only the sugar-tariff rebels of the National Party and one Liberal backbencher, Ken Aldred, broke the strange silence of these years.

As it happened, the arrival of Dr Hewson to the leadership of the opposition coincided with the arrival in Australia of the deepest recession since the end of World War II. In an obvious way the recession was of political benefit to Dr Hewson: the electorate was in posse mood. In a less obvious way, however, the recession proved a lethal threat to a politician in the Hewson style. The nation was in no mood for even more experiment. Moreover, the benefits the good doctor promised were rather theoretical; the medicine he dispensed, the GST, altogether too real.

During the second half of 1992, Dr Hewson became stubborn and unapproachable. He was doing what was right. If the nation did not like what he offered, and to judge by the increasingly alarming opinion polls it did not, so be it.

The story of what happened inside the machinery of the Liberal Party in December 1992 has not yet been revealed. According to some accounts Dr Hewson would not have held the leadership by Christmas if he had not agreed to compromise at the last minute. In what was probably the most difficult moment of his political life *Fightback!* was transformed into *Fightback! 2*.

The recession, he now explained, was deeper than even he had anticipated. Two billion dollars was allocated to tax incentives for business; three billion was found for special government projects. Apparently, after all, one could spend one's way out of a recession. In a democracy, he now remembered, it was vital to listen to the people. Dr Hewson had listened. The people had told him to retain dole payments after nine months of unemployment and, above all, to remove the GST from food.

The changes to *Fightback!* proved insufficient. The electorate was torn between two negative impulses: the desire to punish Paul Keating and the fear of Dr Hewson. Fear proved stronger. The GST was not the only source of anxiety. More deeply, the electorate feared the impact on their lives of the new Hewson style of ideologically driven politics.

With the electorate's unambiguous decision against Dr Hewson on 13 March, the Liberal Party finds itself, quite suddenly, without a plausible program, style or leader. The party will have either to elect a new leader or a new people. Genuine statesmanship within the party is now required. It is hard to see from where it will come. For too long the backbenchers have been following their leader like sheep. The Liberal Party has suffered no mere electoral loss; an era in the history of conservative politics has drawn to its end.

1993

Dr Hewson and Middle Australia

I am not convinced that the truly catastrophic performance of the Liberal Party in the federal election of March 1993 has yet sunk in.

Australian political history tells us that there are two circumstances which turn voters against a government: a serious split in the Cabinet or a sudden economic downturn. During the Keating government both conditions were amply fulfilled. And yet the Liberal Party lost seats to Labor.

Nor was this catastrophe an aberration. The depth of the decline of the federal Liberal Party can be demonstrated thus. Between the election of Menzies in 1949 and the defeat of Fraser in 1983, the Liberals ruled in Canberra for all but three years. If, however, Keating wins the next election the ALP will have enjoyed sixteen consecutive years in office. Surely there is something here to explain.

In recent weeks two interesting insider analyses of the Liberal Party's decline have been mounted. From the left of the party Dr Michael Wooldridge has argued that the root of the Liberals' problem is their failure to attract the votes of fashionable and conspicuous sub-electorates—women, ethnics, greens, gays, the artistic community and so on. From the right, Peter Costello has argued almost precisely the opposite case. For Costello the capture of the ALP by the new class has presented the Liberal Party with a unique opportunity to make inroads into working-class Australia (on the model of the so-called 'Reagan Democrats') which it has, to its cost, thus far failed to grasp.

I have a third, more radical, suggestion to make about the electoral failure of the Liberal Party: namely that since the end of the Fraser government the Liberal Party has gradually lost touch with the socio-economic values of its fundamental base—the vast urban and property-owning middle and lower middle class.

This is not, I will admit, an area where precision is easy. Nevertheless at least initial evidence for this proposition can be provided. I will try to do this by a simple comparison of the values of Dr Hewson, as recorded in his speeches as Liberal Party leader before the last election, and the values of middle Australia as measured by the opinion pollsters.

Under Dr Hewson, the Liberal Party, between 1990 and 1993, stood above all other things for something called individualism. 'The story of human progress,' was for John Hewson 'the story of how we have learned to focus on the individual rather than the clan.' His preferred form of individualism was economistic and rugged. 'I suspect that worries about occupational health, job security, leave loadings, and lump sums,' he told one of his audiences, 'never entered the heads of those who tamed the bush and worked the mines.'

According to Dr Hewson this naturally Australian form of individualism was opposed by a variety of forces which he generally called 'vested interests'. Such vested interests included the trade unions who now exercised their traditional tyranny through the Accord, the 'industrial relations club' and the arbitration system. They also included 'staggeringly pessimistic', inward-looking

Australian businessmen whose handout mentality had been acquired during the long slumber of protectionism. 'It is the historic destiny of the Liberal Party,' Hewson proclaimed in his Deakin lecture, 'to send industrial arbitration and protective tariffs to join White Australia in history's rubbish bin.'

The worst of all vested interests was, however, the public sector and the mentality it fostered. The public sector had 'squeezed out' the private sector, the only source of what Hewson referred to as 'real jobs'. It had 'squashed individual incentive and restricted individual freedom'.

Whitlam was responsible for what Dr Hewson once called AIDS—Acquired Income Dependency Syndrome. The welfare state and the 'Balmain basketweavers' who serviced it, peddled a false idea of compassion, appealing to 'the lowest common denominator'. As he put it: 'Giving people a choice is the compassion that liberates—just giving is the compassion that suffocates.' Hewson favoured small government.

As Dr Hewson understood, to clip the wings of those key vested interests was no small matter. He proclaimed himself the leader of nothing less than a Liberal revolution. 'I think we are about the most significant revolution that this country has seen in decades. We are going to jettison all the bad attitudes and the bad policies that were triggered with the arrival of the age of Whitlam.' Or on another occasion: 'You cannot have too much change and you cannot do it quickly enough.'

The interesting political question concerning the Liberal Party, at the high noon of its commitment to economic rationalism, is how far this program and rhetoric on balance attracted, and how far it repelled or frightened, what might be called middle Australia. Let us take a brief look at the results of some recent opinion polls.

Perhaps the most dramatic discovery is that Australians have been almost entirely untouched by the anti-protectionist sentiments propagated daily over the past ten years by the media, the

Canberra mandarinate, the Labor government and, even more enthusiastically, by the Liberal opposition.

In January 1993 Newspoll asked a sample of 1200 Australians whether they agreed or disagreed with the use of tariffs. Eighty per cent agreed. An even higher proportion, 88 per cent, approved of the provision by government of incentives to Australian business. The same percentage agreed that jobs were indeed being lost because of cheap imports. In September 1993 Newspoll asked a similar sample whether they agreed with the idea of government-procurement policies for Australian business. Ninety-five per cent agreed, 87 per cent strongly.

Against the wisdom of their rulers, then, there are few issues on which Australians are more united than on the value of protection. Dr Hewson's complaints about the slowness of the Labor government's tariff-cutting policies were not, to put it mildly, to the electoral benefit of his party. Nor did it help his party when he characterised government-procurement programs or anti-dumping measures as disguised protectionism. By instinct Australians are more economic nationalist than economic rationalist.

What, then, of the question of small government? While it is perfectly true that many Australians would like their taxation to be lower, this hope is not at all linked to a general desire to wind back the welfare state. Consistently in the polls Australians claim increased welfare spending is more important to them than reduced taxation. On one occasion, in 1988, the Morgan poll put this issue bluntly. Australians were asked to choose between greater economic growth and lower social equity, or greater social equity and lower economic growth. When pushed thus, 63 per cent favoured social equity over economic growth, 33 per cent favoured economic growth over social equity.

And what of trade unionism? Here Australian attitudes appear to be rather ambivalent. In late 1992, on the one hand, 57 per cent of Australians thought that, on balance, trade unions had been good for their country. On the other, 62 per cent thought they had too much power. Eighty-seven per cent thought trade unionism should be voluntary; 78 per cent, however, believed that employees should have the right to strike. Compared with ten years earlier fewer Australians regarded trade unions as a positive force in our history. But then again fewer believed that they had too much power or caused unemployment. Judging by such surveys a party like the Liberal Party, set upon radical industrial relations reform, must negotiate a careful passage between Australians' real concerns about the overweening power of trade unions and their equally real support for their survival. Middle Australia would probably prefer the gradualism of Laurie Brereton to the radicalism of the H. R. Nicholls Society.

Let us examine one final issue: the Liberal Party's commitment to systematic and radical reform. On balance this seems more likely, at least on the basis of the surveys, to ring bells of alarm in middle Australia than to mobilise support.

For Australians are, at present, unusually insecure. Take, as one index, the fear of unemployment. Only 65 per cent now feel their present job is safe. As recently as the mid-1980s 80 per cent felt safe. Thirty-two per cent now see a real possibility of being unemployed in the near future. Only 39 per cent now think that in this circumstance they would quickly find another job. This is not the kind of society which is likely to be attracted to calls for more change and more uncertainty and to programs of radical reform.

Contemporary Australians are, in general, not ideological but existential conservatives. Asked in 1993 what was most important to them 35 per cent said a secure life, 27 per cent a family-centred life, 16 per cent the 'good life', 10 per cent a stimulating life, 8 per cent a life of achievement. An understanding of this temper has eluded the Hewson Liberals.

My conclusion is straightforward. The program and rhetoric of the Liberal Party, as it developed progressively in the decade between 1983 and 1993, was based on a deeply flawed premise: of an electorate suspicious of the state; keen to deconstruct the

Deakinite settlement; hostile to protectionism, the welfare state and moderate trade unionism; enthused by a rhetoric of rugged market individualism.

The falseness of this premise goes a long way towards the explanation of the Liberal Party's decade of impotence.

1993

Labor (Still) in Power

THERE have been, so far at least, only two genuinely illuminating interpretations of Australian politics during the 1980s—Paul Kelly's masterpiece *The End of Certainty* and now Phillip Chubb's television documentary, *Labor in Power*.

They are, however, altogether different kinds of interpretation. Kelly's book is fundamentally optimistic. His purpose is to show how, during the 1980s, a body of radical, free-market ideas—concerning financial and then labour-market deregulation, anti-protectionism, privatisation and so on—gradually worked its way through both Australian political parties, transforming in the process a sleepy, inward-looking, resource-based economy into a vibrant manufacturing, export-oriented, internationally competitive one. Unfortunately for Kelly, the Australia of the early 1990s, at the critical moment of his narrative, settled into a state of what appeared to be semi-permanent recession. Accordingly, his book ended not, as planned, with optimism and self-confidence but in muddle and uncertainty.

Phillip Chubb has, in *Labor in Power*, produced an altogether darker interpretation of the 1980s. He is concerned only secondarily with the transformative economic program of the Labor government. His primary concern is with the protracted power struggle between the prime minister, Bob Hawke and his treasurer, Paul Keating, which was played out, for the most part beneath the surface, from the election of 1984 to the second, successful Keating challenge to Hawke of Christmas 1991. Unlike Paul Kelly, Chubb is essentially a moralist. He has produced a fascinating investigation into the nature (and corruption) of power.

The starting point for Chubb's narrative is Keating's vague, private conviction that in 1980 Hawke had promised to pass to him the Labor prime ministership after something like two terms.

As revealed through the eyes of Chubb, Paul Keating emerges slowly as a politician in the grip of three powerful anti-Hawke emotions: resentment, contempt and, in a curious way, envy. Hawke, he convinced himself, had seized the prime ministerial prize too easily, without having served his required apprenticeship inside either the Labor Party or the parliament. In this, as in so much else, Hawke was a very lucky man. With the true *hauteur* of the Labor Party aristocrat, Keating says Hawke did not need to 'weary him' with the view that he held the prime ministership because of his personal qualities or his 'innate glory'. In his view Hawke's effortless passage to power entitled him merely to a modest run. The arrogance of this comment is, quite simply, breathtaking.

By 1984 Keating's early resentment at Hawke's glide to power was deepened by growing feelings of contempt. His response to the heroin addiction of Hawke's daughter, which paralysed the prime minister during the disastrous election campaign of 1984, was not so much pity as disdain.

For Keating, Hawke's political judgment was, from this moment, fatally impaired. His decision, for example, made on the run in 1984, to hold a post-election tax summit, was preposterous. Hawke's indecisiveness was also by now, largely thanks to Keating, becoming legendary. It was, as Chubb establishes, almost certainly Keating and not Senator Peter Walsh who coined the phrase 'old jelly-back' for the pre-tax-summit Hawke.

By the mid-1980s, Keating saw himself as the real prime minister of Australia and Bob Hawke as an increasingly pathetic pretender. He was no longer willing to cover for Hawke, no longer willing—in a phrase he uses three times—to be Hawke's 'handmaiden'.

This was not the way things appeared to Hawke. Where Keating was driven by a resentment which deepened as his self-confidence soared, Hawke was from the first oblivious to all this, locked as he was into the myth of his own indispensability. Hawke's likeable staffer, Richard Farmer, found something almost 'eerie' in the calm of Bob Hawke on the night of his prime ministerial election. For Hawke, on 5 March 1983, destiny was simply following its predestined course. When, five years later, John Dawkins came to Hawke to ask him to go, he found him not only in a stubborn but also in an almost trance-like state.

Bob Hawke was the embodiment of political narcissism. The adoring people were the mirror into which he gazed deeply. Secure in the love of the people, he felt untouchable. His public persona brought to mind for Neville Wran the Oscar Wilde aphorism: 'the flatterer is seldom interrupted'.

Only the realists of the Hawke camp, the so-called Manchu court—like the dourly anti-romantic Bob Hogg—did the interrupting, trying to rouse Hawke from his dreamy self-absorption, to get him to see how Keating was systematically undermining his authority. With reluctance Hawke was drawn into the rough and tumble of battle with Keating—and then only in an inept and ultimately ineffectual way. In 1988, shortly after the budget which was to bring home the bacon, Hawke damned Keating with faintest praise. Keating was doing a commendable job, but he was by no means indispensable to the Hawke government.

Keating exploded. Graham Richardson, the only remaining political bridge between the Australian prime minister and treasurer, tried to patch up a reconciliation. Keating was unappeasable. By late 1988 the potential danger of their rift had become so obvious that both agreed to swear a formal, secret oath at Kirribilli House, in front of trusted seconds—the bemused Bill Kelty and the bored Sir Peter Abeles. Keating agreed to call off his guerilla campaign; Hawke to hand him the prime ministership of Australia following the election of 1990.

The fact that this deal implied the necessity of misleading the Australian electorate over Hawke's willingness to serve out a fourth term bothered no one. Of greater concern to Keating was the fact that, after the election of 1990, Hawke seemed to suffer from a bout of Kirribilli amnesia. In reality, Hawke was now struggling manfully to find a plausible excuse to break his oath. Eventually he discovered it in Paul Keating's strange, impromptu address to the National Press Club—where he likened himself, much to the amusement of the nation, to Placido Domingo, and where he bemoaned the absence of any great leader, thus far, in the history of Australia.

The final battle was now joined. So nasty had things become that Hawke was putting it around, at least through his staff, that if Keating succeeded in wresting the prime ministership from him, Australia would be ruled by 'a couple' who despised their country. The struggle had now really plumbed the depths.

Not all is dark, however. In *Labor in Power* we are given an unforgettable, and in many ways, endearing portrait of the Third Labor Man, Graham Richardson. At times of parliamentary crisis all phones led to Graham. Like Hawke and Keating, he was part of the tribal right. Much more than them, however, he was almost entirely uninterested in ideology, policy or even consistency. It was he who, from Tokyo, defused the MX-missile crisis—in favour of the left. It was he who forced through the caucus the decision to sell uranium to France, a decision he regarded as politically ludicrous.

Only once, during the 1980s, was Richardson—almost certainly to his own astonishment—bitten by the bug of belief.

He became, for a time at least, a sincere greenie. No doubt this was severely embarrassing to him. Happily he found himself able to justify this unanticipated flight into idealism. Environmentalism, he assured himself, was not only spiritually noble, it was also good politics. His conscience was clear.

In the broader Hawke–Keating struggle, Richardson appears to have been the pivotal figure. Until 1990 he held Keating at bay for Hawke. In the ministerial reshuffle of that year he came to the view that Hawke had hoped to drive him out of politics into the high commissionership at London. Allowing this impression to form in Richardson's mind was one of Hawke's most fateful mistakes.

While these political gods were playing out their power struggles, for those who lived on earth the Australian economy was slowly grinding to a halt. The Treasury was now, as it had never been before in the history of the federation, the dominant force in our political life. 'Treasury,' David Morgan reminds us here, 'always had its own agenda. It got more of its agenda up in the decade of the Hawke–Keating government than for the rest of the post-war period combined.' It found in Keating a vigorous advocate and naive true believer. In the 1980s Australia came as close as it is ever likely to come to having a Treasury-led government.

In 1986 the Treasury came to the view, following the April balance of payments figure, that the economy was 'stuffed'. Keating transferred their warning to the nation with his banana-republic remark. In 1987, after the stock-market crash, Treasury and the Reserve Bank decided to keep monetary policy loose. Once more, Keating obliged, this time engineering the mad credit boom of the late 1980s. Finally, during 1989, again on Treasury and Reserve Bank advice, Keating raised interest rates to almost unprecedented levels. As the nation groaned under their weight, Treasury assured Keating, and he assured us, that there would be a 'soft landing'.

An isolated band of truthsayers—led by the redoubtable John Button—whose feet were firmly planted on earth, warned otherwise. Keating and the Treasury mandarins dismissed the mounting evidence of impending catastrophe as 'anecdotal'. As the Hawke–Keating power struggle approached its climax, the economy was being driven on to disaster.

Apart from a bitter aftertaste, Phillip Chubb's tour de force left me with two abiding impressions. The first concerned the nature of political power in contemporary Australia. While the mythic foundations and the formal structures of our constitutional edifice are solidly democratic, the animating spirit of our political life appears to be becoming increasingly oligarchic. We are ever more powerfully controlled by the narrowly based cabals at the heart of executive government.

Labor in Power is, if nothing else, witness to the need for a revival in the spirit of parliamentarianism. In a truly parliamentary system no national summits of executive governments, big business representatives and trade union bosses would dare to assemble in a parliamentary chamber. In a true parliamentary system no prime minister, even in the heat of debate, could call one of our houses 'unrepresentative swill' and survive.

Another question arose in my mind. During these power struggles what was the Canberra press gallery doing? For almost seven years—apart from the occasional public flare-up between Hawke and Keating—the national press gallery conveyed a convincing and, as it turns out, utterly inaccurate impression of the formidable and effective prime ministerial–treasurer *team* which was in charge of the nation's affairs. How came it that so many were misled by so few for so long about the nature of political reality?

1993

A Voyage of Rediscovery

EVERYONE would agree that, on the eve of its fiftieth anniversary, the federal Liberal Party is in considerable trouble. There would be far less agreement as to its cause. In my view at the heart of the contemporary Liberal Party's difficulties is the question of identity.

It is an oddity of Australian political history that from the time Robert Menzies brought his party to power in 1949 until the time Dr Hewson lost the unlosable election in 1993—with the possible exception of the short and troubled Gorton interlude—the Liberal Party has never faced a real crisis of identity. Under Menzies and his minor successors, Holt and McMahon, the identity of the Liberal Party was clear. It stood for a pragmatic, protectionist and welfarist version of capitalism and against Labor Party socialism. It stood for anticommunism, the British connection and the American alliance against the Labor Party's ambivalence on these questions. Most deeply it defended the values and interests of the expanding suburban middle class and, through its allies—the Country Party and the DLP—the values and interests of the bush and of the most traditional parts of the Catholic working and lower middle class. On the foundation of this identity the Liberal Party governed Australia for almost a quarter-century.

By the early 1970s parts of the Menzies foundation had begun to crumble. Because of the Vietnam War the influence of both anti-Americanism and anti-anticommunism spread, for the first time, beyond the intelligentsia and Labor Party true believers. Because of British entry into the Common Market the material basis of the British link collapsed. Most importantly of all, because of the coming of a kind of middle-class cultural revolution—seen most dramatically in the decline of religion and the rise of sexual liberation—even the most solid social pillars of the Menzies Liberal Party, the great conservative, suburban middle class, became unsteady. It was time for change.

In the short term at least, the disasters of the Whitlam government—not only its economic incompetence but also the comic-opera indiscipline of its ministry (captured by the fleeting appearance of Tirath Khemlani on our national political stage)—masked from the Liberal Party the need for adaptation to a new world. It is no disparagement of Malcolm Fraser's achievement to point out that he won two of his elections and possibly the third because of the shadow Gough Whitlam cast over the back gardens of suburban Australia.

It was only when the Fraser government fell during the drought of 1983 that the Liberal Party, for the first time since its creation, felt the need to rethink its identity. This involved, however, no identity crisis. What was remarkable was how swiftly and smoothly the transformation occurred. Under Andrew Peacock, but even more clearly under John Howard and John Hewson, the Liberal Party abandoned the pragmatic, protectionist and welfarist dimensions of its traditional identity and embraced, in their stead, the most full-blown version of market liberalism Australia had experienced since the 1930s.

During the period from 1983 to 1993 the Liberal leadership routinely spoke of the Fraser government as seven wasted years. It systematically drove the party's economic wets out of the party or underground. It pioneered policy directions—in regard to privatisation, enterprise bargaining and the abandonment of interventionist industry policy—which the Hawke government first attacked as New Right barbarism and later adopted as sheerest commonsense.

Eventually the Liberal Party produced in the economics professor Dr Hewson, and in his blueprint for the transformation of Australia, *Fightback!*, the leader and program perfectly suited to the party's bold, new, post-Fraser economic rationalist identity. If Hewson and *Fightback!* had triumphed in March 1993 the Liberal Party would not, of course, have faced any crisis of identity. As we know, however, they did not succeed. Inevitably as a consequence of this disastrous loss—the strangest in the party's first fifty years—the Liberal Party was plunged into crisis.

On the surface this crisis concerned leadership. Against all political reason the captain, who had singlehandedly steered his ship onto the rocks of catastrophe, retained his post. Insofar as he tried to do anything, Dr Hewson now tried to combine in his person the leadership of the rationalists on the economic front and of the moderates on the cultural front. As a moderate he hinted that he was a republican. As a rationalist he appeared psychologically incapable of burying *Fightback!* Eventually, over *Mabo*, the strain began to show. As a moderate Hewson wanted to appear sympathetic to the Aboriginal cause. Yet as a rationalist he was worried about the impact of *Mabo* on mining. In his confusion, on the day when the parliament passed its *Mabo* legislation, the future 'conscience of the Liberal Party' called the new law, of all things, 'Australia's day of shame'. He had somehow pressed the wrong cliché button.

Unhappily Dr Hewson's identity crisis was not purely personal. It reflected strains which could be found near the centre of the party. Because of the trauma of March 1993, the Liberal Party was forced to abandon the hard edge of its economic-rationalist program and rhetoric. In their hearts most Liberals suspected that it was its radicalism which had driven workers, pensioners, teachers and public servants back to Labor. The Liberal Party was resolved not to repeat this mistake. Yet it was also clear that the sudden disappearance of economic rationalism as a source of identity had left, within the party, a vast ideological black hole. After the shock of 1993 the Liberals knew what they recently had been and what they presently were not. They were far less sure about what they now were.

With the recent victory of the 'progressive conservative' Downer–Costello leadership team some Liberals have hoped that the vacuum left by the collapse of economic rationalism might be filled by a reactive social conservatism. Since the 1993 election, they point out, the agenda of Australian politics has been transformed. It is no longer dominated by economic questions—unemployment, taxation, foreign debt—but by those cultural issues—the republic, Aboriginal reconciliation, women's and gay rights—placed on the agenda by Paul Keating. With the loss of the economic-rationalist identity, is it not possible, they argue, for the new Liberal leadership to challenge Keating over the republic or *Mabo* or the traditional family?

For two reasons I think it is not. The first relates to the media. Contemporary Australian journalists are openly hostile to all expressions of conservatism. It is no accident that since coming to the leadership of the Liberal Party, Alexander Downer has slipped on a number of cultural banana skins—over the Adelaide Club, the republic, *Mabo*, gay rights, the League of Rights—thrown in his path by the press corps and Mr Keating's media minders.

The media, however, is not the only problem. The cultural issues placed on the agenda by Keating are precisely the issues which unite his own party and create confusion within the enemy camp. These are the kind of political issues leaders relish. Questions like the republic or *Mabo* or gay rights obviously divide moderates from conservatives within the Liberal Party. Less obviously they also divide dispositional conservatives along generational lines.

For the older generation of Liberals—like, say, John Howard—opposition to the Keating cultural agenda comes easily. For intelligent younger conservatives, like Alexander Downer or Peter Costello, who came into adulthood during the cultural revolution of the sixties and seventies, the matter is not so simple. They are torn between a nostalgia for the social and moral stability of the Menzies world; a repudiation of many of its ethnic and sexual prejudices; and a clear-sighted recognition that it represents, for better or worse, a world that has been irrevocably lost. Because of the divisions between conservatives and moderates and because of the ambivalence of the younger conservatives the Liberal Party's engagement with the politics of Keating's cultural agenda time and again plays into the hands of the Labor government and its media supporters. As a recipe for the future identity of the party it would prove a disaster.

The new leadership represents the first serious attempt by the Liberal Party, since the election of 1993, to find a passage between the twin perils posed by Hewson's economic rationalism and Keating's cultural agenda. It attempts to turn the political gaze of Australians back to those issues Keating would have us forget—permanent mass unemployment, family breakdown, growing social inequity, the emergence of the underclass, rural impoverishment, business uncertainty and mounting foreign debt. The Liberal Party has now formally abandoned its ill-fated rationalist adventure, avoided the temptations of reactive social conservatism and set out upon a more modest journey of rediscovery—in search of middle Australia.

1994

The Keating Collapse

THE strangeness of the 2 March federal election result has not yet been fully grasped or satisfactorily explained. In 1996 Labor lost in a landslide almost equivalent to the one which buried the Whitlam government of 1975. But, unlike Whitlam, the Keating government on the eve of its catastrophe was disciplined and united. Unlike Whitlam it was generally regarded as economically responsible and competent, having delivered four years of low inflationary growth. And yet Keating was swept from power only marginally less ignominiously than Whitlam. As Alan Ramsey has pointed out, in 1996 the ALP recorded its lowest primary vote in Australia since 1931, in New South Wales since 1906, and in Queensland since federation. What transpired was an electoral catastrophe, without apparent cause.

The first hint about what might have happened came with the news about the excellent performances put in by every single candidate who had been targeted by the Labor leadership and the press gallery on political correctness grounds. In Kalgoorlie the disendorsed former ALP member, the anti-*Mabo*, anti-multicultural, Graeme Campbell, was returned with a slightly larger majority than he had achieved as the endorsed candidate in 1993. In Leichhardt, the National Party candidate, Bob Burgess, who had spoken of citizenship ceremonies as 'dewoggings', increased his party's primary vote from 14 per cent to 20 per cent. In Kennedy, Bob Katter, who had defended Burgess from those 'slanty-eyed ideologues who persecute ordinary average Australians', achieved a swing of 12 per cent, the third highest in the country. But even he was outdone by Pauline Hanson. After having been swiftly disendorsed by the Queensland Liberal Party, for having described the Aborigines, absurdly enough, as Australia's new priviligentsia, she received a swing in Oxley, the ALP's safest Queensland seat, of almost 20 per cent. This was by far the largest swing of the election.

During the campaign virtually every editorialist and serious commentator claimed that the views expressed by the Coalition's politically incorrect brigade were likely to be electorally damaging to themselves and, in the case of Burgess and Katter, to their party. As it turned out, this was the opposite of the truth. The division between the sentiments of Australia's political elites and its ordinary people was far deeper than political observers in the south had imagined. The successes of Campbell, Burgess, Katter and Hanson provided the first solid clue to the mystery of the Keating catastrophe.

The second clue came when attention was paid to the geographic distribution of ALP seats in the newly elected House of Representatives. The ALP was reasonably strong only in Tasmania and the ACT. It almost retained its strength in greater Sydney and Melbourne and in traditional Labor areas nearby, in Newcastle, Wollongong and Geelong. Beyond this base it was badly hit. In Adelaide Labor held two seats. In the newly elected house there were as many independents as there were Labor members from Queensland and Western Australia combined. As importantly, ALP pockets in regional Australia (except for Tasmania) were almost wiped out. Of the fifty-six regional or largely regional seats in Australia the ALP now holds five.

A plausible interpretation of this political geography was advanced by Terry McCrann in the *Australian*. According to him, the 1996 election represented a 'seismic shift' in voting patterns in an Australia which was now divided along a cultural fault-line, which separated the agenda-setting 'Triangle' of Sydney–Melbourne–Canberra from the country beyond. Inside the Triangle, McCrann argued, sufficient voters had been attracted to Mr Keating's 'big picture'—*Mabo*, APEC, Asia—to make the territory marginally pro-Labor. Outside, in the regions and the non-Triangular capitals, voters were singularly uncharmed by the Keating vision and resentful of his government's bossy and coercive ethos of political correctness. They defected in hundreds of thousands to the Coalition. There were now, he claimed, two Australian political nations. Within the Triangle the ALP held thirty of the fifty-four seats; outside it eighteen of ninety-four. Such a division had 'potentially profound implications for the broader dynamics of Australia'.

There are, in my opinion, serious problems with this analysis. McCrann is wrong, firstly, in suggesting novelty for the electoral geography of 1996. In the Whitlam election of 1975 and the post-Whitlam election of 1977 Labor was, roughly speaking, as weak outside the Triangle as it is in 1996. In 1977 it had the same number of seats in Queensland and Western Australia as it has now. It had four more in South Australia, but three fewer in Tasmania. McCrann's two political nations were first sighted not in 1996 but in the mid-1970s. Interestingly, where Whitlam pioneered, Keating followed.

More importantly, in assimilating the Keating vision to the idea of political correctness, McCrann's analysis seems to me somewhat imprecise. What was genuinely innovative in the Keating prime ministership was the way he married the economics of the right—deregulation, free trade and privatisation—with the contemporary social movements of the left—environmentalism, feminism, multiculturalism, Aboriginal and gay rights. This proved a fatal combination. While different parts of the Keating program had strong appeal to both conservative and radical elites, neither part appealed greatly to middle Australia. In its eyes Canberra is quite commonly seen to be governing in the interests not of all Australians but of minorities. The Coalition understood this well. Their slogan 'For All of Us' hit the mark.

Not since Whitlam, although for somewhat different reasons, has the rhetoric and the ideological impulse of an Australian government been more attuned to the preoccupations of the political elites and more remote from the thinking of ordinary Australians than it was under Keating. As a visionary, a kind of politician rarely found in Australia, Paul Keating appealed far more deeply to the nation's intelligentsia than did his predecessor, Bob Hawke. But he was an infinitely less effective politician. His vision—half Manning Clark, half Milton Friedman—went down in middle Australia like a lead balloon. Mr Hawke had a far better instinctive grasp than he about how much progress the punters could take.

The tension between elite and popular opinion was manifest right across Australia. In implying that Keating's big picture went down well in Labor's most traditional heartland—the Triangular working-class suburbs of Sydney and Melbourne, which remained in 1996, as they had after Whitlam, the ALP's most reliable base— Terry McCrann is wrong. But he is probably right to suggest that the impact of the Keating vision was most disastrous for his party beyond the Triangle—in regional Australia, and in Queensland, South Australia and the West.

A third possible clue to the mystery of the Keating catastrophe was provided, for me at least, by one aspect of the outcome of the 1996 Victorian state election which had not shown up so clearly, even in Victoria, in the federal result. In the state election the ALP polled well in the old working-class suburbs of Melbourne's north and west. In the newer settlements of the working class, the outer east and the poorer suburbs of the south, however, the swing was, if anything, to the Liberal Party. It is not impossible that what was glimpsed here was part of an interesting general pattern—the presence in contemporary Australia of two rather distinct working-class political cultures. The first might be described as the culture of an older, geographically immobile working class, whose voting patterns are still rooted in traditional Labor and trade union soil; the second as the culture of a younger, socially and geographically more mobile, more entrepreneurially minded group, which has almost altogether shed the Labor and trade union loyalties of the old manufacturing working class.

The traditional Labor electorates were hardly likely to be attracted to Mr Keating's 'big picture', yet these electorates in 1996 still returned ALP members with sizeable majorities—in the north and west of Melbourne, the south of Sydney, in Wollongong and Newcastle, and in the working-class suburbs to the north of Adelaide. Something different occurred in both regional Australia and in the mining and services-based economies of Queensland and Western Australia. Here the old working-class political culture seems by now to have almost altogether collapsed. The voting habits of the battlers are less and less distinguishable from the voting habits of what is generally called in shorthand 'middle Australia'—the modest, struggling mass of the lower middle class.

The faded political loyalties of this new working class were perhaps seen most dramatically in Queensland—in the 20 per cent swing in Oxley to Pauline Hanson and in the reduction of the ALP presence there to two seats, both with safety margins of less than 2 per cent. These faded loyalties may also help explain the astonishing drift of almost one million votes from Labor to the Coalition between 1993 and 1996. In 1993, when offered the radical economic proposals of Dr Hewson, which included his proposal for the partial dismantling of the welfare state, a substantial section of the battlers of middle Australia, even outside the Triangle, even in Queensland, opted for Keating Labor. When, however, the same electorate was asked to choose in 1996 between a moderate Howard Coalition program and Keating's radical vision, then—except in the stubbornly traditional Labor heartlands of Sydney and Melbourne, the public service electorates of Canberra and in idiosyncratic, green-conscious Tasmania—the new working-class and lower-middle-class voters of middle Australia, in very substantial numbers, quietly changed their minds.

1996

The Strange Personality of Jeffrey Kennett

UNLESS something astonishing happens the Kennett government will be returned in a landslide. Throughout the past year the government's credentials have looked imposing. The finances are in surplus. Business thoroughly approves of what it has done. The grand prix was an outstanding popular success. Most importantly, the Labor opposition is unelectable. And yet, as a kind of protest, I will not be voting for the Coalition.

For three and a half years Victoria has been governed by a premier who has treated his critics with arrogance or disdain, who has refused to engage in public debate on terms other than his own, who has shown little respect for democracy, and a feeble understanding of such basic concepts of good government as the separation of powers, conflict of interest or even the rule of law. In his style of leadership, Kennett has done considerable damage to the political, legal and civic culture of Victoria. Consider the following cases.

In August 1993 Kennett told the general public that he was

pleased that the police had finally arrested the murderer of three young women. At the time the man had not been found guilty. The premier's comments looked as if they might imperil the prospect of a fair trial and, therefore, of a successful prosecution. The Director of Public Prosecutions, Bernard Bongiorno, announced that he was considering an action against the premier for contempt.

That evening Bongiorno was summoned to the home of the attorney-general, Jan Wade. On two or three occasions the telephone rang. Bongiorno became aware that the caller was the premier. He felt that he was being pressured not to proceed.

Some weeks later Bongiorno in fact decided not to proceed. His reason may have been that the murderer had entered a guilty plea. Yet the conflict between the DPP and the premier was not yet over. Behind Bongiorno's back the government began drafting legislation for the restructuring of the office of the DPP. The draft legislation gave the deputy director veto power over his director. It also stripped the DPP of his capacity to lay charges of contempt. When this draft legislation leaked, the first of these proposals was killed off by the near-unanimous opinion of Victoria's lawyers. The second, concerning contempt, was duly enacted. Kennett had his revenge. Later that year Mr Bongiorno resigned as DPP.

But it is not only the idea of the separation of powers which escapes Kennett. The very concept of democracy has a surprisingly pale hold on his imagination.

In August last year the premier floated at a business breakfast the idea of placing the non-elected commissioners who had run the Melbourne City Council since 1993 on a more or less permanent footing. This idea found little support. Yet Mr Kennett was not discouraged. Shortly after, he suggested scrapping by-elections in the case of governments with five-seat majorities or more. Kennett conceives of government as a higher form of management. As the CEO of what he has come to call Australia's fifth largest company, by-elections clearly seem to him a waste of time.

So do certain kinds of public debate. As early as 1992 a

conflict arose between the premier and the ABC's '7.30 Report'. For the next three years, even after apologies were offered, Kennett refused to appear on this program or to allow his ministers to appear. Late last year the Victorian-based '7.30 Report' was scrapped. Kennett now extended his boycott to the new national and state programs which replaced it. In his judgment his government has more to lose than to gain by appearing on ABC television's current affairs programs.

Kennett's attitude strikes me as fundamentally undemocratic and faintly unconstitutional. Current affairs television is one of the most important ways citizens now observe their governments being scrutinised. I am simply astonished that Victorians have tolerated this boycott for so long. I am even more astonished that they accepted, without a whimper of protest, Kennett's decision not to debate the Victorian opposition leader, John Brumby, during the course of the election campaign.

But not only the robustness of the democratic culture is under threat in Victoria. So is the rule of law. During the life of both the Kirner and Kennett governments citizens have been increasingly deprived of the right to defend their interests before the courts. The most disturbing instance arose over the legislation establishing the grand prix authority.

A year ago massive earthwork occurred at Albert Park. Residents nearby discovered that their homes were being seriously damaged. They also discovered that the grand prix legislation foreclosed their ability to take action for compensation at law. Kennett was not unmoved by their plight. He offered his personal guarantee that damage would be compensated. He would err, he promised, on the side of generosity.

These comments astonished me. I had always assumed that the idea of the rule of law went deep in Australia. And yet here was a premier who genuinely regarded his personal pledge as a more reliable security than a citizen's right to pursue his or her interests before the courts.

Recently a most serious issue—the bidding process over the contract for Victoria's casino—has returned to haunt Kennett. I am of course in no position to know whether or nor the tender process was pure. All that I know is that Sally Neighbour, a 'Four Corners' journalist, reported that she had spoken with an employee of the casino authority who, she claimed, had told her that during the bidding process telephone calls were made to members of the Victorian Cabinet divulging confidential information about the rival bids. This person was willing to give evidence before a court.

Victorians already know that two of Jeff Kennett's friends—one of whom is the Treasurer of the Liberal Party—won the casino licence. They also know that last year, due to the premier's spirited intervention, the casino was allowed to double the number of its gaming tables while police investigations into the company that owns the casino were being pursued.

I know it is a hopeless gesture. But as long as Victoria is governed by a premier who thinks that an appropriate answer to the 'Four Corners' allegation is to label the ABC 'leeches' on the productive forces of society, he will not have my vote.

1996

Lying in Politics

THE 1996 federal election campaign must have been one of the most peculiar in recent Australian history. As things have turned out, the most important issue of discussion ought to have been the commonwealth's budget deficit. Yet this was the one issue of the campaign which could not be seriously discussed.

For its own political reasons, the Keating government refused to reveal to the public Treasury's deficit forecasts. To reveal these forecasts would have doomed the government to even more certain defeat. Labor decided to pretend that no serious deficit was in prospect.

Oddly enough, it suited the opposition to collude in this evasion. It was true that the opposition pressured the government to release the forecasts, knowing it would not. The refusal made the government look bad. Yet even without the forecasts the opposition knew for certain that when it took government it would be informed that there would be a serious budget deficit in the coming year. It was not only that every independent analyst agreed on this point. Even more decisively if there was no deficit in prospect it was inconceivable that the government would not have released the Treasury forecasts.

Nevertheless, despite this knowledge, the opposition went to the people on the assumption of a balanced budget, promising solemnly to make no major spending cuts to Labor's popular programs. The opposition feared that if it had told the electorate the truth, namely that it would be obliged to renege on its spending promises when it discovered that it had inherited a budget deficit, its honesty would be used by the prime minister to destroy John Howard in much the same ruthless way he had used the GST to destroy John Hewson. Faced with a choice between risk and mendacity, the opposition chose mendacity. It is not difficult to understand why.

The election campaign was transformed by this strange political logic into a farce, a mock struggle between parties who shared an understanding of the true fiscal situation and an interest in keeping this knowledge to themselves. Together the government and opposition agreed to mislead the Australian people about the one question which was certain to affect their lives in the immediate future, namely the question of how the party which was elected intended to deal with the domestic budget deficit it was certain to inherit.

When the Coalition was elected it was inevitable that it would be obliged to choose between honouring its promises or following its policy instincts. Equally inevitably it opted for its version of fiscal responsibility rather than for keeping its word. Its first budget was a litany of broken pledges in labour-market programs, research and development, export-enhancement schemes, Medicare, superannuation, university and ABC funding. What has been genuinely interesting to me is the fact that editorialists and political commentators have shown little hesitation in commending John Howard on his choice. Judging by the post-budget discussions one would have to conclude that most political insiders in Australia no longer regard the idea of honesty as a cardinal political virtue.

It might have been one thing for a hard-bitten political realist, like Paddy McGuinness, to remind his readers, as he did, of the inevitability of political lies and of the wisdom of an electorate willing to choose to be governed by the party it can trust to break its irresponsible promises. It is altogether another thing when a generally uncynical politician like John Howard expressed pride that he has been able to keep at least seven or eight out of every ten political promises he had offered the Australian people in order to get to power. The fact that Mr Howard felt able to speak like this, and that virtually no one was shocked by his words, is evidence of how feeble the idea of honesty in politics has become. Clearly as a nation we now regard policy responsibility as vital, and policy honesty as an optional extra.

As a consequence, since the budget, certain awkward questions about the relationship between honesty and democratic public life have not even seemed worth discussing. Let me raise here only the most obvious. If politicians are entitled, when faced with the choice between an uncomfortable truth and a plausible lie, to choose the plausible lie, if when such lies are discovered the discovery is cost-free, if we are to accept that pre-election pledges are merely the tactical moves of a political game, I do not see how we are to prevent the drift of the citizenry to a general state of political cynicism. Or to put the point another way. If lying gradually comes to seem an acceptable political means to a worthwhile end, what will prevent democracy degenerating into a struggle between elites whose relationship to the electorate goes no deeper than the conduct of an auction, every three or four years, in search of the votes of a largely indifferent and ignorant population?

1996

Trivial Pursuits

WHAT are we to make of the issue that dominated our national politics in the spring of 1997: the Travel Rorts Affair? For my part, before its shocking conclusion, I had come to think of it as a relatively trivial and ugly and ungracious game—a kind of moral contact sport—in which we had all been condemned, as participants or commentators or spectators, to play our prescribed parts.

The game was, of course, sparked by our most seasoned political journalist, Laurie Oakes. From the interstices of the Canberra public service a leak had sprung. Although in appearance spontaneous, the release of the leak had in fact been precisely timed for the scheduled return of the main teams to the national arena of politics, the federal parliament. Outsiders like myself would probably never learn who was responsible for this leak, or what were the obscure political scores which were thereby being settled.

The rules of the game occasioned by this leak soon became clear to all players. For longer than anyone could remember parliamentarians had been, in different ways, using travel allowances as an income supplementary scheme. (I was told of this twenty years ago when I applied for a political job I thankfully failed to get.) Some practices—for example claiming a travel allowance while sleeping at the home of a family member or friend—were within the rules. Others—for example claiming a travel allowance while sleeping in the comfort of one's own bed—were not.

The purpose of the game was also clear. It was to identify as many as possible of those political opponents who had made false or embarrassing claims. As a result of the Oakes leak it was relatively simple to prove that the Minister for Transport, John Sharp, had made certain false claims, and also relatively easy to prove that the Minister for Administrative Services, David Jull, had helped Sharp conceal such claims from the public gaze. By the time the inevitable had occurred and Sharp and Jull had resigned, Labor led the Coalition two goals to nil. The contest now turned to the future of the Minister for Science and Technology, Peter McGauran. McGauran had made some rather extravagant claims that were within the rules and one or two rather trifling claims which were not. After a day of skirmishing he too resigned. By the common agreement of the commentators Simon Crean was the outstanding player. Kim Beazley's performance as opposition leader, we were told, was solid but lacked flair. There was something in his demeanour which expressed an inner reserve about what was taking place. For this he was widely regarded, although not by me, as somewhat weak.

Around this time something slightly unexpected occurred. For reasons that remain unclear one of the defrocked ministers, David Jull, let it be known that a member of his staff had informed members of Howard's staff of Sharp's indiscretion. For a moment it looked as if the prime minister might have misled the parliament. If this had been proved John Howard would have been required to resign. The game would have been over. It was not to be. Howard's long-time adviser, Grahame Morris, argued that he had kept the Jull intelligence to himself. It was therefore he who resigned. The game's reward for taking out a prime ministerial adviser was unclear. All that was clear was that in this first week all the scoring had been on the Labor side.

On the following weekend the leaders of both teams travelled to Melbourne to participate in the preliminaries to a decidedly less depressing sporting contest, the AFL Grand Final. Both appeared comfortable and relaxed. Beazley joked that he had walked from Perth to Melbourne and stayed overnight in a tent. Howard replied that such intelligence was not required. Beazley's every move had been watched. These good-natured comments underlined the fundamental civility of Australian political life. They also revealed that both team leaders recognised that what was being transacted in Canberra, with apparent deadly seriousness, was in the end merely a sporting contest by other means.

Over the Grand Final weekend the Coalition regrouped. It now discovered a target of its own, the Labor Party's Shadow Finance Minister, Senator Nick Sherry. Sherry had claimed a city travel allowance while spending evenings in his mother's home, fifty kilometres from Hobart. To the general amusement of the political nation he was mocked by Peter Costello as the Bedouin of Burnie and as the possum of Opossum Bay. These words delivered to Nick Sherry the political equivalent of what is called in the language of Australian football a 'shirt front', a perfectly legitimate but perfectly lethal knockout blow.

In parliamentary combat of the kind we had witnessed over the previous fortnight it is assumed that all players are capable of absorbing and surviving vast doses of moral punishment. Usually this assumption is either sound or at least appears on the surface to be so. In the case of Nick Sherry it was not. Having given his life to politics, Sherry now probably thought he faced the prospect of becoming nationally prominent, for the first time in his life, not as a political leader but as a figure of scandal and of fun. He imagined his name, and the name of his Labor Party father, would be mud. Something about the description of him as a homeless Bedouin seems to have triggered deep feelings of loneliness and vulnerability. He decided there was no alternative but to take his life.

With Nick Sherry's attempted suicide the political game came very abruptly to an end. Everyone suddenly awoke, as if from a bad dream. One Tasmanian senator, the Catholic conservative Brian Harradine, spoke of the need for healing and reconciliation, and of an evil spirit which had inhabited the parliament. Another, the radical environmentalist Bob Brown, who had expressed throughout the fortnight his distaste for the conversion of the national parliament to a bullring, called for fundamental change in the way politics in Australia is pursued. It is unlikely that the hopes of either Harradine or Brown will be fulfilled.

What of the leaders? On the day of the attempted suicide John Howard issued a brief press release expressing shock. He decided, in my opinion wrongly, not to appear before the television cameras to offer his interpretation of the attempted suicide and the events of the past fortnight. He left this task to Kim Beazley. Beazley, again in my opinion, spoke superbly. It was, he said, the democratic duty of the opposition to hold the government to account. It was no less the duty of the government to do the same in regard to the opposition. For Sherry's attempted suicide neither politicians nor the media were to blame. There were no easy morals to be drawn. Beazley spoke soberly and sadly, as a man capable of recognising, simultaneously, the unavoidability of what had transpired over the past fortnight and also its profound futility.

And what of the onlookers, the Australian citizens? They were compelled to watch, passively as spectators, a fortnight of precious parliamentary time being spent on an unseemly scandal over minor corruption in the political class, ending in the resignation of three government ministers and, infinitely more seriously, in the attempted suicide of one of their shadows. Some of these citizens are out of work. Many fear losing their jobs or their businesses or for the job and life prospects of their children. If they are on the land, many face ruin. Many are finding it increasingly difficult to cobble together for themselves or their families a decent material life. Is there really in Australian politics, they must wonder, no better way? This, too, is my question. Like others, I can find no easy answer.

1997

PART THREE

THE NEW POLITICS OF RACE

Our First Anti-Politician

THERE is no disagreement that the Pauline Hanson phenomenon represents something new and significant in Australian political life. There is, however, very considerable disagreement about how her rather startling appearance at the centre of our politics can be explained and even greater disagreement about what, in the longer term, it might mean.

It is tempting to think that the national obsession with Pauline Hanson can be explained simply as nothing more than the consequence of her rather peculiar election to the House of Representatives—as a disendorsed candidate willing to express unfashionable views about Aboriginal privilege and Asian migration. Such a simple explanation cannot, however, be true. Graeme Campbell was elected, as the member for Kalgoorlie, in precisely the same way and on precisely the same program. Yet, although he is a more sophisticated and seasoned politician than Pauline Hanson, he has failed completely to capture the public imagination.

The distance between our fascination with the member for Oxley and our indifference to the member for Kalgoorlie provides a clue to the riddle of Pauline Hanson. Graeme Campbell represents in the public mind merely another politician, albeit one with a set of unfashionable, right-wing views. Pauline Hanson has come to represent something much deeper—a widespread hostility in the electorate to the political process and parliamentary politics. Pauline Hanson is not merely another politican; she is our first *anti-politician*.

There can be no doubt that for many ordinary Australians Pauline Hanson possesses that magical quality which political scientists, since Max Weber, have called charisma. When she walks in suburban streets or shopping malls people cheer her progress and wish to shake her by the hand. When a rather lacklustre right-wing politician is planning to launch a new party—it is Ted Drane I have in mind—she is invited to the party's foundation and asked whether she might be willing to endorse its parliamentary candidates, one by one. It is as if, somehow, by her mere presence, some magic might rub off.

Yet if Pauline Hanson possesses charisma it is of an extremely peculiar kind, a kind which I have come to call negative charisma. We think of a charismatic politician as eloquent. Pauline Hanson is, by contrast, almost painfully inarticulate. We think of charismatic politicians as inspiring. Pauline Hanson's mood is of sullen resentment and stubborn defiance. Her negative charisma is expressive not of hope for the future but of bitterness about the present. In her inarticulateness, in her sulkiness, in her ignorance—for which she is not only forgiven but, I suspect, admired—she has become for a considerable part of Australia (for millions if the opinion polls are to be believed) a symbol of nostalgia for an old world which has been lost and of deep-seated discontent with the new world which has taken its place. As our first elected anti-politician, Pauline Hanson expresses in her mood the anxieties and the grievances of a far from negligible section of traditional Australia.

Yet Pauline Hanson is an anti-politician in a more specific sense. Since her election she has come to express the anti-parliamentary and anti-Canberra suspicions of her broad constituency. When she delivered her maiden speech—one of the few maiden speeches of recent years which has had a real political impact—she delivered it to an almost empty house. The parliament had, as it were, boycotted her. When, in response to this speech and its influence in the land, her parliamentary colleagues passed a bi-partisan anti-Hanson motion deploring racism, she, in turn, boycotted them by flying out of Canberra to seek refuge in the 'real world'—a working-class market in the western suburbs of Melbourne. The symbolic meaning could not have been more plain.

By now the question on everyone's lips was whether the astonishing popular following Hanson had been able to attract would be likely to reshape Australian party politics, by the creation of a new party of the populist right. If my analysis of the Hanson phenomenon is roughly accurate this seems unlikely. As an anti-politician and an emblem of middle Australia's discontents, Pauline Hanson's unwillingness to reason or to debate or to explain may be part of her attraction. As leader of a new political party—unless Australia has become a completely different country from the one I imagine I inhabit—the danger to us of her limitations will eventually become transparent. It might be one thing for Australians to experience the pleasure of a temporary, rather thoughtless, cultural *Schadenfreude*, by applauding Pauline Hanson's defiance of respectable opinion. It would be altogether another if, at this moment in our history, a serious political force organised around anti-Asian sentiment were to emerge.

As we have discovered recently, it is simply not possible for Australia to quarantine a domestic political mood—based on nostalgia and irritation—from our international relations with the rather prickly governments and public opinions of the regions in which we happen to live. In contemporary Europe fringe anti-immigrant parties are merely ugly. In contemporary

Australia the emergence of equivalent parties would be a disaster. It was self-evident from the first moment that Pauline Hanson attracted interest, by playing with racial politics, that Australia's long-term strategic interests were at stake. As a consequence of this kind of politics not only Australians of Asian birth but all Australians were likely to be harmed. The failure of the Howard government to respond at once to the Hanson threat—by reminding middle Australia unambiguously about how much we stood to lose if an anti-Asian breeze blew up in this country—represents to my mind the most important miscalculation it has made so far in its brief life.

1996

Hanson and the Populist Right

THE most important question of Australian politics today is whether Pauline Hanson will translate from a phenomenon into a political party. Last year I was of the view that this was unlikely. Today I am not sure.

Every twenty years or so Australia seems to spawn a new political party. It may turn out that the appearance of Pauline Hanson as a factor in our politics is not the result of a freak accident but of something deep going on in our society, something no less disruptive than the Cold War tensions which gave birth to the DLP, and no less significant than that sea change in the values of a stratum of the middle class which has enabled the Australian Democrats to outlive the circumstances of their foundation and to endure.

In order to understand the rise of Pauline Hanson it seems to me useful to look abroad, in particular to the emergence of Hanson-like, radical right-wing politics in western and central Europe over the past decade or so. My guide in this journey is an excellent recent book, *Radical Right-Wing Populism in Western*

Europe, written by the American political scientist Hans-Georg Betz. Betz has suggested to me that where Europe has led, Australia may now be following.

Since the mid-1980s right-wing populist parties have been a factor in the electoral politics of Austria, France, Belgium, Germany, Switzerland, Norway and Denmark. In Austria the Freedom Party of Jörg Haider has captured more than 20 per cent of the national vote; in France the National Front of Jean-Marie Le Pen some 15 per cent. In Belgium as a whole, the ultra-right Vlaams Block receives about 8 per cent of the national vote and a considerably higher proportion in the Flemish lands. In Denmark and Norway support for the so-called Progress parties seems to have stabilised at about 6 per cent. The political atmosphere in three of Europe's oldest cities—Vienna, Paris and Antwerp—is already largely determined by the presence of a powerful radical right.

What lies behind the rise of this populist right in Europe? According to Betz these parties provide vehicles for the political articulation of three distinct moods or opinions which pervade contemporary Europe. The first is of a profound anti-political cynicism. Politicians are now viewed by a very large part of the European citizenry as untrustworthy, as motivated by self-interest rather than the public good, as out of touch with the views and values of ordinary people, as utterly incapable of perceiving let alone solving society's problems. Anti-political cynicism combines with a deep layer of personal insecurity. People have much reduced confidence in their own or their society's economic prospects. They are fearful of losing their jobs, and, if this happens, of never recovering employment. They fear falling victim to crime. They believe that the world that will be bequeathed to their children will be far worse than the world they were born into.

These moods, in turn, combine with deep-seated xenophobia. By the early 1990s a majority of Europeans believed there were too many foreigners and, especially, too many Africans and Asians who had settled in Europe as migrants or refugees. These foreigners were blamed by many for the rise in unemployment and crime. They were suspected of rorting Europe's generous social-welfare systems. The idea that welfare benefits should not be extended to foreigners became so common that it was given a label by political analysts: 'welfare state chauvinism'.

The rise of an unembarrassed xenophobia lies at the heart of the electoral success of the radical populist right. Many of these parties began their lives as pre-Thatcherite, 'neo-liberal' parties, defending an idea of enterprise culture, attacking trade unions, deriding the welfare state, deploring income-tax levels. On this program they did not greatly prosper. In the mid-1980s, after the remarkable electoral breakthrough of the anti-immigrant National Front in the French presidential elections of 1984, right-wing populism changed direction. The parties became openly xenophobic. Muslim migrants from North Africa were these parties' most common target. Both the French National Front and the Austrian Freedom Party began now to advocate programs of discrimination and even repatriation aimed against their immigrants.

In this movement from neo-liberal populism to xenophobia the radical right not only grew. It also changed its electoral base, drawing its most important support not so much now from the private enterprise middle class as from the working or, even more, the non-working lower class. The parallels of all this with Australian populism's transition from the Joh-for-Canberra flat-tax campaign of 1987 to the election of Pauline Hanson in blue-collar Oxley and her astonishing rise to national prominence on an anti-Asian, anti-Aboriginal and anti-political rhetoric seem almost self-evident.

What is remarkable about the rise of Pauline Hanson is not so much that it has occurred but, rather, how long it had taken for some equivalent to the European populist right to emerge here. Since the collapse of capitalism's golden age—the period between 1950 and 1973—advanced industrial societies have been buffeted by wave after wave of profound social and economic change.

Many people, in particular those with capital or higher education or marketable skills, have flourished as never before. Others—without capital or significant education or skill—have been consigned, in our new 'civilisation of unemployment', to a more or less permanent position at the bottom of the social pile. Even those presently in jobs or in small business or on the land have been obliged to accustom themselves, in the giddy pace of change, to insecurity in many forms—to traditional fears like redundancy and bankruptcy and to new anxieties like market-driven demands for endless reskilling or abrupt mid-life changes in career. It seems to me altogether unsurprising that in present circumstances those who find themselves reduced to social oblivion or prey to insecurity should begin to feel like strangers in their own land. It seems to me just as unsurprising that they should be willing, in their resentment at the impotence or callousness of the political class, in their envy of the successful elites, and in their disenchantment with the ruthless pace of change, to turn to plausible bigots like Jean-Marie Le Pen or sincere fools like Pauline Hanson.

Inter-war fascism was described in a classic formulation as the mobilisation of those who felt themselves the losers in the process of modernisation. For its part, contemporary right-wing populism might be described, rather similarly, as the mobilisation of those for whom the era of globalisation has offered, thus far, not prosperity or hope but the threat of meaninglessness and social fear.

1997

Pauline Hanson's Truth

I HAVE often wondered, idly, what a politically significant extremism of the right might look like in contemporary Australia. After reading what looks like the One Nation Party's manifesto, *Pauline Hanson: The Truth*, I have a clearer idea.

The manifesto begins with the movement's sacred texts—Hanson's speeches and press releases. It concludes with the words delivered by Bruce Whiteside at the launch of the Pauline Hanson Support Movement. Australia, we discover, has found its redemptive leader. This 'slip of a girl' is the voice of the people, Australia's Joan of Arc or, alternatively, our Moses. Through her courage she has given us the chance to destroy the anti-Australian diseases of multiculturalism, Aboriginalism and Asianisation which have been imposed upon us. Will we let this moment of possible salvation pass? Or will we join the Hanson army and march by her side?

The strangeness of all this is nothing in comparison with the long middle section of the manifesto, written, apparently, by a disaffected right-wing academic who has decided to remain anonymous. Let us call him X. His contribution is a work of pure political paranoia. His analysis of contemporary Australia centres on the existence of a threatening enemy. As it turns out, the enemy of X's imagination is the left-liberal intelligentsia, the so-called 'new-class' elite. The new class dominates the media, the universities and, above all, the High Court. It is 'decadent' and 'cosmopolitan'. Its 'degenerate, oppressive and evil ideology' is imbued with a 'sickly, sticky, stinking false-altruism'.

This 'false-altruism' is a disguise. Behind appearances the new class comprises self-conscious traitors to Australia. X quotes at length from a passage of Cicero. A nation can survive folly but not treason. The traitor moves secretly among the people. He speaks to 'the baseness that lies in the hearts of all men'. He 'rots the soul of the nation'. A nation can better withstand the murderer than the traitor. The new-class elites have, in fact, a plan. They have already imposed their 'absolute power over us'. But there is more to come. They have 'deliberately earmarked Anglo-Saxon Australia for destruction'. How is this plan to be carried out? X suggests the existence of three strategies.

The first is Asianisation. At the behest of the secret forces dominating the new world order, the new-class elites have decided to open Australia to the surplus population of Asia, particularly of China and India. X imagines Australia in 2050. It now has a population of 1.8 billion. Its capital is called Vuo Wah. Its president is a lesbian called Poona Li Hung, who has been chosen by the World Government. A crime has been committed by a 'crazed blond haired man, of a seemingly insignificant minority racial group tottering on extinction'.

X assures us that the real enemy of old Australia is not the Asian. He assures us that Hanson is not a racist. And yet passages in his chapters concerning the Asianisation of Australia contain some of the most vicious examples of anti-Asian racism I have ever seen in print in Australia. X informs us at one point that stories of Aboriginal genocide are absurd and that 'the real "genocide" which is occurring in Australia today is the dispossession of the majority of Anglo-Australians. In our cities girls as young as fourteen sell sex for as little as ten dollars to buy drugs from Asian gangs'.

If the first strategy for the new-class destruction of Australia is Asianisation, the second strategy is what X calls 'Maboism'—the deliberate destruction of Anglo-Australia by handing it over to the Aborigines. In the course of his discussion of 'Maboism', X, already famously, quotes at length from two books, by Hector Holthouse and Daisy Bates, with their detailed accounts of Aboriginal cannibalism. His purpose is, on the surface, to debunk new-class 'romantic primitivism'. More deeply, it is to dispose of the idea that non-indigenous Australians might have reason to feel uneasy about Aboriginal dispossession. Surely only decadent new-class intellectuals could think that the 'legal' occupation of a continent inhabited by cannibals could have left a legacy of shame?

X also engages in a long anthropological excursion whose purpose is to show that the Aborigines were not even the original inhabitants of this continent and that, indeed, the 'stench' of genocide—of the original inhabitants of Australia by the Aborigines—hung around the continent 30,000 years ago. He believes Anglo-Australia has always treated the Aborigines 'very well'. Taking babies from their mothers was, for example, for their own good. Australians did not even use machine-guns and planes to wipe out the Aborigines, as they might have. Case closed. Hanson is not anti-Aboriginal but 'a great fighter for Aboriginal self-worth and dignity'. To deny this is a 'vile and unforgivable insult'.

If the ultimate new-class strategy of 'Maboism' is, then, to 'break down' Australian society so that it can be 'remoulded' to the plans of the secret world government for the transformation of Australia into the dumping ground of the surplus populations of Asia, the immediate tactic is the disarmament of this country. This explains the contemporary meaning of attempts at gun control.

Because of such things as Asian drug dealers, gangs of black rapists, and even an unknown force that is involved in an international sex trade in 'blonde and blue-eyed' pretty young Nordic women, our cities are descending into fearful dens of crime. Ordinary Australians who, unlike the new-class elites, do not live in leafy suburbs, need to defend themselves.

This, however, is not the real story behind the 'gun banners'. Something more sinister is, in fact, going on. 'Behind the gun controllers is the black claw of the internationalist elite of the New World Order.' X understands what it is aiming at: 'The groundwork for a global gulag, a cosmopolitan police state, has already been put in place.'

In the struggle to prevent this global gulag the new class is, of course, the main enemy. But the established political parties—Liberal, National, Labor, Democrat—are almost as bad. All have been corrupted beyond redemption, taken over by left-liberal ideas. Only the extraordinary courage and the 'intuitive genius' of that great Australian, Hanson, can now, at the eleventh hour, save us from the terrible fate awaiting us.

If *Pauline Hanson: The Truth* were merely the work of a handful of cranks, it would be of little interest or concern. But it is not. It is, rather, the publication of a support movement that stands behind a political party which is gaining a foothold in country Australia, which has the sympathy of very many Australians, and which, according to the most recent opinion poll, has the same level of support as the Australian Democrats.

In my view, the time for Coalition politicians and the conservative intelligentsia to declare themselves unambiguously against the Hanson phenomenon has come.

It is no longer plausible for Coalition leaders to wait until the Hanson movement burns itself out. I urge John Howard, Peter Costello and Tim Fischer to take the time to read *Pauline Hanson: The Truth* and to speak plainly to Australian citizens about their moral and political response. I also urge members of Australia's conservative intelligentsia to read it. Many will find their own ideas—on the new class, political correctness, *Mabo*, multiculturalism, Asian migration, the High Court—absorbed, simplified, systematised and radicalised.

Because of this, I do not believe it is now illegitimate to ask the conservative intelligentsia whether they agree with me in condemning the Hanson movement. Do they support the political movement bearing Hanson's name? Are they neutral in regard to it? Or will they publicly oppose it?

1997

The Counter-Revolution in Sensibility

CONSERVATIVE politicians in Australia are involved in a debate of some significance for the future of this country. The question might appear rather narrow. Should the Coalition parties place Pauline Hanson and the One Nation Party at the bottom of their tickets at the next federal election? In fact, its implication runs deep.

It seems to be generally agreed that, with the victory of Hanson in the seat of Oxley last year, a new element entered our politics. There is considerable disagreement, however, about what precisely this new element was. In my opinion, the election of Hanson was the sign that a kind of counter-revolution in Australian political sensibility might have arrived.

One dimension of this potential counter-revolution concerns relations between the European settlers and Aborigines. Since the 1970s Australians have been involved in a process we call reconciliation. It has taken various forms: acknowledging indigenous land rights; experimenting with forms of Aboriginal political self-determination; uncovering and acknowledging past wrongs. Many Australians have never accepted the value of this process. Many are now turning their backs on it. They bitterly oppose *Wik*. They regard ATSIC as nothing but corrupt. They regard concern with past wrongdoing as obsessive brooding, as black-armband history. For such people, the reconciliation process has never been accepted or has now turned sour. Hansonism is the political expression of their sourness.

The second great cultural shift in Australia, to which Hansonism is a response, is the repudiation of the White Australia Policy and the acceptance, since the 1970s, of high levels of immigration from Asia. To judge by the opinion polls of the past twenty years and the explosion of press and popular interest whenever dissident voices are heard—Geoffrey Blainey in 1984, John Howard in 1988, Hanson in 1996—it would seem that many Australians have never accepted the idea of a non-discriminatory immigration policy. Anti-Asian stories, that Asians are stealing Australian jobs or creating ghetto cultures, are now widespread. When, in her maiden speech, Hanson said that Australia was being swamped by Asians and when she allowed the most repugnant anti-Asian racism to be published in *The Truth* under her name, she became the rallying point for an anti-Asian bigotry in Australia.

But not only that. A third dimension of the post-1970s Australian revolution in sensibility concerned the idea of multiculturalism. Before the 1970s immigrants to Australia were expected to assimilate to the dominant Anglo-Celtic culture. With the triumph of the idea of multiculturalism, this kind of assimilation expectation was abandoned. Non-British migrants could now become fully Australian without being required to assimilate to a provincial variant of the British cultural norm. Multiculturalism allowed non-British migrants to feel more truly at home in Australia. Unfortunately, it made many old Australians feel less securely at home. Hansonism is the expression of Anglo-anxiety in the age of multiculturalism.

In becoming the rallying point for those Australians who were sceptical about the process of Aboriginal reconciliation and uneasy with the levels of Asian immigration and the idea of multiculturalism, Hanson placed before Coalition politicians a genuinely difficult problem. It is a problem which those politicians have not yet resolved.

The relationship between the Hansonite agenda and the Coalition is a complex one. Part of the agenda—her ideas about reducing Asian immigration, and withdrawing from engagement with Asia—is a potential source of conflict not so much between Coalition politicians as between these politicians and their followers. From my observations, Coalition parliamentarians are no less convinced than were their ALP predecessors of the grave strategic danger to Australia were an anti-Asian breeze to blow up here over migration questions. All know that a retreat from Asia would ensure our economic and diplomatic isolation from the region where we live.

The ambiguities in the Coalition over Hansonism arise elsewhere—over those parts of the Hanson agenda concerned with reconciliation and multiculturalism. Over these issues Coalition politicians are deeply divided, both from their parties' memberships and from each other.

There are within the Coalition parties, especially among the younger members of the Liberal Party, many genuine heirs to the progressivist Deakinite tradition. Such politicians have shared in the revolution which has reshaped attitudes to race and ethnicity since the 1970s. They represent within the Coalition parties the force of an unambiguous opposition to Hansonism. Their natural leader is Australia's last Deakinite prime minister, Malcolm Fraser.

The majority of Coalition politicians do not, so far as I can see, belong in that tradition. Many seem to regard the non-Asian parts of the Hanson agenda—the supposed excesses of the reconciliation process and of multiculturalism—with more than a little sympathy. Many regard Hanson as a passing phenomenon of no great significance, or even as a typical ABC beat-up. Many see in her an understandable reaction to the regime of political correctness imposed upon us by Paul Keating. In the Hanson debate the animus of many Coalition politicians—and of their supporters in the press, like Frank Devine or Christopher Pearson—seems to be directed far more strongly against the enemies of Hanson than her supporters. The natural leader of this kind of anti-anti-Hansonism is John Howard. Given what is at stake in this debate, Mr Howard's reticence and ambivalence on the Hanson front have astonished me.

Within the Coalition a battle over Hanson may soon be joined. The narrow issue will be Hanson's position on the Coalition ticket, the more general issue the Coalition's attitude to the Aboriginal question and ethnicity in Australia. The manner in which the Hanson question is debated and how it is ultimately decided will tell us a good deal about the balance of forces within conservative politics today.

1997

PART FOUR

POLITICAL CULTURE

Thoughts on Australia

I am the son of European migrants. One of my parents was born in Berlin, the other in Vienna. Both were Jewish. In the late 1930s, just before the beginning of World War II, they separately made their way to Australia as political refugees. Like most other countries in the world Australia had not at first responded generously to the Jewish refugee crisis. But at the eleventh hour there was a change of heart. My parents were among its beneficiaries. They met here late in the war and married. Neither set eyes on their parents again, all of whom disappeared during the horrors of what eventually became known as the Holocaust. Without conspicuous material success, they picked up their lives as best they could in Melbourne. For a brief period, in this curious new land to which they had fled, I think they found something approaching happiness.

During my childhood the official policy of the Australian government in regard to wave after wave of European migration was something called assimilation. At present this policy is judged harshly, supposedly because it was based on a demand that migrants abandon their cultural roots. I do not remember it so. The home I grew up in—the music, the books, the visitors, the talk—reflected the culture of Central Europe. There was not the slightest sense that there was anything wrong with this. On the other hand, in the neighbourhood I grew up in and the old Australian primary school I attended, I can remember no single instance—not one—where the oddity of my background led to any social unpleasantness, let alone any act of discrimination. This may not have been the experience of other migrant children during the supposedly dark age of assimilation, but it was mine.

Gradually, and without the slightest self-consciousness, I absorbed aspects of the culture of the country in which I had, more or less accidentally, been born. I remember my first-grade teacher weeping in front of us when our regular morning playtime broadcast was interrupted by a solemn male voice announcing the death of King George VI. I was not moved by the death of the king, of whose existence I was only dimly aware at the time, but by the depth and sincerity of my teacher's grief. While I recall vividly the visit of Queen Elizabeth in 1954, I have no recollection whatsoever of the electoral struggles of that year between Menzies and Evatt or of the Petrov affair. I do remember, however, the stories some of our neighbours told me of the suffering of Australian troops in Burma or Thailand and of their refusal to buy the cheap and shoddy Japanese goods—how times have changed—beginning to appear in the shops.

I recall some minor outbreaks of sectarianism, at the time altogether beyond my ken—like the argument between some of my Protestant schoolmates and a group of children from the local Catholic school over the sacrament of transubstantiation, or the alarming moment when one of my Presbyterian neighbours stormed towards her newly acquired television set in order to turn off the film it was showing. The film was called *It's a Great Day for the Irish*. Nothing in our Central European home had prepared me for any of this.

Above all I remember the sport—not only the playing but the undeserved sharing in the splendid achievements. I was too late for Frank Sedgman, but old enough to spend summer after summer seeing Lew Hoad and Rod Laver and Ken Rosewall retaining the Davis Cup. I was too late for Donald Bradman, but old enough to remember when young Norm O'Neill was to be our next Don Bradman which, alas, he never was. I spent every winter playing football until dusk, poorly but passionately, and listening each Saturday to the radio, to bear witness to the performance of my beloved Geelong. The obscure footballers of those days—Ron Hovey, George McGrath, Fred Wooller—assumed for me the status of mysterious Greek gods.

I cannot say that I ever quite ceased to feel to some extent an outsider in this world. I remember at a friend's birthday party a motherly summons to come inside to escape the 'mozzies'. I was the only one who didn't know what she meant. Nonetheless this was the world, outside the home, I came to understand and, unselfconsciously, to love. In this very concrete way I came to be an Australian.

It would be many years before I could provide some form of reasoned explanation for my attachment to this country. If I were now asked to justify this attachment I would reply by pointing to three features of our national make-up.

My first choice will cause annoyance in some quarters. And yet, as the child of Central European migrants, who has spent much of his adult life in ruminations on the destructiveness of political conditions in Europe during the twentieth century, I cannot budge. My first choice is our British legacy. If Australia had been first colonised by Chinese or Spaniards or Frenchmen or Germans or Russians—and even more if for the first three-quarters of its history it had been settled overwhelmingly by immigrants from this original country of colonisation—it would be, in almost every conceivable way, a different country from the one it is now. The Britons who settled Australia brought with them, inescapably, a complex, intricate and unique civilisational pattern, which had evolved over hundreds of years on the other side of the world. Non-Aboriginal Australia did not begin *de novo*. It was, from the first day of settlement, hundreds of years old.

The cultural baggage Arthur Phillip and those who followed him brought with them included language (in some ways the deepest inheritance of all); literature; the understanding of the rule of law; a tenacious notion of private property; distrust of the tyrannical state; belief in, and experience of, an idiosyncratic form of parliamentary government; political parties, trade unions and social clubs; a passion for sports and hobbies; social tolerance and suspicion of fanaticism; a slight feeling of superiority to foreigners; a certain Protestant sectarianism and Irish Catholic anti-establishmentarianism; a self-deprecating humour; an expectation of ample meals; the pub; little interest in cuisine. Need I go on?

Notwithstanding the anti-British edge of some versions of multicultural ideology and of some rather traditional Irish anti-Britishness (emanating at present from Paul Keating), the foundations of Australian civilisation remain, and will remain for a very long time, stubbornly British. I am sure that, in fact if not in theory, the British foundation of Australian civilisation is one of its strongest attractions for most immigrants from Europe, the Middle East or Asia.

And yet Australian civilisation is more complex than this account suggests. This brings me to the second source of what I take to be central to the Australian tradition. While the immigrants to Australia carried with them much that was British, they also, in coming here, consciously shed a part of that cultural baggage. The Britain from which our settlers came was a hierarchical society where the idea of class remained a powerful force in social life. Australia, by contrast, was settled by wave after wave of lower-middle-class or working-class British and Irish men and women who had no love of class privilege and who saw in Australia a means of escape from a deferential society. Through their influence, in Australia, the British cultural heritage was importantly modified by an ethos of egalitarianism.

Until very recently at least, Australia lacked the extremes of wealth and poverty known to Britain, Europe and the United States. Until very recently it was, as a culture, instinctively hostile to social snobbery, pretension and privilege. There might be members of racing or cricket clubs, but they were not notably better treated as spectators than non-members. More deeply, until very recently, Australia contrived a social system—based around full employment, all-round protectionism, minimum wages and the impartial judicial arbitration of industrial disputes between employers and employees—which was the despair of both Marxists and laissez-faire economists, but which underpinned the egalitarian branch of Britishness which flourished here.

This egalitarian ethos was shared until the 1980s by both the Labor and non-Labor political parties. Indeed one of the peculiarities of our nation's history is that this system was established by the great liberal Alfred Deakin and most effectively administered by the great conservative Sir Robert Menzies. Although most of us would agree that aspects of this 'settled policy' require reform, it is far from clear to me that we have yet, as a nation, come to understand how much of the traditional system must be thrown overboard, what precise balance of policies should take its place, and what we stand to gain and lose in the process.

The third great force shaping Australian civilisation is more intangible than the first two but, I think, no less important. I call it space. In a manner not possible in the closer settlements of Britain, Europe and Asia, Australia has offered to its inhabitants, both farmers and urban dwellers, the kind of possibility of land-ownership open only to the privileged in the old world. Until very recently, when some of these dreams have begun to fade, Australia has been a kind of common man's paradise, where peasants or rural labourers could become farmers and where city workers could aspire to generous-sized houses set on substantial suburban blocks with room to raise poultry or run a dog or cultivate a garden. Most Australians have access to sports fields or tennis courts or public golf links and to the beach or the bush.

Freedom is a complex idea. In part it is reliant on political institutions and civil liberties. But in part, as well, it may rest on the availability of elbow room and privacy; on the capacity to play, tinker and potter; to raise a family in comfortable surrounds. The very real appeal of Australian life—its relaxation, its cheerfulness, its quiet optimism—has been, in my view and my experience, intimately connected with this sense of space.

1993

The Young Menzies

ROBERT Menzies, the subject of Allan Martin's biography, was born in Jeparit in 1894 into the modest, small-town, Protestant middle class.* The ethos of the home of James and Kate Menzies combined respect for learning and hard work with belief in civic duty and, above all else, fierce and unquestioning family loyalty. On Robert's mother's Sampson side there was Cornwall and a strain of trade unionism; on his father's side Scotland, Calvinism and respectable conservatism. While the Menzies strand dominated Robert's public career, its sternness was ultimately softened by the labourist consciousness that he encountered in early debate with his beloved maternal grandfather.

Federation Australia was a thin society of relatively frictionless upward mobility. Through native wit, diligence and the scholarship trail the young Robert made the social journey from Jeparit

---

Robert Menzies: A Life, Volume 1, 1894–1943, Allan Martin, Melbourne University Press, 1993.

to the University of Melbourne without the kind of social or psychic strain which would have attended such a journey in England. The man who graduated cum laude in law at the end of World War I was handsome, respectable, moralistic and superior. Only one shadow fell across his brilliance. Despite a commission in the Melbourne University Rifle Club, and despite his strong support for Billy Hughes' conscription referenda, he had not volunteered to serve his country at war. Already his university detractors were drawing attention to this fact. Nothing could have caused Menzies more pain.

Allan Martin's biography resolves the question of Menzies' war service once and for all. During the Great War the Menzies family had settled in Melbourne; James was pursuing a career in the Victorian parliament. The family had, at this time, been devastated by the elopement of their one daughter, Belle, with an unsuitable soldier. At a family conference, regarded by all its members as absolutely binding, it was determined that the two eldest brothers should join the AIF, while the youngest, Robert, should support his parents. Despite the pain the issue caused him, Robert could not, would not, reveal why he had not volunteered. When a former student of the university wrote a bitter letter from the trenches complaining about the 'presposterous rot' being published in *Melbourne University Magazine* about the agonising question of whether to volunteer or graduate, Menzies the law student insisted that it be published. In response, he hinted obscurely of his plight: 'the path of duty does not always lead to the recruiting depot—duty has to many in this respect been a hard taskmaster'.

The failure to volunteer did not blight Menzies' early legal career. On graduation he served an apprenticeship at the feet of Australia's greatest jurist, Owen Dixon, who became thereafter a lifelong friend and political supporter. Already by his mid-twenties, he had made a successful appearance at the High Court. Even Father was impressed. 'You know my dear,' Menzies reported him as saying to his wife, 'I have been underestimating Robert.' Despite his interrogatory skills, Menzies' deepest interest was not in criminal but constitutional law. With Owen Dixon, he won the Engineers' Case, which represented a landmark extension of commonwealth powers. With the encouragement of certain conservative Melbourne businessmen who had organised themselves in 1926 into a federal union, he threw his weight into a referendum campaign to deny the commonwealth, and Stanley Bruce, extended arbitration powers. This was, according to one reading, the turning point in Menzies' career; his initiation into politics.

Menzies later described this entrance as a response to the call of public duty. Perhaps so. But clearly also, and more deeply, political battle had stirred the blood. In 1927 he took a Victorian upper house seat and, without delay, a minor ministry, from which he promptly resigned on a matter of 'high principle'—the extension of a loan to the Amalgamated Co-operative Freezing Works. Menzies was, from the first, an unforgiving public finance man.

By late 1929—at the time when the Great Depression was beginning to be felt—Menzies moved to the Victorian lower house. More importantly, by this time he had drifted to the centre of the Melbourne business and political establishment, to a group centred on the shadowy National Union (reputed to run the Nationalist Party), the Melbourne Club and Mount Macedon. Martin's biography makes it clear that Menzies' great patron was the kindly Melbourne Club-Macedonian stockbroker, Staniforth Ricketson. Through his political support and financial assistance, young Menzies passed rapidly into the inner sanctum of Melbourne conservatism.

The years of Menzies' real political initiation, 1929–31, were of course among the most turbulent in the history of Australian politics. The Scullin government was brutally divided between three responses to the depression it had inherited: the debt repudiationism of the NSW premier, J. T. Lang; the credit expansionism of Scullin's first, scandal-besieged treasurer, E. G. Theodore; and the orthodox deflationism of Joseph Lyons. It was the task of the Melbourne conservatives during these years to destroy both Lang and Theodore and to detach Lyons from Scullin. The centrepoint of this political process was the emotional campaign of 1930 to 'convert' a loan of £28 million, a campaign brilliantly described by Martin. The campaign, joined by Lyons, was for respectable Middle Australia a kind of financial Gallipoli. The repugnance within this world to the postponement, let alone repudiation, of debt repayment ran deep. The national day set aside for the campaign's conclusion was called 'All for Australia Day'. The campaign was an outstanding success. The loan had been oversubscribed by two million pounds; Australia's honour had been saved; Lyons had made himself, through his involvement in it, the natural anti-Labor leader of Australia. He now soon resigned from the Scullin government. A small group of conservatives convinced him to accept, and Latham to release, the leadership of a revitalised non-Labor movement, based around a series of anti-Lang citizens' leagues and the old Nationalist Party. The new party called itself the United Australia Party.

Martin's biography makes it clear that, alongside his mentor Ricketson, Menzies was a critical actor in the complex negotiations and fierce campaigns which together reconstructed Australian conservative politics. It also shows Menzies' political performance at its least attractive. Where Lyons' defence of deflation and fiscal propriety was homely and humane, Menzies', by contrast, was legalistic and pompous.

One of Menzies' great themes in these years was 'the sanctity of contracts'. Their sanctity rendered him quite unmoved by all parliamentary measures to relieve the distress of the indebted. 'Humanity,' on one occasion he informed the Victorian house, 'is not greater than finance.' It was a not uncharacteristic turn of phrase. Even more unfortunate was a speech (which became notorious) in which he argued that rather than escaping its financial troubles by 'abandoning traditional standards of honesty, of justice, of fair play, of resolute endeavour, it would be far better for Australia that every citizen within her boundaries should die of starvation during the next six months'. Allan Martin complains that this passage is usually quoted out of context. Perhaps. But there is no context that could redeem it. We are reminded that Menzies was still a very young man. It was social attitudes like this which led John Cain Snr to call the young Menzies the most 'dyed-in-the-wool Tory' Australian parliaments had seen in fifty years.

This was, however, at best a half-truth. When he entered the Victorian lower house in 1929 a sympathetic portrait had called attention to 'a critical Liberal strain that may have derived from his maternal grandpa'. When he entered the federal parliament, five years later, having inherited both the seat of Kooyong and the attorney-generalship from John Latham, his later solicitor-general, Kenneth Bailey, remarked upon or perhaps reminded him of his 'robust liberalism'. The remainder of his political career represented a search for balance between the strands of the conservative and the liberal within his nature.

Allan Martin calls the young Robert Menzies 'the quintessential representative of the Melbourne bourgeoisie'. He was also, however, the quintessential inter-war Australian-Briton. The Australian-Briton was, characteristically, a Protestant of mixed English-Scottish-Welsh-Cornish (and perhaps Irish) ancestry. He or she felt an intense loyalty to two 'countries', Australia and the United Kingdom, and to one overarching and unifying idea, the British Empire. The Australian-Briton was not torn between conflicting loyalties to Australia and Britain but felt, rather, that the attachment to one deepened the tie to the other. The kind of attachment which the Australian-Briton felt to his or her two countries was, of course, importantly different. Britain was, for many Australian-Britons, Home—the source of law, institutions, language, literature, custom. But it was also, for many, a country of the mind, which might never be visited throughout a lifetime. Australia, despite its strange, originally alien landscape, was for them not Home but home—the site of genuine experience, of family, neighbourhood, work. Not the least virtue of this biography is its sensitive and sympathetic portrayal, through Robert Menzies, of what this complex Australian-British identity once meant.

As commonwealth attorney-general, Menzies travelled to Britain in 1935, 1936 and 1938. On the first occasion in particular, as his breathless diary indicated, Menzies was swept away by a naive and unaffected enthusiasm for Home—the grandeur of Westminster, the picturesqueness of the Cotswolds, the immaterialism of All Souls. He was also swept away by pride at his great political, legal and social success. On his first visit Menzies never quite shed the innocence of the all-conquering provincial. After his grandest triumph, his oration at the conference of the Empire Parliamentary Association, his thoughts turned home. 'I think,' he recorded in his diary, 'of Mother and Father listening in 12,000 miles away and trust not to dishonour them and get to my feet, and *mirabile dictu*, get away with it.' Nor did he quite grasp, on this first visit, the manner in which the British establishment was deliberately cultivating him. After meeting Menzies in Australia the *éminence grise* of the Committee for Imperial Defence, Maurice Hankey, telegraphed Stanley Baldwin: 'We ought to make much of him. He is a strong man and very pro-British, and most anxious to meet our leading men.'

Gradually in the later visits of 1936 and 1938—where Menzies was involved in the demanding and tedious post-Ottawa trade negotiations over Argentinian beef and tariff protection for Australian manufacture—his naivety about Home came to be tempered by a certain realistic disillusion about the role of imperial idealism where economic matters were concerned. He negotiated toughly over trade on behalf of his government, without being deflected in the slightest from imperial loyalty (and, as it happens, an altogether uncritical support for Chamberlain's appeasement policy). Menzies was unproblematically loyal to both the British Empire and to Australia. Only a later generation would discover in this kind of double loyalty something shameful. In so doing they—and most importantly the late Manning Clark—took it as their task not to illumine but to argue against Australian history.

Joseph Lyons once explained in a letter to his formidable wife, Enid: 'We induced Menzies to come [to Canberra] in the expectation that he would succeed me.' During Menzies' second trip to England in 1936 Lyons was even more explicit. He promised Menzies he would 'press' for the changeover on his return. Lyons, however, led the UAP to the 1937 election. After Menzies' third trip, in late October 1938, something in him may have snapped. Allan Martin is characteristically careful here. Menzies, he argues, experienced now 'a seeming rush of ambition, the inwardness of which was and probably will always remain ambiguous'.

The first possible expression of this rush of ambition was a post-Munich speech in which he argued that democracies needed leadership as inspiring as that of the dictator countries. Most of the nation's press and, *a fortiori*, an enraged Enid Lyons took this as implied criticism of the prime minister. Menzies to the end denied it. Whatever the case, five months later, to the general approval of the press, he resigned from the Lyons government over a matter of principle—the bloody-minded Country Party obstruction of Dick Casey's far-sighted national insurance scheme. Had Menzies somehow learnt of the approach Lyons had recently made to Stanley Bruce in London urging his return to the Australian prime ministership? Martin does not know.

A little over three weeks after Menzies' resignation Lyons was dead. What followed is powerfully described by Martin. Dr Earle Page, the leader of the Country Party, had announced he would not serve in a Menzies Cabinet. On 19 April 1939 he rose in the parliament to explain his decision. Twenty-four days earlier, Page claimed, Menzies had departed the Lyons government at a time of national crisis; twenty-four weeks earlier he had launched what had appeared to be an attack on his leader; twenty-four years earlier he had failed to serve his country at war. The house was in uproar. During the speech Pattie Menzies left the visitors' gallery;

she would never acknowledge Page again. Fadden dissociated himself from his leader. Menzies defended himself as best he could. James and Kate Menzies soon flew to Canberra to defend the honour of their son. Kate told the *Daily Telegraph* that the family had compelled their youngest 'to look after us'. She regarded Bob as 'the bravest of all my boys'.

In the upshot Menzies took the prime ministership from Stanley Bruce, the National Union candidate (backed by Casey) whose terms were impossible, and from the aged Billy Hughes. In regard to Page, however, Menzies had already paid a heavy price for years of ill-disguised contempt.

Within six months of the Menzies prime ministership, Germany had invaded Poland, Britain had declared war on Germany and 'as a consequence' Australia was, as Menzies pointed out, also at war. Allan Martin shows, in one of his rare authorial interventions, that not one parliamentarian opposed Menzies' consequentialist logic, let alone his Cabinet's decision. No one regarded this as an 'other people's war'.

As it turned out, despite considerable success in laying the administrative ground for Australian mobilisation, the first year of the war was for Menzies a distinctly miserable time. Under great pressure from Britain and the New Zealand government, Australian troops were dispatched to the Middle East against his wishes. During the period of the Nazi–Soviet pact, communist-led unions created trouble, especially on the coalfields. Menzies was beset by a whispering campaign from his supposed allies in politics and the press about his alleged failure as a war leader. Most shatteringly of all, in August 1940, he lost three of his closest political friends in an air crash—Street, Gullett and Fairbairn. His mood at this moment was captured in an extraordinarily bitter letter he composed, but most likely did not post, to the editor of the *Sydney Morning Herald*. 'Every campaign has been personally abhorrent to me. I have waded through the sewer of personal abuse...I sometimes curse the day I entered politics.'

By early 1941 the situation in the Pacific was darkening. With John Curtin's Labor Party now balancing the UAP in the House of Representatives but refusing to form a national government, and parts of his own disaffected backbench in almost open rebellion, it was probably with some relief that Menzies embarked upon his fourth trip to London. Its purpose was to concentrate the minds of the British military on the alarming state of Singapore and Far Eastern defences. By the time he arrived, this mission—which Bruce had presciently warned was unlikely to bear fruit—was to some extent overtaken by preparations for the ill-fated Greek campaign. Allan Martin's assessment of Menzies' role here is characteristically precise. Menzies, he argues, was not informed of the campaign until he arrived in London. He did not, as some have alleged, keep General Blamey in the dark. From the first he regarded the campaign less favourably than Churchill and more favourably than Bruce. His demands for Australian Cabinet approval were, in effect, all but ignored. Approval was sought three days after the first Australian units had been dispatched to Greece.

From his first encounter in 1935, Menzies' relations with Churchill had been ambivalent. During the visit of early 1941 they deteriorated sharply. Menzies came to believe that Churchill's judgment was erratic, that his temperament was dictatorial, and that he had by now surrounded himself with spineless yes-men in the War Cabinet. Towards the end of his visit, Menzies began to do the anti-Churchill political rounds, grumbling with the embittered Lloyd George, the cantankerous Beaverbrook, the dispossessed Hankey. According to Martin's account, it seems clear that Menzies, while in London and for several months thereafter, did dream of holding down a permanent War Cabinet post in London, as the South African Jan Smuts had done in World War I. Churchill denied him this dream. It also is clear that, *pace* David Day, he did not plot for himself a path to the British prime ministership. With a combination of delicacy and firmness, Martin shows the Day thesis to be nonsense.

As Menzies approached Australia in late May 1941 he confided to his diary: 'A sick feeling of repugnance and apprehension grows in me.' In part this may have reflected his unrealised War Cabinet ambitions; in part his disgust at having to return from the spirit of common endeavour and common sacrifice of Blitz Britain to the safety of a hedonistic, squabbling country. On arrival Menzies did not conceal his dismay with his country. He forfeited altogether thereby his last prime ministerial authority.

Allan Martin's biography reveals, as I understand it for the first time, Menzies' own account of the plot that undid his leadership. Somehow these interesting details seem almost irrelevant. From the moment of his return home in 1941 his prime ministership was doomed. Even his strongest supporters knew that this most gifted of Australian politicians had been brought down by some strange incapacity to win the confidence of his fellows or to disguise from them the sense of his own superiority. He was, rightly, in August 1941, dispatched by them to the wilderness. When he inherited the leadership of the shattered rump of the UAP after the election of 1943—the point at which the first volume of Martin's biography concludes—it was altogether unclear whether Menzies had emerged from the wilderness or his colleagues had joined him there.

Martin's first volume of Menzies is a genuinely fine book—elegant, absorbing, timely, fair-minded and scrupulous. There are, however, two lines of criticism which I would level against it—one minor and one major.

The minor line of criticism is largely aesthetic. It seemed to me, in the reading, that the decision to conclude the first volume of Menzies' biography in 1943 was, from the artistic but also from the analytical point of view, a mistake. The savage and humiliating loss of the prime ministership in August 1941 was the pivotal point in Menzies' career: the point towards which the balance of his early political virtues and vices inexorably led him; the point from which he had to discover in himself the spiritual energy, the courage and wisdom on which to rebuild his political fortunes. The greatness of Menzies is found not in what is revealed in this volume but in his subsequent capacity to transcend the loss of 1941. In this book, for these reasons, the two post-1941 chapters seemed to me something of an anticlimax.

The major line of criticism goes deeper. To put the matter simply: as an historian Allan Martin seems, to me at least, too non-interventionist. Let two examples suffice. I approached this biography with the hope of coming to understand the evolution of Menzies' early socio-economic ideas. What I discovered was a Menzies who in 1930 was able to say 'humanity is not greater than finance'; who in 1934 appeared to a Britisher 'contemptuous of soft and soppy policies' but who in the same year delivered his maiden speech on the evil of unemployment; who in 1938 was an enthusiastic supporter of tariff protection for Australian manufacturing; who in 1939 resigned from the Lyons government over its failure to deliver national insurance; and who, in 1943, in his famous 'Forgotten People' speech, distanced himself from both socialism and old laissez-faire. What I was unable to discover from Martin's biography was how exactly the pieces of this jigsaw fitted together. Or again. I also approached this biography (my appetite whetted by Judith Brett's recent psycho-political study of Menzies) with some hope of assessing her claims about the dynamics of his family life and how they may have affected his political style and his relations with his country and his colleagues. While throughout Martin's book there are interesting snippets on Menzies' private life, there is nothing analytic or systematic. Two additional, non-narrative chapters—one on the mind of Robert Menzies, another on his non-public life—would, I think, have deepened our understanding of him.

I do not, however, wish to cavil. No one living in a country which regards Manning Clark as its greatest historian can afford to undervalue an Allan Martin.

1993

Why I Am Not a Republican

IT is now abundantly clear that when Mr Keating retired to the backbench between the first and second challenges to Mr Hawke no new grand economic strategy, which might fill the spiritual void created by his loss of faith in the Treasury line, occurred to him. Instead, in its place, was born the ambition to fulfil an historic destiny by becoming the father of the Australian republic. At first, Mr Keating tested the water on the question of the flag. When that did not ruin him, he openly made his bid for the republic.

History is, generally, not shaped by the mass of ordinary people but by relatively small groups who care passionately. Three groups in Australia care passionately for the republic. The first, of course, are the self-conscious Irish. Their folk memory is suffused with stories of harsh British rule in Ireland—of Cromwell and the Famine and the Easter Rising of 1916—and of the sectarian struggles and the Protestant ascendancy in Australia. Irish Australians are instinctively both anti-British and anti-monarchy. It is no accident that the first Australian prime minister who raised the issue of republicanism seriously was a *Keating*, that the leader of the movement was a *Keneally*, the editor of the conservative newspaper which supported the cause a *Kelly*, and the first Liberal Party leader who broke ranks on the issue a *Fahey*. For the first time in our history the Australian elite is generously (and rightly) peopled by descendants of the Irish. In part at least, republicanism is their revenge.

The Irish Australian elite is not alone. The republican cause is of passionate interest to two other groups—the ethnic intelligentsia and the left. The ethnic intelligentsia have a variety of particular reasons, drawn from political struggles in their ancestral homelands, for cheering on republicanism. The kind of historical memory that makes the Irish anti-British, makes many Australian Greeks anti-monarchy and many Arabs anti-colonial. The ethnic intelligentsia, however, also share a general enthusiasm for what one might call the multicultural project, at whose core is the aspiration to overturn all British cultural symbols in this country with a new symbolism based on a mental picture of Australia as a 'mosaic' of immigrant and indigenous 'contributions'. For the ethnic intelligentsia a victory of republicanism would represent the official burial of British Australia and the formal triumph of its desired successor: Australia Multicultural.

The third source of support for the republican cause is the left. While the left intelligentsia share some of the anti-British *ressentiment* of the Irish and the enthusiasm for the multicultural project of the ethnics, in addition they see in the republican movement a potent weapon in their protracted cultural struggle against insufferable Australian-establishment conservatism. The left associates constitutional monarchy with imperial loyalty, cultural cringe, the Singapore 'betrayal', the Melbourne Club, Sir Robert Menzies' monarchism, Sir John Kerr and 1975. For the left the victory of republicanism would represent belated compensation for a century of almost incomprehensible Australian conservatism.

To borrow the presiding metaphor of the comic final volume of Manning Clark's *History of Australia*, it would see the uprooting of the 'old dead tree' of Australia's British connection and its replacement by the 'young tree green' of an authentic Australian nationalism.

There has been until now, so far as I am able to see, only one powerful argument advanced in favour of the abandonment of constitutional monarchy and the embrace of the republic—that put forward by John Hirst in *Quadrant* in September 1991. Hirst argued for a minimal republican program: the governor-general as head of state, elected by a college of federal and state parliamentarians. According to him, such a change was required because, with the fading of the once-real aura of the British monarchy in Australia, a symbolic vacuum had been created at the heart of our political culture. This vacuum was being filled by the fads and fashions of the day. Only under a republican constitution could a sturdy civic culture be recreated, capable of recognising our debt to Britain and of drawing to itself the allegiance of the young.

On one issue Hirst was right. There can be little doubt that the symbolic power of the monarchy in contemporary Australia is all but dead, and little chance that it can be revived. On the broader cultural question, however, I think Hirst is wrong. As the tide of republicanism has risen in Australia, the movement has rapidly been commandeered by those who see it not as a means for reviving our civic culture but as a vehicle for reshaping our constitution and society, rewriting our history or twisting the knife in the heart of the Menzies tradition. The victory of republicanism would not mean, as things stand, an antidote against the fashions of the day but a significant triumph for them. So long as this remains the case, I shall resist the republican drum.

1993

On the Manning Clark Affair

ON 8 May 1991 I lunched with Peter Ryan. (I have consulted a diary to establish the exact date.) One of the topics for discussion was Manning Clark. The subject of Clark had clearly been weighing heavily on his mind. He spoke of his intention to write an essay about his old friend whose *History of Australia* he had published when he ran Melbourne University Press. It would not be flattering. Ryan was already imagining the anger of Manning and the social ostracism which would be visited upon him by Clark's vast network of friends and admirers. Never mind, it *had* to be done.

A fortnight following our lunch Manning Clark died unexpectedly. I heard no more of this essay for some eighteen months until Peter Ryan inquired as to whether I might be interested in considering a piece on Manning Clark for publication in *Quadrant*. I said that indeed I was interested. It was this essay which eventually arrived on my desk and which was published in *Quadrant* in 1993.

To my considerable surprise Ryan's essay provoked, almost instantly, a major national controversy in which even the prime minister, Paul Keating, has become involved. Predictably enough, I suppose the early rounds of the controversy have focused more on the propriety of Peter Ryan for writing the essay than of the infinitely more important question of the status of Manning Clark.

Because Ryan's essay appeared two years after Manning Clark's death, Ryan was openly accused (by Professor Stuart Macintyre, for example) of 'personal cowardice'. This, of course, is an extremely serious accusation. It is also, almost self-evidently, false. As Peter Ryan makes clear, his essay on Manning Clark was written with his eyes fully open to the social price he would be obliged to pay as a consequence. Whatever else may be said against it, its publication required considerable bravery from Ryan, and of a kind only infrequently encountered in the academy.

Given the courageous kind of man I know Peter Ryan to be—in part on the basis of his self-effacing memoir of his war experience in New Guinea—I have no doubt that he would have preferred to have had the essay that was bubbling up in him published when we lunched in May 1991 rather than after Manning Clark's death.

At the very least Macintyre and others cannot deny that this is an open question. Accusations of cowardice against a man who risked death in the New Guinea jungles, and who is now risking a kind of social death in the circles of the intelligentsia, should not be levelled so lightly.

In the first blows of the controversy Peter Ryan was accused not merely of cowardice for delaying his publication until after Manning Clark's death but also of a kind of sacrilege for launching what Robert Hughes called, in characteristically pontifical style, an attack upon the dead. This accusation seems to me simply nonsensical. Manning Clark died more than two years before Ryan's essay appeared. Is it seriously being suggested that critical examination of the work of the man who is regarded as Australia's foremost historian, and as one of its most important thinkers, should be placed under a semi-permanent moratorium? Is it being suggested that only those who are enthusiastic about his work and thought should be permitted to speak?

Some of the critics of Peter Ryan have in mind, in criticising him, the pain his essay will cause Manning Clark's family. This is a serious issue. No doubt the pain is genuine. The anger felt in the family towards Ryan (which was expressed by Clark's widow with some restraint and grace) is only too easy to understand. I have no doubt that Peter Ryan does indeed understand all this. The question, however, is whether or not considerations such as these should stand in the way of free and open discussion of one of the central figures in our history.

I do not think so. Nor, it appears, did Manning Clark. Shortly after Sir Robert Menzies' death, he described Menzies as a 'hollow man' and as a 'nothing'. In his general *History*, he portrayed him as an Anglophile lickspittle who had devoted his life to service of the 'Old Dead Tree' of empire. Did Manning have in mind the feelings of Dame Pattie and the children? Did he regard their certain pain as a ground for self-censorship? Despite the feelings of the Menzies family, Manning Clark, I assume, thought that he was obliged to tell the truth, as he saw it, about a central figure in our history. In his *Quadrant* essay, Ryan has done no more and no less.

The final accusation levelled against Peter Ryan's essay is that the criticism of Manning Clark it contains is, because it is purely *ad hominem*, of no consequence.

In part, this claim (first advanced by Robert Hughes—before he had read the essay!) is simply false. The second half of Ryan's essay is devoted to a sustained criticism of the work—to its factual inaccuracies, its clichés, its bathos, its frozen 1940s University of Melbourne Labour Club leftism, its imperceptiveness concerning character, and so on.

More deeply the accusation of *ad hominem* misses altogether what is genuinely serious in much, although not all, of the anecdotal material in the Ryan piece. According to his analysis the faults in Clark's character—his extraordinary unwillingness to listen to criticism, his self-absorption, above all his determination to fabricate for himself a grand prophetic persona—led him into the squandering of his fine talents as teacher and writer.

In a curious way Ryan's portrait of Manning Clark is reminiscent of Clark's own style of portraiture. If I grasp Ryan correctly, he observed in what he regarded as Manning Clark's long decline as an historian the working out of what Clark might have called his fatal flaw—extraordinary vanity.

Nor can the evidence for such a claim—the interconnection between character and work—be simply brushed aside. Listen, for example, to the strange final words of the last chapter of Clark's concluding volume:

> The time was coming when an Australian voice would be heard in the age when men and women lived without faith either in God or in the capacity of human beings for better things. The time was coming when an Australian voice would be heard on the great debate on what it has all been for. The time was coming when an Australian voice would be heard telling the story of who Australians were and what they might be. A new discovery of Australia was about to begin…

By now Manning Clark had become the hero of his own *History*.

It is not only Peter Ryan who has been criticised for this essay on Clark. *Quadrant* has also been taken to task for its role in this affair. According to Professor Macintyre and several others, *Quadrant* has been 'hunting' after Manning Clark for fifteen years.

What is the evidence here? So far as I can remember in the twelve years prior to my editorship *Quadrant* published only two significant articles on Manning Clark, one by John Carroll and one by Claudio Veliz. Given that *Quadrant* is the only conservative literary journal in Australia and that the final volumes of Clark's history are contemptuous and scathing of the conservative tradition in this country, the fact that these essays are less than kind is hardly surprising or evidence of a 'hunt'.

In the first three years of my editorship of *Quadrant* we published nothing on Clark except a short assessment at his death by John Barrett. This year we have published two pieces—a general essay on Australian history by John Hirst, which begins with a short but penetrating critique of Manning Clark, and Ryan's essay.

Although I did not commission either piece, after their arrival I was genuinely hopeful that *Quadrant* might become the forum for a lively debate about the status of Clark's *History* and of its strengths and weaknesses. Thus far, the Hirst article has occasioned no response from Australia's academic historians. When the dust settles it will be interesting to see whether the public controversy the Ryan essay has excited will divert them from their private exchanges or arouse them from their slumber. Whether the academic historians like it or not the question of Manning Clark seems to many thoughtful members of the general public a matter of real importance.

Professor Macintyre has labelled my claim to be interested in stimulating a discussion on Manning Clark 'duplicitous'. From where his high-minded omniscience in this matter comes I do not know. I am as genuinely committed to the debate on Manning Clark as I was in 1991 to the idea of opening the pages of *Quadrant* to a discussion of economic rationalism. I suppose the only difference is that this time a different part of the political spectrum will disapprove.

If the academic historians deign to enter this debate it will be of considerable interest. Thus far, in the media controversy at least, those who have been willing to talk have not felt able to defend Manning Clark on the conventional grounds of, let us say, balance, reliability, methodological rigour or, dare I say it, truthfulness.

In general their argument seems to be that Manning Clark was a great visionary and imaginative writer who must be judged by standards other than those more usually applied to academic historians. No doubt such a defence could be mounted intelligently. But it will have to show rather than assert the power of the imagination that controls the work. And it will have to show rather than assert the depth of its vision.

1993

The Whitlam Whirlwind

IN December 1972 Gough Whitlam led the Australian Labor Party to power after twenty-three years of unbroken conservative rule. On 11 November 1975 the Governor-General of Australia, Sir John Kerr, dismissed him. Within the Westminster system this was the first time since 1783 that the Crown or its representative had dismissed a government which had not broken the law and which commanded a majority in the lower house of the parliament.

The Australian political nation is still bitterly divided over the rights and wrongs of the dismissal, the most dramatic event in modern Australia's otherwise rather soporific postwar history. If the issue of the dismissal stubbornly refuses to die it is not because of the constitutional instabilities it left. Despite dire predictions there were none. It is rather because the differences between left and right over the place of Whitlam in the course of Australian history have never been resolved.

In 1967 Gough Whitlam won the Labor leadership. He revived his party's fortunes almost alone. Because his background placed him firmly within the professional middle class and because his serious political enemies came, almost entirely, from the doctrinaire left, before 1972 many thought of Whitlam as a pragmatist or even an opportunist, who had made his home in the Labor Party more or less by accident. They were quite wrong. Whitlam was a modernising reformer of genuinely radical bent. As a convinced centralist he conceived an ambitious constitutional blueprint for the movement of power in Australia from the states to the commonwealth. And, as a convinced socialist, he was the architect of a vast and costly program of egalitarian reform in areas of interest to him—social welfare, health, education, transport, urban planning and the arts.

Yet Whitlamism, before 1972, was more than the Australian version of Fabian socialism adapted to the Keynesian age. The years of Whitlam's leadership of the Labor opposition were also the years in which Australia, alongside all the advanced industrial democracies, experienced the first stirrings of the profound cultural revolution, in shorthand the sixties, which was destined to dissolve forever the old certainties on which attitudes to sexuality, male–female relations, race, hierarchy, authority, the natural environment, had for generations been based. Whitlam might have assumed the leadership of the Labor Party as a welfare state socialist. But by the early 1970s he had become, in addition, something rather different—the symbol of cultural hope for a new generation of university students and left-liberal intelligentsia, which had been politically mobilised and unified by opposition to the Vietnam War.

Although he was not really part of this generation, it was the progressivist Whig in him that allowed Whitlam to adapt to its mood. In 1972 he and his party campaigned under the extraordinarily successful slogan, 'It's Time'. It was the slogan of a new political elite-in-embryo, which felt that with the advent of Whitlam it had arrived at the threshold of power. A strange kind of youthful euphoria attended the election of the Whitlam government in December 1972.

Once in place the Whitlam Cabinet set about its transformative task with relish. In its first year this Cabinet made well over one thousand decisions, at a rate of more than twenty per week. Before Whitlam, in 1972, 700 pages of legislation passed the parliament; in 1973 2,200. Nor was legislation the only form of Whitlamite busyness. Once in office, Whitlam established more than a hundred expert commissions to report on every aspect of national life—from uranium mining to human relationships. He constructed for his government what two early analysts nicely labelled a statistical model of achievement.

By Australian standards the Whitlam government was not only extremely busy but also extremely radical. In the area of health, after almost three years of bitter struggle with the medical profession, it established Australia's first universal system of insurance. This was, by far, Whitlam's most popular and most enduring legacy. In the area of education, the Whitlam government vastly increased the size of commonwealth spending and the scope of commonwealth involvement. With Whitlam Australian education experienced three prodigal years. In the area of social welfare, the Whitlam government expanded commonwealth initiatives and expenditures at so rapid a pace it is scarcely an exaggeration to speak of Gough Whitlam as the father of the contemporary Australian welfare state. The transformation of the Australian state under Whitlam is most startlingly revealed in the figures. In 1972 public expenditure in Australia was 32 per cent of GDP. After three years of Whitlam it had risen to 39 per cent.

The Whitlam whirlwind affected far more than the size and nature of the Australian state. With Whitlam the history of Aboriginal land rights begins. Under Whitlam, for the first time, the Australian government became a significant patron of the arts. Australia's long march from cultural cringe to cultural strut had begun. Under Whitlam Australians were blessed, or cursed, by a new no-fault divorce law. With his support, the women's movement entered a fruitful partnership with the Australian bureaucracy. Femocracy was born. Due to his enthusiasm, Australia's only significant colony, Papua New Guinea, took an early, some still say premature, road to independence. Under Whitlam some remaining symbols of Australia's British connection—the imperial honours system, 'God Save the Queen' as the national anthem, state government appeals to the Privy Council—were overturned. In December 1972, after three of its Cabinet ministers described President Nixon as mad, Australia lost its reputation, very suddenly, as the United States' most reliable and predictable ally. It was never, under Whitlam, regained. Before Watergate overtook him, Nixon may have been seriously considering the removal of US military bases from Australian soil.

To attempt to do so much on so many different fronts in so short a time was no small thing. But to do so while deliberately offending so many powerful interests was to take a very real political risk. Yet Whitlam was a risk-taker of heroic proportions. His government offended farmers by withdrawing from them many traditional subsidies. It alienated domestic manufacturers by a sudden 25 per cent across-the-board tariff cut. It alarmed foreign mining companies with ambitious schemes for Australian control of resources and energy; doctors with its introduction of Medibank; lawyers with its plans for legal aid. State governments bitterly resisted the commonwealth's unwanted intrusions into their traditional spheres. The defence and intelligence establishment no less bitterly resented Whitlam's ostentatiously independent and, as they saw it, naively pro-communist and offensively anti-American foreign policy line. Not surprisingly the opposition parties became the rallying point of an intense and broad-based hostility to Whitlam.

In the life of the Whitlam government the middle of 1974 was the turning point. Whitlam won an early election but failed to gain the one thing he needed—control of the Senate. More importantly, the booming Australian economy, which had thus far sustained Whitlam, despite soaring inflation, finally broke. The most dramatic evidence of the collapse was in the labour market.

In June 1974 83,000 Australians were recorded as out of work; in December 1974 240,000. This was the worst employment outcome in Australia since the Great Depression. The Australian economy moved into deep recession. Stagflation was, undoubtedly, not an Australian domestic but a global phenomenon. No advanced industrial economy would escape its effects. Yet within Australia—because the end of what Eric Hobsbawm calls capitalism's Golden Age coincided with the arrival of Whitlam and his reforms—the new Labor government would be held by its many enemies, from that day to this, as mainly or even solely responsible for Australia's post-Golden Age economic woes. An extraordinarily powerful conservative myth—that the Whitlam government was the worst in Australia's history—took hold.

This myth was rendered particularly plausible because of the fact that, in the second half of 1974, at the moment of the ecoomic crash, the Cabinet's left briefly took control of Australia's economic affairs. Treasury, supported at first by Whitlam, advised a deflationary 'short, sharp shock' solution to the stagflation problem. The left opted instead for a high-spending Keynesian solution. The government decided on an overall increase in expenditure of four billion dollars or 32 per cent. Health spending increased 30 per cent; education 78 per cent; urban and regional affairs 173 per cent. Most observers regarded this budget as wildly irresponsible. More importantly, at this moment, relations between the Cabinet and Treasury almost altogether broke down.

This breakdown in relations marked the beginning of Whitlam's end. By late 1974 Treasury was aware of two half-baked schemes for the raising of vast petro-dollar Arab loans by unconventional means. From Treasury and elsewhere details of these loans adventures were leaked to the opposition, led now by its most formidable figure, Malcolm Fraser. These leaks were the most consequential in Australia's political history. At a time when the Whitlam government was increasingly electorally vulnerable, due to the sharp economic downturn and the general public's growing irritation with the grandiosity of the Whitlam style, the scandal of the loans affair was deployed very effectively by the opposition and the press to call into question not merely the capacity and probity of the Whitlam government but its very legitimacy. By the second half of 1975 many Australians genuinely believed that Whitlam was driving their country to ruin.

In July 1975 Whitlam was obliged to dismiss Jim Cairns, the deputy prime minister, from his Cabinet for misleading the house over the loans affair. In October he was obliged, for similar reasons, to ask Rex Connor, his mining minister, to resign. The opposition now moved in for the kill. Its tactic was the blocking of supply in the Senate. This was the first time in Australia's history that supply had been thus withheld.

Whitlam faced obvious catastrophe if forced to an election. He decided to resist. He spoke of 1975 as Australia's version of Britain's House of Lords crisis of 1909. He was determined to break the Senate's money power once and for all. For four weeks the nerve of both the government and opposition held. No one knew how the crisis would be resolved. All anyone knew was that if no one gave way, by the end of November, supply would be gone.

In thinking about the political situation he faced, Whitlam had not included the governor-general in his calculations. Whitlam thought Kerr had no option but to accept the advice of his prime minister, whatever that might be. Sir John Kerr was unwilling to see himself as Whitlam's rubber stamp. He was intensely interested in the legal conundrum of the reserve powers of the Crown. He feared for his country and for his own reputation if supply were to run out while the Senate crisis was unresolved. He also feared that if he spoke frankly with his prime minister about his concerns Whitlam might approach the Queen to have him removed.

By the end of the first week of November 1975 Kerr was moving towards his fateful decision. On 9 November he requested the opinion of the Chief Justice of the High Court, the former

Menzies minister, Sir Garfield Barwick. Barwick handed Kerr a brief note recommending dismissal. Two of Barwick's fellow judges seem to have accepted such a view. All this confirmed Kerr in the course of action he was already determined to take.

On 11 November Whitlam went to Government House with a request for a half-Senate election. To Whitlam's complete astonishment, Kerr handed him, instead, his notice of dismissal. Kerr received Fraser at once. Fraser agreed to act as caretaker prime minister until an election was held. Five weeks later this election took place. Its result came as no surprise. Whitlam and the Labor Party were defeated in one of the great landslides of Australian political history.

Since the dismissal, there have been only two schools of thought concerning 1975. Conservatives still argue that Whitlam was justly destroyed and by legal means. His government got what it richly deserved. The left still argues that Whitlam was unjustly destroyed, by illegal means, because its reform agenda threatened the interests of the privileged classes. Conservatives altogether underestimate Whitlam's real liberating cultural achievement. They exaggerate the degree of his government's economic culpability. For its part the left altogether underestimates the astonishing political clumsiness and the dangerous indifference to obstacles and social interests Whitlam displayed throughout the period of his rule.

Gough Whitlam himself has made two important contributions to the debate over his government and its fate. In 1979 *The Truth of the Matter* was published, a one-sided and bitchy yet powerfully argued case against Kerr. In 1985 he produced his magnum opus, *The Whitlam Government*, an extraordinarily self-centred and deeply tedious but nonetheless indispensable account of what he took to be his government's outstanding record of achievement.

In 1997 there is a third volume, *Abiding Interests*. It contains a loosely connected set of essays concerning the events of 1975; Whitlam's post-1975 life, especially as Australian Ambassador to

UNESCO; and his current opinions about some questions that dominated his time in government—international relations in Asia and Europe, Aboriginal land rights, medical insurance in Australia, environmental politics, democratic electoral reform. Many of these essays show Whitlam at his boastful and pedantic worst. At one moment, when he is pontificating, with real ignorance, on the breakup of Yugoslavia, he cannot refrain from reciting a brief history of the Balkans. None of these essays, more importantly, add anything substantial to our understanding of Whitlam or his government.

One of the essays in *Abiding Interests* is entitled 'Clues to a Coup'. It consists of little more than anti-Barwick gossip. Nonetheless there is in *Abiding Interests* one real, if unintended, clue to the turn of events in 1975. Only a genuine narcissist could imagine that there are readers eager to read such gossip or to hear a former prime minister's blow by blow account of his years as Australia's representative at UNESCO. Yet this, undoubtedly, is what Whitlam believes. As an author, Whitlam's willingness to inflict boredom is almost cruel. His political narcissism might have given him the boldness to undertake, more or less single-handedly, the transformation of his country. But it also helps explain one of his most important and puzzling shortcomings as Australian prime minister—his almost total unawareness of the existence of others.

1997

The Kerr Conundrum

PAUL Kelly is the pre-eminent Australian political journalist of his generation. The only book that rivalled his first study, *The Unmaking of Gough*, was *The Whitlam Venture* by Kelly's peer of the previous generation, Alan Reid. Nothing, however, even remotely rivalled Kelly's tour de force on the Hawke years, *The End of Certainty*, his finest achievement to date. Now, with *November 1975*, he has produced the most penetrating analysis of the dramas which overtook Australian politics in the spring of 1975.*

November 1975 is in essence a study of political character under conditions of crisis. Its analytical novelty lies in Kelly's decision to make its central focus not the leader of the opposition, Malcolm Fraser, or even the prime minister, Gough Whitlam, but the governor-general, Sir John Kerr. Kelly's Kerr emerges as a working-class lad who, despite outstanding success in the law,

---

*November 1975: The Inside Story of Australia's Greatest Political Crisis, Paul Kelly, Allen & Unwin, 1995.

never quite succeeded in overcoming his desire to please his social or legal superiors or his fear of earning their disapproval. Boundingly ambitious, but too timid to abandon law for a career in politics, he saw himself throughout his life as a man of destiny. At time of crisis a governor-general such as this—whose formality, courtesy and bonhomie masked deep layers of weakness, insecurity and suspicion—proved a political disaster.

Sir John Kerr's self-conception as governor-general was grandiose. On his appointment he returned to a book of his first patron, Dr Evatt, *The King and His Dominions*, where the doctrine of the reserve powers was defended, and to the works of a Canadian academic jurist, Dr Eugene Forsey, a reserve powers maximalist. Kerr was perhaps the only eminent Australian of his generation who, before November 1975, regarded the question of the reserve powers as one of the burning issues of Australian constitutional life.

Within months of assuming office Kerr was becoming concerned at his treatment at the hands of his prime minister. He was genuinely disturbed that he had not been invited to attend an Executive Council meeting of 13 December 1974 where four Whitlam ministers agreed to authorise the search for a four-billion-dollar loan for 'temporary purposes'. Although Kerr agreed to sign the minute authorising the loan quest, he regarded the legal argument buttressing the 'temporary purposes' phrase as laughable and the offhand manner in which he had been treated in this affair as offensive. He had no intention of becoming a 'rubber stamp' for the Whitlam government. By the autumn of 1975, when the loans affair had grown into a major political scandal, Kerr became prickly, defensive of the dignity of his office, wary of another Whitlam snub.

On all this Kelly is highly interesting. Kerr, he argues, did have a genuine cause for grievance about how he had been treated on 13 December. He did have legitimate grounds for concern over the propriety and legality of the loans decision. But he was quite wrong, or so Kelly believes, in keeping his grievances and concerns to himself. It was Kerr's right to expect frank consultation from his prime minister. It was his duty to offer frank advice and warning. Instead he chose simply to smoulder and to brood. This was not only unmanly. When a major constitutional crisis blew up later that year, it proved a fateful choice.

How is this crisis of 1975 to be explained? There is, as Kelly argues, a contradiction at the heart of the Australian constitution. According to the principle of responsible government, which we inherited from Westminster, governments are made and unmade on the floor of the lower house of our parliament, the House of Representatives. According to the principle of federalism, which we borrowed and adapted from the United States in order to clinch the federation deal, our upper house, the Senate, has the legal power to block supply and eventually, therefore, to unmake a government which retains the confidence of the House of Representatives. On 14 October 1975—following the resignation of the Minister for Energy and Natural Resources, Rex Connor, the loans affair's last victim—the opposition announced its decision to block supply in the Senate. For the first time in our history, a political crisis exposed the responsibilist–federalist contradiction at the constitution's core.

It is one of the oddities of Paul Kelly's book—and it must be said one of its limitations—that he is not really interested, except peripherally, in the question overshadowing the politics of 1975, namely why it was that for the first three years of the Whitlam government its opponents had never come to regard its exercise of power as legitimate. Those chiefly interested in this question will not find their answer in Kelly. He is almost exclusively concerned with a narrower question—namely why it was that the great political crisis of October–November 1975 became for Gough Whitlam not his greatest political triumph but his most catastrophic defeat. Kelly's explanation here focuses on the failure, at the moment of crisis, of the Whitlam–Kerr relationship and on the success of the third man, Malcolm Fraser, in exploiting this failure politically.

According to Kelly, Whitlam's failure was relatively straightforward. In concentrating on the task of breaking the will of the opposition in the Senate and in achieving what he had come to see as an historic people's victory over the reactionary forces of the Senate and the states, Whitlam simply took the political passivity and malleability of Sir John Kerr for granted. Whitlam did not believe a reserve power still resided in the governor-general. He did not believe the governor-general had any alternative but to accept his advice, whatever that might be. He did not even feel obliged to take his governor-general into his confidence during the crisis to explain his political strategy, or to refrain from light-hearted banter—'casual intimidation' Kelly calls it—about the possibility of dismissing him from office should he prove difficult. For Whitlam, in short, at this moment of crisis, Kerr was simply not a political consideration. Not only did Whitlam regard Kerr as a cipher; he was not even psychologically shrewd enough to see that it was politically necessary for his opinion to be concealed.

For the governor-general—according to his own estimation the most important public figure in the country—to be taken thus for granted was mightily displeasing. Clifton Pugh, who was painting Kerr's portrait at the time, saw his face turn crimson with rage when he heard Whitlam inform a television audience that his governor-general had absolutely no alternative but to accept his advice. But more than Kerr's *amour-propre* was wounded. As Kelly shows in convincing detail, by late October 1975 Kerr was haunted by a fear that if he should speak frankly with his prime minister about his political doubts and anxieties he might be sacked. In Kelly's version of events, the resolution of the greatest crisis in the nation's political history was, in the end, vitally influenced by a bad case of vice-regal employment insecurity.

By November Sir John Kerr felt alone, a bundle of nerves, fretting about the future of his nation and his person. It is, in

Kelly's version, to Malcolm Fraser's great political credit that, by this time, he had won the confidence of the governor-general by treating him with nothing more than fitting frankness and due courtesy. A sixty-minute interview between Kerr and Fraser in late October transformed, according to Kelly, the atmosphere of Australian politics. By this time Kerr was completely entrenched in his determination not to discuss political questions with his prime minister. He had decided long ago that Whitlam would not listen to reason. He was fearful that a frank conversation would rob him of his job. He had rationalised this fear by arguing to himself that his dismissal would imperil the nation by drawing the Queen into an ugly antipodean constitutional crisis.

After taking legal advice from the Chief Justice, Sir Garfield Barwick, a clear plan of action formed in Kerr's mind. He would not now even entertain a Whitlam proposal for a half-Senate election, which could not be held before supply was exhausted on 27 November. He would summon Whitlam and dismiss him. After checking on the telephone on the morning of 11 November that his terms were acceptable, he would summon Fraser and appoint him as caretaker prime minister. This is what transpired in the early afternoon of 11 November 1975—the most consequential political transaction in the history of the Australian federation.

In *November 1975* Paul Kelly is highly critical of Sir John Kerr's performance—essentially on three grounds. Kerr's intervention, he argues, was founded firstly on false law. While there was no question of an Australian government contriving to rule without supply, and no question that it was within the power of the Senate to block supply, there was simply no requirement for a government to resign or call an election—as both Barwick and Kerr believed—at the moment supply was denied it in the Senate. In the period before supply dried up it was perfectly legal for the Whitlam government to attempt to avoid a general election by political manoeuvre. A political resolution of the deadlock of the houses was, of course, what Whitlam was still trying to achieve on 11 November.

Sir John Kerr and his supporters (myself included) have long argued that, while supply would not run out until 27 November, 11 November was the final date for action by the governor-general because that was the last possible date for the calling of a pre-Christmas election. But as Kelly shows persuasively, this political logic is nonsensical. The decisive date for the securing of supply was not the date of the election but the date on which the decision to hold an election was made. Supply could have been secured if Whitlam had announced as late as 27 November that he intended to call a general election in the new year or if, on that day, Kerr had dismissed Whitlam and appointed Fraser as a caretaker prime minister on the same terms as he did on 11 November. By dismissing Whitlam on 11 November Kerr deprived him of a fortnight or so for political manoeuvre. And, as Kelly's mustering of the evidence convincingly shows, it is very far from obvious that the Coalition's Senate nerves would have held firm during this fortnight. This is no small matter. The breaking of even one or two senators might have rendered the November crisis a Whitlam triumph rather than a Whitlam disaster.

Which leads to Paul Kelly's most penetrating and persuasive criticism of Sir John Kerr. In 1867, in one of the most important passages of British constitutional theory, Walter Bagehot defined the outer limits of the power of the sovereign under Westminster as the right to be consulted, the right to advise, the right to warn. In *November 1975* Paul Kelly emerges as a convinced Bagehotian. Not only does he affirm the right of the governor-general to be consulted by his prime minister. In the case of the reserve powers he transforms the idea of sovereign rights—to advise and warn—into duties. For Kelly, and for at least half the Australian political nation in 1975, it was inconceivable that the governor-general should exercise his ultimate reserve powers without first discussing the vital questions with his prime minister, without first advising and warning openly and frankly of the course of action he intended to pursue in the absence of a political resolution to the deadlock of the houses. Kelly's robust Bagehotianism is constitutionally innovative, but for my part I find it altogether persuasive.

Paul Kelly is of course one of Australia's leading republicans. He understands that even a transition to the republic will not resolve the tension between the responsibilist and federalist impulses in our constitution. But at least, as he argues, the transition to a republic will protect the Australian head of state from the kind of tenure insecurity that niggled at Sir John Kerr during the November crisis. For, as Kelly points out, a governor-general dismissible at the will of the prime minister is less secure than either an hereditary monarch or a president elected by the people or the parliament. The coming of a republic will not by itself save us from another 1975. But it will protect its president from any temptation to repeat, during the crisis, the furtive behaviour of Sir John Kerr.

1995

Why I Am No Longer Not a Republican

I

Almost two years ago I wrote about why I was not a republican. Gradually, over these past two years, my thoughts on the issue have changed. Two developments have intervened. The first is the behaviour of the younger generation of the British royal family. In the greatest of all taxonomies of the English constitution, Walter Bagehot divided its fundamental institutions into two categories—the efficient, most importantly the Cabinet and the Commons; and the dignified, the monarchy and the Lords. In essence he argued that the political system worked through its efficient institutions but won the allegiance of the populace through the magic of its dignified institutions. In the past two years we have seen all magic drained away from the British royal house. In Britain itself, because of the weight of history, the house of Windsor may survive its younger inhabitants. But in Australia, where the fact of even a dignified monarch as our head of state has come to appear distinctly anachronistic, the appearance of a notably undignified one as her successor strikes me as nearly lethal to the monarchical cause.

But there is more to my conversion than this. Over the past two years it has become clear that even our staunch monarchists have come to believe that the present system is, in the long term, living on borrowed time. Recently John Howard, the most natural defender of the monarchy in this country, argued that if there was a referendum on the republic this year he would vote for the monarchy but that, if there was to be a referendum in five years, he could not say. Such an attitude is, I think, now typical among the more intelligent members of the monarchical party. But it is also an attitude deadly to their cause. An institution whose long-term future remains at least an open question—as the monarchy in Australia was a mere five years ago—is still alive. An institution whose removal seems, even to its supporters, only a matter of time is, in important respects, already dead.

My de-conversion from the anti-republican cause is not, however, merely negative. I have also come to think the movement to republicanism may bring with it certain benefits. I was very taken by a remark made last year by the former governor-general, Sir Zelman Cowen. Sir Zelman said that of all the things he had done as governor-general nothing was of more importance to him than the speeches he delivered. In these speeches, he explained in a striking phrase, he had sought to 'interpret the nation to itself'. I was taken with Zelman Cowen's remark for two rather different reasons. In part I simply agreed with him. I am sure that the nation does indeed thirst for sober and wise reflection, on fundamental questions affecting our national life, which are generated from within the political system, but which are not spoiled by the smell of party-political contest.

But I am also sure that under our present arrangements the speeches of the governor-general cannot quench that thirst. Ever since the constitutional struggle of the seventeenth century between monarch and parliament, the citizens in British-style systems have been on a kind of permanent alert against political interventions by their heads of state. For this reason, within the Westminster system, the expression of anything which resembles an interesting political opinion from a head of state appears faintly unconstitutional. It seems to me that if we were to move to a republic this aspect of our political culture might gradually change and that such a change would be no bad thing.

In contemporary Europe certain non-executive presidents—most notably Richard von Weizsäcker of Germany and Vaclav Havel of the Czech Republic—have played, precisely through their speeches, a kind of constructive political role which is at present outside our constitutional practice or imagination. As presidents they have spoken of matters fundamental to their nation's identity—in the case of Weizsäcker on the question of the Holocaust, in the case of Havel on the dilemmas of democratic politics after totalitarianism—and, as importantly, in a tone and with a complexity that can only deepen the political culture of their nations. Both have shown how a non-executive president can provide an antidote to the corrosive political cynicism of our times.

One possible advantage of our movement to the republic is that an institution along the lines of the European non-executive presidency at its best may gradually evolve here. To elect a president by some indirect process—perhaps, like the Germans, through an electoral college of federal and state parliamentarians—will invest the office of head of state with a different history and a different kind of authority than is presently the case with the governor-general. Eventually we may learn to listen, with interest and attention, to what our president has to say.

There is another reason which favours an indirectly elected president over a prime-ministerially appointed governor-general. There is, as 1975 revealed, one major fault in our constitution. According to our law the Senate has the power to block or defer supply and to force the government of the day to an election. According, however, to the sentiment of a considerable part of the political nation the use of such a power appears improper or even unconstitutional. If anything, the events of 1975 deepened this fault. On the one hand, it strengthened the legal case for the Senate's right to block supply. On the other, it strengthened the repugnance of one half of the political nation to its use.

Given that this fault is not likely to be resolved in the near future and given that we may again face a crisis similar to 1975, it is clear that an indirectly elected presidency would be an office far better equipped to handle the politics of such a crisis than was the governor-general. An indirectly elected President Kerr, removable only by the vote of the same electoral college, would not in 1975 have needed to fear that a warning to the prime minister—that he would not tolerate an attempt to rule without supply—might lead to his own dismissal and the destruction of the reserve powers. A President Kerr need not have feared speaking openly to the nation about the constitutional dilemma he faced. A President Kerr could have negotiated and sought legal advice far more openly than he did. If, in short, in 1975 our head of state had been an indirectly elected president, he could have acted in the open. The sense of furtiveness, and of shock, surrounding the politics of the dismissal could have been avoided.

Paradoxically, then, the move to an indirectly elected presidency, which many conservatives presently oppose, is most likely to strengthen the reserve powers, which many republicans presently resent. Even more paradoxically, if we can learn from examples like Weizsäcker and Havel, the move to the presidency may provide us with the kind of dignified head of state which Walter Bagehot thought to be vital to our form of constitution, and which the present system of absentee monarch and appointed viceroy has become increasingly incapable of supplying.

In the long term the future of the movement towards an Australian republic will be determined more by John Howard (or his heirs and successors) than by Paul Keating. Keating has placed the issue of the Australian republic at the centre of our politics. He has chosen a committee to examine republican options; soon his government will respond to its report. And he has continuously needled the Coalition, as only he is able, on the question of the republic. Yet this marks the limit of what he can do. So long as the Coalition remains opposed, there will be no Australian republic. The Australian people are loath to pass at referendum even trivial proposals for constitutional change. The question of the republic is not trivial. Without bipartisan support there is not the slightest prospect of Australia becoming a republic.

II

So far as I can see thus far there have been only two serious arguments mounted within the Coalition in defence of our present constitutional arrangements. The first is an argument about utility, expressed, most colourfully, in the language of instinctive conservatism—'if it ain't broke, don't fix it'. On the surface this is an attractive argument. No doubt our constitutional arrangements do work well enough. And where there are faults—for instance the abiding uncertainty about the Senate's use of its powers to block supply—these will not be corrected by the move to the republic. Yet on closer inspection this argument seems to me to miss the point. Those who support the movement from monarchy to republic are arguing not about the efficacy of our present constitution but about its symbolic content, and in particular about the mismatch between contemporary Australian identity and the British monarchical inheritance.

Less than fifty years ago, because the vast majority of Australians felt themselves to be part of a broader British civilisation, the attachment to the Crown, on all sides of politics and between the generations, was deep and real. Today—in part because of the drift of economic and defence realities, in part because of the impact of immigration, in part perhaps because of the general disenchantment of the times—such sentiments have become feebler and feebler. The symbolism of the British Crown has been emptied of resonance. Only for a part of the older generation of Australians can the British monarchy provide a rich and living source of allegiance and affection. For most of the younger generation the retention of the British Crown at the symbolic centre of our polity is puzzling, meaningless, odd.

There is, however, another serious strand to the conservative argument for the maintenance of constitutional monarchy in Australia. This argument suggests that minimalist republicanism is an illusion and that it is impossible to tamper with the symbolic periphery of the constitution without fundamentally transforming the workings of its non-symbolic core. Conservative Coalition scepticism about the minimalist republican program focuses on two key difficulties: the manner by which the head of state is to be elected; and the future, under the republic, of what have come to be called the head of state's reserve powers.

When the minimalist republican program was launched most of its supporters favoured the election of the president by two-thirds majority of an electoral college comprising the two federal houses. Since then, however, public opinion polls have shown that the overwhelming majority of Australians favour presidential election by direct popular vote. If popular opinion had its way here the president would be the only directly elected figure in our polity.

As anti-republican conservatives have correctly pointed out, the direct election of the president has the potential to alter, in an unwanted and unpredictable way, the balance in the constitution between the head of state and the prime minister. What, however, they have failed to see is that this does not amount to a case against republicanism. There is nothing to prevent the Coalition making the question of an indirectly elected presidency the absolute condition of its support for the republic at referendum. Nor need its arguments be unpersuasive. Most Australians support the idea of direct presidential election because they do not wish party politicians to make their choice for them. Yet no process is more likely to allow party politicians to dominate the presidency than a nationwide electoral contest between party political machines. It should not prove too difficult for the Coalition to persuade the electorate that indirect election is the most reliable route to achievement of a dignified, non-party president.

The conservative anti-republican case also rests on fears that, somehow or other, the reserve powers of the head of state will be swept aside in the rush towards republicanism. Once again these fears seem insubstantial. As was seen in the report of Paul Keating's Republican Advisory Committee, the real argument within the camp of minimalist republicanism is not over the retention of the reserve powers. The real argument is between those, like Malcolm Turnbull, who wish to draft a codified system of reserve powers and to make their use justiciable before the High Court, and those, like George Winterton, who wish to leave the present conventions concerning the reserve powers—including even their ambiguities—essentially untouched and uncodified. For complex reasons I believe conservative republicans should strongly support Winterton. Moreover, as I have argued earlier, far from sweeping away the reserve powers the movement from an appointed governor-general, dismissible at the pleasure of the prime minister, to an indirectly elected president, with a security of tenure, would, if anything, strengthen the capacity of a republican head of state to act decisively and openly should a crisis resembling 1975 ever return.

As I see it, so long as the leadership of the Coalition remains wedded to the constitutional monarchy Australia will never become a republic. Its veto is de facto absolute. Yet so long as it remains outside the republican debate it will be constantly vulnerable to the expert taunting of the prime minister and to the charge of being out of joint with the times. If, however, the Coalition does eventually enter the national conversation wholeheartedly it will be in a position to help ensure that, in the movement to the republic, the balances of our constitution remain firm and that its symbolism, once more, as in the days of British Australia, takes hold of the public imagination.

1995

The Manning Clark Affair II

ON 24 August, Brisbane's *Courier-Mail* revealed that Australia's most famous historian, Manning Clark, had been the recipient of the Soviet Union's highest honour, the Order of Lenin. The better part of eight pages was devoted to the story. Clearly the *Courier-Mail* believed that its revelation was of the greatest cultural and political significance.

If the *Courier-Mail*'s allegations were true, Australia's understanding of itself would never be quite the same again. If they were false, not only had an extremely serious injustice been done but, in the ill-feeling generated, the very possibility of conducting a genuine discussion of the only Manning Clark question that matters— the value of Manning Clark's work and thought—had been jeopardised again.

The *Courier-Mail*'s case rested on three kinds of evidence. The first were the eyewitnesses. According to the anticommunist journalist Peter Kelly, a mutual friend of his and Clark's, the late Geoffrey Fairbairn, had seen Clark wearing a medal he thought to be the Order of Lenin at a Soviet embassy function sometime in the 1970s. Fairbairn swore Kelly to secrecy. Clark was his teacher, his colleague and his friend.

The second eyewitness was the great Australian poet, Les Murray. In 1970, he had dropped in on a private dinner in Canberra at the home of fellow poet David Campbell. Murray saw a Soviet medal on Clark's chest. He, too, thought it to be the Order of Lenin and was shocked. Like Fairbairn, he understood that tens of millions of innocent lives had been destroyed in the grotesque Soviet experiment.

The *Courier-Mail*'s investigation proceeded over many months and was fundamental to Clark's good name. If he had indeed received an Order of Lenin, he would be regarded by many Australians at best as disloyal. And yet, until the evening before the story broke, not one member of the *Courier-Mail*'s staff appears to have made contact with the Clark family. As we shall see, if they had done so, the identity of the medal Fairbairn and Murray had seen might have been cleared up in a matter of moments.

Nor does it seem that the *Courier-Mail* took even the most obvious steps to check whether Murray could be certain that he had seen an Order of Lenin and not perhaps some other Soviet medal bearing Lenin's portrait.

Instead of sending an independent journalist to Dymphna Clark or Murray, the *Courier-Mail* dispatched its associate editor, Wayne Smith, to the Australian Archives in search of evidence that might reveal clues to Clark's clandestine relations with Soviet intelligence. What Smith stumbled upon in Clark's Australian Security Intelligence Organisation file provided the second string in the *Courier-Mail*'s evidentiary bow.

Smith discovered that Clark had maintained a long friendship with the communist political scientist Ian Milner, an External Affairs spy who had defected to Prague in 1950. Some discovery. Far from the relationship being secret, Clark had written extensively about Milner in his autobiography, *The Quest for Grace*.

Smith also discovered that Clark had taught English to the Soviet ambassador, Nikolai Lifanov, in the early 1950s. According to reports, Lifanov's English was excellent. Was there then not something sinister in Clark's embassy visits? Almost certainly there was not. If Clark's early 1950s Soviet connection had a security significance, he would not have met with Lifanov but with the head of intelligence, Vladimir Petrov. Petrov had never heard of him.

Every Smith discovery in the ASIO file is open to similar non-sinister interpretation. It is most likely that Clark received numbers of communist friends at his Canberra home because, as Clark never disguised, very many of his friends were communists. It is most likely that he travelled to the Soviet Union on four occasions because, in regard to the nature of the Soviet Union, he remained for a very long time a hopelessly foolish optimist, one who believed that Soviet communism might mend its ways and win some kind of victory over the doomed societies of corrupt capitalism. This was no state secret. It was, in fact, the subject matter of his book *Meeting Soviet Man*.

The *Courier-Mail* discovered nothing either new or noteworthy in Clark's ASIO file to suggest he was a worthy recipient of the Order of Lenin. The Soviet Union, before Mikhail Gorbachev, was a serious totalitarian state. Such medals were not handed out as a reward for friendly visits to philistine ambassadors or for writing purple prose about Lenin's love of humanity. They were at least the Soviet equivalent of a knighthood.

Having decided that Clark had been awarded the Order of Lenin, the *Courier-Mail* approached two genuine experts in the field of Soviet intelligence—Brian Crozier, a battle-hardened anti-Soviet activist, and Oleg Gordievsky, a senior KGB defector and double agent. What was problematic about Crozier and Gordievsky was not their expertise but their judgment. It is impossible to think of two former Cold Warriors less inclined to scepticism. Gordievsky believes that president Franklin D. Roosevelt's key foreign policy adviser, Harry Hopkins, was a *conscious* Soviet agent of influence.

Crozier once suspected that the impeccably anticommunist scholar Leonard Schapiro might be an agent of the KGB.

But it was worse than that. Crozier and Gordievsky were asked the wrong question. Neither it seems was asked to help the *Courier-Mail* decide whether or not Clark had been awarded an Order of Lenin. Rather, they were asked what Clark must have done in order to have been worthy of so high an award. Crozier thought he must have been 'an overt and conscious agent of influence'; Gordievsky, 'a very, very important' one. His former KGB colleague in Moscow, Colonel Mikhail Lyubimov, went even further. He was sure that Clark would not have received the Order of Lenin unless he had been not a mere agent of influence but a very important spy. Lyubimov was probably right. Yet the *Courier-Mail*, presumably through embarrassment, removed his completely logical assessment from its second edition of 24 August.

Within a day or two of publication, the wheels began to fall off the *Courier-Mail*'s exclusive. The Clark family let it be known that Manning had indeed received a Soviet medal in 1970. It bore a Lenin profile and, they claimed, had been awarded to him on the occasion of a lecture he had given to mark the centenary of Lenin's birth. It seemed highly plausible that this was the medal Fairbairn and Murray had seen. Geoffrey Dutton remembered joking about the medal in question with his old friend.

The editor-in-chief of the *Courier-Mail*, Chris Mitchell, insisted now that his newspaper had never made the absurd allegation that Clark was a spy. All they had suggested was that he was an 'agent of influence'. Perhaps, an editorial on 31 August hinted, he had merely been an unconscious one.

The wheels were now off. On 24 August, the *Courier-Mail* had announced that Australia's most famous historian was in fact 'an undiscovered member of the communist world's elite'. On 31 August it was merely 'an open question…whether Manning Clark was an agent of influence'. On 24 August, the *Courier-Mail* had opened its eight-page exclusive with these words: 'Professor

Manning Clark was awarded the Soviet Union's highest honour, the Order of Lenin'. By 31 August, it thought it 'a pity' that the 'side debate about whether or not Manning Clark had been awarded the Order of Lenin' had obscured the real Clark question. I cannot but agree. My only difference with the *Courier-Mail* is this. It blames others for allowing the real Clark question to be obscured yet again. For my part, I blame the newspaper.

II

The question raised most immediately by the current controversy is Clark's peculiar relationship to the Soviet Union and the communist movement. This question has both an emblematic and individual significance. It points to a kind of blindness that Clark shared with an entire generation of the Australian left and provides a clue to deep flaws in his thought and work.

As he tells us in *The Quest for Grace*, Clark became interested in the communist movement when he went to Melbourne University in the mid-1930s. Part of what attracted him was communist demystification of the king-and-empire loyalism of Melbourne's Protestant, bourgeois establishment. A pamphlet that he read in 1934, which argued that capitalist societies rested on fascism and war, hit him with the force of revelation. He began to haunt the International Bookshop. He became convinced that history was indeed, as Karl Marx had said and as his parents' socially unequal marriage confirmed, the story of class oppression and class war. He also became convinced that in the great story of the liberation of humanity from oppression, the Russian Revolution of 1917 was a shining event and that the bourgeois world into which he had been born was unjust, evil and corrupt, doomed to disappear from the face of the earth. It is no exaggeration to say that he dragged these beliefs after him for the next half-century or more.

Clark tells us he never joined the Communist Party. He was repelled by the dogmatism and bullying he encountered there. Communist self-certainty was, for Clark, the mirror image of bourgeois smugness. But his resistance to a final embrace of communism went deeper than this. Communism would never satisfy his religious yearning. The figure of Christ beckoned him throughout his life. In 1937, as he listened to the Spanish Civil War debate at the University of Melbourne, the image of Christ, conjured by B. A. Santamaria, pulled him in one direction; the idea of the Enlightenment, invoked by Nettie Palmer, in another. He explained in *The Quest for Grace*:

> From that night to the present day, I will never be able to decide which side I am on—the side of Catholic Truth, or the side of the Enlightenment. I will go on wanting the Marxists to discover the image of Christ and the Catholics to see the need to destroy our corrupt society.

Throughout his life, as he explained time and again, it was his hope to reconcile the words of Christ with the revolution of 1917.

There was nothing in his writing to suggest that this hope was, given the history of communism, absurd and obscene. During Clark's own lifetime, communist regimes, most violently in Stalin's Russia and Mao's China, had dispatched to horrible deaths more than a hundred million innocent human beings. Clark never understood that, from a human point of view, 1917 was more easily linked with 1933 than with 1789. This is the plain truth that Clark never faced—the bloody muddle at the centre of his thought. It was a muddle he shared with an entire generation of the left and one which provides a clue to the present collapse of the left in Australia and the west.

III

In October 1958, Clark took his first trip to the Soviet Union. He went at a peculiarly unfortunate time. Just months before he left, the communist leader of the Hungarian uprising of 1956, Imre Nagy, had been executed by Soviet leaders. On the eve of his departure, the great Russian writer Boris Pasternak, who had been awarded the Nobel Prize, was expelled from the Soviet Writers' Union, and covered with calumny so ferocious and vile it still has the power to shock and dismay. Clark travelled as part of a delegation representing the Fellowship of Australian Writers. There was no reason to think that after the assault on Pasternak he was even tempted to stay away.

The book that Clark wrote about his tour, *Meeting Soviet Man*, is now rarely read and even more rarely understood. In a recent exchange, columnist Gerard Henderson described it as a 'tract', journalist Warren Osmond as a 'thoughtful' account of the post-Stalin thaw. It is neither. *Meeting Soviet Man* is one of the least polemical but also one of the most foolish and naive books any western visitor to the Soviet Union would ever write.

In it, Clark did not deny the crimes of Stalin, the millions of deaths during collectivisation, the murder of political opponents. Rather, he wondered idly why a figure so dark in heart as Stalin had been able to inherit the Russian Revolution from the noble Lenin. He had no answer. He regarded Stalin as a kind of Dostoevskian Grand Inquisitor, a man who believed the bodies of innocents would manure the soil for the future happiness of humanity. Clark knew this involved millions. Yet the Stalin question that interested him most deeply was this: 'Did he feel sorry?'

Clark was far from easy with all aspects even of post-Stalin Russia. He was vaguely unnerved by the attack on Pasternak, which he called 'spiritual popery'. Yet he wondered whether his unease was not misplaced, whether he was merely suffering from a bad case of 'bourgeois liberalism'. With less ambiguity, he disapproved of the Soviet propensity to rewrite its history and intuited a kind of spiritual emptiness in the Soviet people he met, an absence of 'inner life'. He even allowed one seriously subversive thought to cross his mind. Might not the darkest prophecies of Dostoevski—about the murderousness of the revolutionaries after the death of God—be right after all?

Such thoughts did not persist. The longer Clark stayed in the

Soviet Union—only three weeks, but he was a quick learner—the greater became his certainty that something of immense significance for the future of humanity was being transacted. Clark experienced everywhere in the Soviet Union great 'uplift'. In the west one felt nothing but 'cynicism, madness, despair'; in the Soviet Union, purpose and optimism, 'common faith, common hope'. After a visit to the Tolstoy Museum at Tasnaya Polyana, he was finally sure. He knew now he was in a country that was 'recapturing its being and the ideals of 1917'.

The key was the splendid figure of Lenin. History's Lenin had exterminated his class enemies, destroyed his political opponents, established the secret police force and the first concentration camps, sent several hundred thousand Russians to their graves. Clark's Lenin was, by contrast, 'Christ-like at least in his compassion'. At the prospect of 'a classless society...of people loving and trembling for each other', Clark's Lenin was 'as excited and lovable as a little child'. If the present Soviet leaders could only express remorse for the errors of the Stalinist past—the muddying of the waters, as he called it—then the memory of Lenin's unerring intellectual grasp and the sureness of his moral touch would, he was convinced, restore to the revolution its good name. Indeed Clark believed that, although the west did not yet see it, the great resurrection had already begun. He felt profoundly fortunate to have been able to travel in the Soviet Union at such a time. At the midpoint of his tour, he had written home: 'With more charity towards those who do not share its faith, it could become the first [society] to create equality and brotherhood. I believe it will.' His tour had convinced him that the two figures in Russian history he most loved, Lenin and Dostoevski, could be reconciled after all. 'No one whom Dostoevski has caught by the throat and the heart could be indifferent to Lenin.' His tour had convinced him, too, that with the revival of the idea of 1917 the end of the terrible era of bourgeois capitalism was at hand.

IV

Clark visited the Soviet Union again—in 1964, 1970 (two years after Warsaw Pact tanks put an end to the Prague Spring) and in 1973. Although, so far as I know, he published nothing about these experiences, it is clear that the dreams of 1960 slowly faded. During the Order of Lenin controversy, the Clark family released extracts from the diary he kept during his 1970 visit. They show a Clark whose eyes are now open to aspects of Soviet reality. From that time until his death, whenever Clark discussed Soviet-style societies, he added, as a kind of incantation, the charges of greyness and conformism to his old accusation of spiritual popery.

And yet, oddly enough, although the hopes he had acquired as a young man had died, the negative underbelly of these hopes—the moral conviction that he lived in a wicked and corrupt bourgeois-capitalist world and the historical conviction that such a society was doomed to revolutionary overthrow—grew, if anything, more fierce.

Let me illustrate. For many Australians, the Menzies era—with its quiet optimism, full employment, steadily rising living standards, its well-balanced farming and manufacturing economy, university expansion, flourishing of the arts, astonishing successes in world sport—looks now like a golden age. For Clark, somewhat differently, the Menzies years were of unrelieved gloom or, as he put it in 1973, 'of unleavened bread'. Clark developed, as a mannerism, the strange habit of characterising an entire historical era through ruminations on its leading politician. He portrayed Robert Menzies as a man whose tragedy was that he devoted his talents and his life to the defence of a dying world—of bourgeois capitalism at home, the British monarchy and United States imperialism abroad. Clark also was in the habit of seeking out Australian visionaries—Prometheans, he called them—who might be able to rescue his country from its fathomless dullness. Clark saw in Gough Whitlam just such a man. His hopes were on fire. Yet, as early as 1973, he wondered whether 'they'—the bourgeois establishment or 'Yarraside', as he called it in his private code—could tolerate the hopes Whitlam excited or whether they might not trap him, bring him down.

As it happened, on 11 November 1975, they did. Even worse, on 13 December, the Australian people overwhelmingly elected the arch-conspirator Malcolm Fraser. 'Are we,' Clark now asked, 'a nation of bastards?'

What was interesting about Clark's response to November 1975 was not the anger he felt. Many democrats were deeply shaken by the unwillingness of conservative political forces, after twenty-three unbroken years of rule, to allow Whitlam even an uninterrupted three. What was strange was the way in which, at his moment of fury, Clark had nothing to draw upon, in his analysis of November 1975, but the Marxism–Leninism of his youth.

In part, Clark explained the destruction of the Whitlam government through the standard communist critique of the contradictions of democratic socialism. As a typical democratic socialist Whitlam believed, Clark argued, that capitalist society could be genuinely reformed without seizing economic power from the bourgeoisie. He wrote in the *Australian* in January 1976:

> There, perhaps, lay the key to the great dilemma, the insoluble problem of the Whitlam government and possibly of any reformist, social democratic government: namely how to remove all the moral infamy, injustice, and the inequalities of a capitalist society while still preserving the essential feature of such a society, the private ownership of the means of production, distribution, and exchange.

Like Scullin and Chifley, Whitlam had tried to manage more humanely the bourgeois state. Like them, he failed.

Clark was, however, convinced that the conspirators of November 1975 were living on borrowed time. The end of parliamentary government was approaching. Australia was, he thought, one of the three or four most reactionary societies on earth—in the same category as racist South Africa or fascist Spain. Such societies could not survive the progressive march of the people's democracies.

Concerning our future, Clark entertained at this time two fantasies. According to one of them, he envisaged the communist revolutionary left seizing power in Australia. His vision of this Leninist future was no longer gentle or caring but of the dispensation of a harsh and spartan justice to the enemies of the people. According to the other fantasy, he envisaged the people's victory bringing down the curtain on the short drama of European civilisation in the Antipodes. He took consolation from the fear gripping other intelligent Australians:

> ...we, too, like the other reactionary societies in South-East Asia and elsewhere, were about to be wiped off the face of the earth, that the peoples of the world, carried away as they were and are by a hope of better things for mankind, would not let us survive...[that] we would either be eliminated...as though we had never been, or mercifully, and with quite undeserved charity, be given a chance to return to the place whence we came, that precious graveyard of the contemporary world, the United Kingdom and Western Europe.

V

All this waving of fists and gnashing of teeth might not have mattered much were it not for the way in which it coloured and in the end subdued his historical vision. When Clark embarked upon his general history, he thought it would concern the struggle to create a civilisation from the clash between the great forces of Catholicism, Protestantism and the Enlightenment. It was the originality and grandeur of this conception that excited virtually the entire generation of Australian historians who came to maturity in the 1960s. By the time he reached his last volume in 1987, however, the vision had shrunk terribly—into something astonishingly simple and banal. This shrinkage was the real cost Clark paid for his unresolved lifelong flirtation with communism.

There were by now for Clark, in the inter-war period, two Australias. One was the Australia of Yarraside—the graziers and businessmen, the professors and pastors. The interest of this Australia was in the profitability of the capitalist economy. Its religion was Protestant; its morals were puritan; its loyalty to empire and king. In the political sphere it was served by class representatives such as Stanley Bruce, scholarship boys such as Robert Menzies or Labor traitors such as Billy Hughes and Joe Lyons. These Austral-Britons represented the 'Old Dead Tree'.

The second Australia was made up of those able to imagine a better world: social revolutionaries, inspired by 1917; poets dreaming of an authentic Australian culture and nationalism; Labor visionaries, such as Curtin or Chifley, whose light on the hill had not yet been extinguished. They represented the 'Young Tree Green'.

Throughout his final volume Clark 'barracks', there is no other word than John Hirst's, for the visionaries, nationalists and life-enhancers against the straiteners and life-deniers of Yarraside. Yet, as he knew, time and again his team was destined to lose. Why? In part the creed of the revolutionaries, he argues, was wrong, drawn from alien sources, not from the suburbs or the bush. In part the ALP was a great disappointment. Out of power it succumbed to grubby electoral pragmatism; in power to the hopeless task of better managing the capitalist state on behalf of the bourgeoisie. And, in part, the people were to blame. They had been bourgeoisified by material comforts. Their eyes scarcely rose above their quarter-acre block. Time and again their conservative instincts destroyed the hopes of those who had imagined for Australia a brighter future. In the final volume of his history, Clark gives an almost unrelievedly gloomy portrait of his country. He also gives us, in my opinion, a remarkably shallow one.

I wish not to be misunderstood here. The problem with Manning Clark's history is not that it is informed by Marxism. The problem is rather that it is informed by the kind of Marxism–Leninism—with its crude historical determinism and class against class polemics—which he had picked up in the Communist Party pamphlets of his youth and which, for some reason, he never subjected to hard thought. Historians with a far more serious grasp of Marxism than he, and a far stronger allegiance to the Soviet Union, have nevertheless been responsible for some of our century's most impressive historical work.

The comparison between the final volume of Eric Hobsbawm's series on the economic history of capitalism since the French Revolution, *Age of Extremes*, and of Clark's *A History of Australia* is painful. With Hobsbawm, Marxism is undeniably a powerful analytical tool. With Clark, a kind of surface Marxism, dressed up in the garb of Old Testament prophet, turns the twentieth-century history of this country into an almost comically partisan and melodramatic morality play.

It is, in my opinion, these hard questions about Manning Clark's thought and his work and not furphies about Orders of Lenin secretly awarded that we still need to discuss.

1996

Bob Santamaria

IT can be said of relatively few Australian political figures that they leave a lasting impression on their country's history and moral life. It is this, however, which can truly be said of B. A. Santamaria, one of this country's most remarkable public men.

Santamaria was the child of a large and close and tumultuous Italian migrant peasant family who ran a greengrocery in Brunswick. In the early 1930s, through his native wit and the no-nonsense education he received at the hands of the Christian Brothers, Santamaria was able to make his way up Sydney Road to the University of Melbourne, where he was an outstanding student of history, political science and law.

The 1930s were a fiercely ideological time. Santamaria found his home not on the communist left or the Protestant right, but inside the Campion Society, with its politics of Catholic revivalism. It was as a young Catholic warrior that Santamaria, in March 1937, in a university debate on the Spanish Civil War ignited an audience, which included the young Manning Clark, with his pro-Franco battle cry, 'Long live Christ, the King!' It was as a young Catholic idealist that he established the *Catholic Worker*, a monthly, to convey papal social justice doctrine to the masses. And it was as a Catholic loyalist at that time that he encountered the man he admired most of all and who would shape his life—the Irish prelate, Archbishop Daniel Mannix.

In 1937 Mannix offered Santamaria a post in the secretariat of Catholic Action, which was to be the focus of a politically activist Catholicism. It did not even occur to Santamaria to turn this offer down. Although his acceptance determined the course of his life, shortly before his death Santamaria still wondered, terribly, whether it might not, after all, have been a mistake.

As a part of his work in the secretariat of Catholic Action Santamaria, for some fifteen years, drafted the annual social justice statements of the Catholic bishops of Australia. From this work he crystallised a distinctive version of Australian political Catholicism—which upheld the virtues of Christian piety, duty, family, work, rural community and small business against the vices of communism, big business, secularism and soulless modernity. To this vision Santamaria remained loyal for the rest of his life.

In August 1941 Santamaria was approached by an ALP leader in Victoria, H. M. Cremean. Would it not be possible, he wondered, to organise a struggle against the influence of the communists in the trade unions? Santamaria thought it might. From the raw material of Catholic activists and trade union parish Catholics, and with the strong support of Mannix, Santamaria created now what became known as the Catholic Social Studies Movement, or simply the Movement.

The Movement had the support of the bishops. In turn it became the animating force behind the so-called Industrial Groups created by sections of the ALP. Santamaria displayed in this work toughness and real organisational genius. In 1945 the Communist Party had a majority of votes at the congress of the ACTU. By the early 1950s its grip on most of the strategic unions had been broken. Santamaria had been the behind-the-scenes Bonaparte of this campaign. So successful had it been that he thought that a return to a 'normal life' might soon be possible.

Fate now intervened. In 1951 the leadership of the ALP fell to a brilliant but erratic, ruthless and suspicious intellectual, Dr H. V. Evatt. He was willing to court Santamaria to help bring him to power. Santamaria found Evatt's courtship unsettling and disgusting. After a secret meeting, before the election of 1954, he confided to his wife that he had discovered in Evatt a theological impossibility—a man without a soul. Mannix, ever the political realist, encouraged him nonetheless to persist in these talks.

As it turned out, Dr Evatt narrowly lost the 1954 election. The loss unbalanced his mind. He blamed it upon a wicked conspiracy involving Prime Minister Menzies, Brigadier Spry of ASIO, the Soviet defectors Vladimir and Evdokia Petrov, and Bob Santamaria's Movement. In October 1954 Evatt made his fateful move, for the expulsion of the Santamaria forces from the ALP. Within six months, by the most dubious of methods, at the ALP conference in Hobart, he had succeeded. Santamaria now found himself unexpectedly the intellectual leader of a new political party, which eventually called itself the DLP.

It was not only the ALP that split about the question of Santamaria. The Catholic Church also divided, essentially between the hierarchies of Sydney and Melbourne. The Movement was a lay association, but under loose ecclesiastical control. Sydney, led by Bishop James Carroll, took its case against the Movement to Rome. After a trial so secret Santamaria learnt of its having taken place only a quarter-century later, the Vatican in effect instructed the Movement to dissolve. For a deeply loyal Catholic like Santamaria, this Vatican ruling was probably the most bitter blow life was ever to deal.

But Santamaria fought on. By 1958 he found himself, as a

consequence of these two devastating political defeats at Hobart and at Rome, the ideological driving force of a new political party and the charismatic leader of a new lay Catholic association, which called itself the National Civic Council and which was, in effect, the old Movement reborn.

The DLP was a significant influence in Australian politics for two decades. By the disciplined delivery of its second preferences it was a vital factor in keeping the coalition governments of Robert Menzies and his successors in power. The price it asked, in return, was for the maintenance of a hawkish anticommunist foreign policy abroad and for state aid for Catholic schools at home. From Santamaria's point of view both achievements left a bitter aftertaste. The war in Vietnam was ignominiously lost. The parochial Catholic school system was revolutionised by the progressivist wave that swamped traditional Catholicism after the Second Vatican Council.

The DLP collapsed rather suddenly in 1974. It was killed off in part by the discrediting of militant anticommunism at the end of the Vietnam War, and in part by the rapid disappearance of the social type that had provided the DLP with its electoral base—the dutiful Catholic of the working or lower middle class. This social type had been unable to withstand the great post-1960s cultural revolution that transformed Australia, alongside all societies of the western world.

Santamaria saw in this cultural revolution—in particular in the decline of religion and family, and the rise of promiscuity and pornography, of abortion and euthanasia—the symptoms of steep civilisational decline. The west had, he thought, moved from its Christian period to the Enlightenment, and from the Enlightenment to the Kingdom of Nothing. An image that invaded his writing more and more was of the fall of the Roman Empire. He saw his Movement supporters as an isolated and embattled remnant, standing up, rather hopelessly, against the barbarian advance. Santamaria lived now, psychologically speaking, at a time of permanent crisis. His mood was of stubborn resistance and of stoical defeat.

For Bob Santamaria, in his final decade, only one thing changed. During the Cold War, Santamaria, like most anticommunists, had not dwelt much on an old Campion theme—the inhumanity of capitalist civilisation. In the 1990s, after the collapse of the Soviet Empire, it was to this question that he, increasingly less tentatively, returned. Santamaria argued, with what we can now see as a considerable prescience, that the international finance system was out of control. He was astounded that an economists' ideology, dominant in Canberra, was so lightly allowing farms and manufacturing businesses to be destroyed. He was appalled by a growing acceptance of permanent (male) unemployment and of radical social inequality. From time to time Santamaria spoke now of the naked economic self-interest of the capitalist class, with a savagery that had once been voiced only by his enemies of the old left. Not surprisingly, it was with a number of such enemies—Clyde Cameron, Jim McClelland, Bernie Taft and Jim Cairns—that in his last years, as an old Cold Warrior, he laid down his arms and concluded a fitting and rather moving peace.

What legacy does Santamaria, then, leave? He was a modest and realistic man. He knew that throughout his life he had swum, without much hope, against a great secular tide. He entered public life in the 1930s to help build in Australia a more Christian society. He left it at a time when that society was far less Christian than it had ever been. It was true that for two decades he helped, during its darkest days, to keep the ALP from power. Santamaria did not regret this. He would, however, hardly have considered it an achievement of lasting worth.

What he did truly achieve lies elsewhere. For sixty years, almost every day, Bob Santamaria gave his life to the service of the public good. During these years he brought to his work the qualities of intelligence, courage, selflessness, persistence and loyalty.

Many people may disagree with his vision of the good. Few will dispute that he showed in his life, in a manner almost without parallel in his time, the civic virtues vital to its achievement. With Bob Santamaria's death we have lost one of our genuinely great public figures.

1998

The Republic's Unanswered Question

I was surprised by how interesting and affecting an occasion the Constitutional Convention turned out to be.

With the rigid predictability of parliamentary life our political palates have become rather jaded. To observe an assembly where party discipline did not dominate, where speeches from the floor really mattered and where the outcomes of votes were not known in advance, was a politically refreshing experience.

But there was more to it than this. The convention debates were marked throughout by seriousness, civility, vitality, optimism and good humour. As an observer of these debates, I was particularly struck by how much we have gained from two of the great cultural shifts of recent times—the triumph of the multicultural idea and the emergence of an Aboriginal political class. Neither the ethnic nor the Aboriginal participation at the convention seemed at all tokenistic as they might have even two decades ago.

Nor, so far as I could see, was there anything even remotely patronising in the attention paid to the views of the younger delegates. If anything the reverse. Psychologically speaking, the decisive blow struck against the ultra-minimalist republican model came when Richard McGarvie's proposal to restrict participation in his constitutional council to persons aged between sixty-five and seventy-nine was drowned in laughter. To judge by the convention, Australia is, in spirit, a young nation still.

The Constitutional Convention struck me, then, first of all, as a very attractive gathering of contemporary Australia in all its diversity—of conservatives and radicals; of young and old; of Anglomorphs, ethnics and Aborigines; of politicians, professionals and media personalities. It was only gradually that I began to sense in this gathering a missing element. Eventually I put my finger on what it was—the voice of ordinary Australians. On reflection this absence struck me as of great potential significance.

Like most members of the politically interested class, the class which reads the quality press and follows public affairs on the ABC, I found the proceedings of the convention riveting and, on occasions, moving. I strongly suspect, however, that for very large numbers of Australians the convention was, at best, a matter of indifference and, at worst, an occasion for cynicism with regard to the self-interested antics of politicians, old fogies and glitterati.

In Australia the most salient political division seems to me now not the one which separates left from right but the one which separates the world of the elite from the world of ordinary people. I cannot help wondering if whether, in the end, the lack of connection between these worlds might not now more than anything else threaten the success of the republican project.

The political problem can be put thus. At the convention the moderate republican case, for the election of the president by a vote of the politicians and not of the people, prevailed. It is not difficult to see why it had to be so. History tells us that referendums which are opposed by one of the two major political parties do not pass. If the convention had supported a popularly elected president the republican referendum would, almost certainly, have been opposed not only by the National Party but also by most leading figures among the Liberals.

Under these conditions, unless history is no guide, the proposal for a directly elected president could not possibly succeed at referendum. In holding out against this model the Australian Republican Movement was not stubborn or inflexible but realistic.

Unfortunately—and this is where the trench line which separates the world of the elite from that of ordinary people becomes important—every opinion poll taken in recent times makes it abundantly clear that the overwhelming majority of Australians, if they are to have a republic, insist upon a president chosen not by politicians but by themselves.

Why? It seems to me implausible to believe that this determination to have a popularly elected president arises from constitutional considerations of any kind—either from agreement with radical republicans about the need for a more democratic political system or disagreement with moderate republicans about the dangers to the Westminster system a directly elected president might ultimately pose. My guess is that the stubborn determination to have a people's president or none at all arises from different considerations altogether. It seems to me to arise most deeply from contemporary disaffection with politicians and the political process; from the sour and sullen popular mood that has gradually taken root in Australia in the era of globalisation and permanent economic insecurity; from, in short, precisely the same set of factors that help explain the short-lived explosion of popular enthusiasm for the anti-politics of Pauline Hanson in the months following the election of March 1996.

On the question of the popularly elected president for once the hopes of the radical left and the mood of ordinary Australians coincide. It is this coincidence which places before the moderate republican movement a new and rather daunting challenge.

Over the next eighteen months the moderate republicans must somehow convince Australian electors that the severing of the final link with Britain is a matter of real moment in the history of Australia. They must somehow convince them that the sole practical means of achieving this end is to agree to allow the despised politicians to choose their president. If they do not succeed in this, there exists now a very real danger that a curious de facto alliance between conservative monarchists, utopian radicals and the popular distemper will be formed. If that happens the splendid republican victory achieved at the convention may be lost.

1998

PART FIVE

ECHOES OF THE HOLOCAUST

The Road to Auschwitz

THE great historian of English law, F. W. Maitland, once felt compelled to remind his readers of the fact that events which are now in the past were once in the future. No formulation could capture more exactly the problem faced by the historian of Hitler and the Jews. When Hitler took power in Germany in 1933 the Final Solution was still in the future. The task of the historian of the Holocaust is to reveal to us the road that led from 1933 to Auschwitz, without allowing that road to seem either more pre-determined or more haphazard, straighter or more crooked, than it in fact was. To judge by *Nazi Germany & the Jews*, the first of a two-volume history of the Holocaust, no one seems more likely to succeed in this task—of showing how the unthinkable became possible and how the possible became real—than Saul Friedländer.* As the success of Daniel Goldhagen's *Hitler's Willing*

---

*Nazi Germany & the Jews: The Years of Persecution, Saul Friedländer, Weidenfeld & Nicolson, 1997.

Executioners shows, the reading public hopes to discover a road to Auschwitz which is relatively straight. In Friedländer's more complex, mature and tentative book it will not find such a road.

Friedländer's road to Auschwitz begins with the Nazi onslaught on the Jews of Germany in the early months of 1933. Its primary aim was to destroy Jewish influence over German culture. The arts were very rapidly 'de-Judaised'. Books of Jewish authors were ceremonially burned. Jews were removed from academic posts, from the civil service, from the boards of great German companies. A leading German newspaper explained the whole process of elite cultural cleansing thus: 'A self-respecting nation… cannot leave its higher activities in the hands of people of racially foreign origin.'

As a result of the convergence of a deeply rooted tradition of Christian hostility to the Jews—as Christ-killers and stubborn rejectors of his message of redemption—with the more recent outburst of anti-modernist and almost invariably anti-Semitic 'cultural pessimism', the German conservative elite embraced the Nazi assault on 'the undue influence of the Jews' with genuine enthusiasm.

What Friedländer shows here is well known. What he also shows and what is less well known is how timid, pathetic and foolish was the mainstream German Jewish response to this threat. The Jews were advised by their leaders to 'wait calmly' until the Nazi storm passed. They were, tragically, advised against 'hasty emigration'. With the encouragement of the chief rabbi of Germany, Leo Baeck, a book was compiled detailing the positive contribution of the Jews to Germany's development. Inside the Gestapo this book was greeted with withering contempt. 'The naive reader,' it reported, 'would get the impression that the whole of German culture up to the National Socialist revolution was carried by Jews.' With Nazi encouragement a separate Jewish cultural organisation was formed, the *Kulturbund*. In a Jewish population of 500,000 it soon boasted a membership of 180,000.

The regime forbade polluting Jewish performance of the greatest Germans—Schiller in 1934, Goethe in 1936, Beethoven in 1937, Mozart in 1938. Nonetheless the *Kulturbund* flourished. When the Berlin tram arrived at Charlottenstrasse, the conductor's cry was: 'Jewish culture—everybody off!' The leftist émigré Kurt Tucholsky thought his fellow Jews' greatest ambition was to prove to the Germans they could still, in times of adversity, produce a fine theatre.

In September 1935 Jewish cultural segregation was formalised in the Nuremberg laws. Jews were now excluded from German citizenship. But as Germany was a 'legal state' a precise definition of the Jew was required. After Hitler's intervention the question was settled thus. Those with three or four Jewish grandparents were 'full Jews'. Those with two Jewish grandparents who did not attend synagogue or who had not married a Jew were 'mixed bloods of the first degree'. Those with one Jewish grandparent 'mixed bloods of the second degree'. Marriage or sexual relations between Aryans and Jews were strictly forbidden. First-degree mixed bloods were encouraged to marry Jews. Second-degree mixed bloods were encouraged to marry Aryans. In extramarital sexual matters the laws now reflected what Friedländer calls the Nazi pornographic imagination. Aryan women under the age of forty-five were prohibited from working as domestics in Jewish homes. Jewish doctors were prohibited from conducting genital examinations of Aryan women. Jews were banned from municipal swimming pools.

The influence of eugenics was not restricted to Jewish policy. Before the war the Nazi state had already sterilised 300,000 Germans suffering from hereditary diseases or mental illness. By this time the state was moving from sterilisation toward euthanasia. In late 1938 Hitler personally issued instructions to his physician, Karl Brandt, to kill a retarded baby by the name of Knauer, which had been born without limbs. By August 1939 the extension of this first action—a euthanasia campaign targeting certain types of inmates of Germany's mental asylums—was set to proceed. As Friedländer argues, Nazi Jewish policy and the Nazi policies of sterilisation and euthanasia developed, as expressions of eugenics, along separate but parallel paths. It was only after the invasion of the Soviet Union, when the staff who had disposed of the mentally ill were transferred to the Jewish extermination centres in the east, that these paths would meet.

In late 1935 and early 1936 Nazi policy towards the Jews changed gear—with a shift in emphasis from cultural segregation to encouraged emigration through a graduated program of economic pressure and expropriation. 'Aryanisation', it was called. For the Nazis the preferred destination for Jewish emigration was Palestine. Friedländer captures nicely the Nazi ambivalence towards Zionism. Within the frame of Nazi conspiracy theories the Zionist state had long been seen as the base from which the Jewish quest for world power would be launched. Within the frame of Nazi racial thought a separate Jewish state outside Europe appeared a fittingly *völkisch* solution to the Jewish problem. Because of this latter consideration, in the era of encouraged emigration, the Zionists were undoubtedly the kind of Jews with whom the Nazis preferred to deal.

In 1938 pressures on the Jews of Germany to emigrate intensified. In July 1938 a new wave of violence erupted. In November, following the assassination of a German diplomat in Paris by a seventeen-year-old Jew, Grynszpan, whose parents had been thrown out of Germany to a camp on the Polish–German border, anti-Jewish violence exploded. For the Jews of Germany *Kristallnacht* —a semi-spontaneous, semi-orchestrated pogrom, as Friedländer decisively shows—was the true turning point. Göring was put in charge of post-*Kristallnacht* anti-Jewish operations by Hitler. The Jews were ordered to pay a one-billion-mark fine as recompense for the Parisian outrage, and to pay the cost of demolishing the synagogues which had been destroyed. Those Jewish schoolchildren who remained in the German school system were expelled. Jews were forbidden access to German social welfare. Their dead could no longer be buried in German public cemeteries. All had to take designated Jewish names. Most importantly, all Jewish business in Germany was finally closed down. Many younger Jews now scrambled to get out of Germany. My mother was one of these. One hundred and eighty thousand, predominantly older Jews—including my maternal grandparents—remained. When war broke out it was this battered, isolated, bewildered, defenceless remnant that waited upon their fate.

II

What was the role of Hitler in the evolution, between 1933 and 1939, of Nazi policy towards the Jews? It is on this question that Friedländer makes his most significant contribution. In recent years historians have argued over the question of Hitler's role in the Holocaust. Earlier historians—known now as 'intentionalists'—generally believed not only that Hitler dictated every stage of Nazi policy towards the Jews but also that from the moment he entered politics a plan to exterminate the Jews of Europe was fully formed in his mind. Some more recent historians—known as 'functionalists'—have raised doubts about this version of events. They deny to Hitler the kind of pivotal role the older school of historians took for granted and place more emphasis on the role of bureaucracy. They deny that in 1933 a blueprint for the Holocaust already existed in the mind of either Hitler or his inner circle.

Friedländer's relation to this debate is complex. On the one hand he acknowledges that one part of the case of the older historians is genuinely implausible and must be discarded. If Hitler always intended to rid the world of the Jews, why did the Nazi state before September 1939 encourage the emigration of its Jews to parts of the world where it was unlikely German power would ever reach? On the other hand, and more importantly, he gives a genuine depth and complexity to that part of the older version—concerning the centrality of Hitler to the Holocaust—which remains, in essence, true. Friedländer's restatement of the intentionalist case goes something like this.

Before he came to power Hitler's world-view had been shaped by a particular stream of anti-Semitism, preached by the Wagnerian Bayreuth circle. Hitler believed he had discovered in their version of the supposed struggle between the two pure races—the Aryan and the Jew—the key to world history. His anti-Semitism was starkly Manichaean. The Aryans were in his mind the cultural creators; the Jews the cultural destroyers. His anti-Semitism was also conspiratorial, formed by the tsarist forgery, *The Protocols of the Elders of Zion*. Bolshevism represented for Hitler a covertly Jewish political movement. The Bolshevik seizure of power in the old Russian Empire represented for him part of the Jewish bid for world power and world destruction. His anti-Semitism was, finally, apocalyptic. Hitler's deepest purpose in entering politics was to save the world by waging war against the Aryan's eternal enemy—the Jew. For the Hitlerian world-view Friedländer coins the useful term 'redemptive anti-Semitism'.

In 1933 no one yet understood what Hitler's redemptive anti-Semitism portended. No one here includes Hitler. At the core of Friedländer's interpretation, far more plausible than in the earlier intentionalist interpretations like Lucy Dawidowicz's *The War against the Jews*, is his understanding of the indeterminacy in Hitler's own mind about the ultimate destination of his Jewish policy. Office did not release Hitler from the grip of the redemptive anti-Semitic world-view. It did, however, at first, set strict limits on what he could do. Friedländer shows the irreducible tension between Hitler's policy pragmatism and ideological rigidity on the Jewish front. Even more importantly, and with a greater subtlety than I have ever before encountered in histories of the Holocaust, he shows the ways in which, over time, the gulf between Hitler's private world-view and the Nazi state's Jewish policy gradually and inexorably closed.

In the early years of policy caution, Hitler's deeper ambitions on the question of the destruction of the Jews did not go beyond occasional, often cryptic, private remarks. Yet as the regime became entrenched, and as the weakness of its enemies became more clear and as Hitler's self-confidence grew, the language in which the discussion of the Jewish question was framed became, increasingly, more rage-filled, more radical, more frank.

In 1936, in the year of the Franco-Soviet Pact and the struggle between left and right in the Spanish Civil War, Hitler and his circle drew directly on a Protocols-style language about Bolshevism as a manifestation of the Jewish bid for world power and world destruction. By late 1938 and early 1939, as tension with the western democracies grew, the idea of Jewish extermination, if it came to war, was already in the air.

On 30 January 1939 Hitler offered, in the Reichstag, a solemn warning and prophecy. If international Jewry should again plunge Europe into war, the result would be not the bolshevisation of the globe but the annihilation of the Jews. Unlike Lucy Dawidowicz, Friedländer does not interpret this prophecy as a simple statement of intent. Even less, however, does he see in it mere rhetorical hot air. For him, with speech like this, the idea of the Final Solution was moving from the realm of the private and the unthinkable to the public and the possible. 'No program of extermination had been worked out, no clear intentions could be identified...[But] a series of radical threats against the Jews were increasingly integrated with the vision of a redemptive final battle for the salvation of Aryan humanity.' The gulf which had once separated ideology and policy was narrowing. We reach the point, at the conclusion of Friedländer's fine first volume, where the fate of the Jewish remnant in Germany becomes part of a larger story—the annihilation of the Jews of Europe in the Holocaust.

1997

David Irving

IN 1993 a reporter from the *Age* telephoned. He informed me that the federal government had banned the British historian, David Irving, from visiting Australia. What did I think?

I said that I opposed the ban. My opposition was not, to put it mildly, based on admiration for the work of David Irving. Nor was it based on a view that to impose a political ban on a potential visitor to Australia is always wrong. I would not, for example, oppose the banning, in present Balkans circumstances, of visits to Australia by pan-Serb fanatics or pro-Ustashe Croats.

My opposition to the ban was not based on principle but on practical considerations. Knowing a little of Australia and of Irving's recent history I assumed he and his supporters would be capable of using the ban to make him a civil liberties martyr.

While a visit from Irving would be a low-key affair—perhaps providing aid and comfort to tiny bands of young neo-Nazi thugs and to the ageing anti-Semites still hovering around Eric Butler's League of Rights—a non-visit would, by contrast, be a sensation.

The media and the civil libertarians would, most likely, take up his cause. Many Australians who became interested in the case would see him as merely a dissident historian, whose views on Hitler, Churchill or the Jews deserved serious consideration. If he was wrong, they would think, why could he not be debated and refuted? Some would see the ban as yet another example of the political power of the Jewish lobby in Australia.

For all these reasons I thought the ban on Irving was likely to do more harm than good. Others disagreed.

Who, however, is this David Irving about whom Australians have been arguing over the past months? Until the mid-1970s he could still be regarded merely as a prolific, non-academic, usually right-wing, military historian, with a specialty in World War II.

The turning point for Irving came in 1977 when he published his most substantial work thus far, *Hitler's War*. In it he argued that Hitler—the most viciously anti-Semitic political leader in the history of Europe—had not ordered the mass extermination of European Jewry, had not known of his SS subordinates' enactment of his policy and had indeed tried wherever possible to help the Jews. The evidentiary basis for these astonishing claims were one or two ambiguous scraps of evidence which were savagely distorted, and the well-known lack of a written order from Hitler on the question of the Final Solution.

Following *Hitler's War* Irving ceased to be taken seriously by fellow historians. He began to seek out, and to be sought out by, altogether different company—by the neo-fascist fringe in Germany, France, Britain and the United States, and in particular by those devoted to exposing the 'myth' of the Jewish Holocaust.

At the same time, Irving's historical views were becoming increasingly ugly and bizarre. In 1980 he published a book on the 1956 revolution in Hungary. It portrayed the anticommunist revolution as, in essence, an anti-Semitic uprising of Hungarian gentiles against their Jewish-Bolshevik overlords.

In 1987 Irving launched in Australia a new biography of Churchill, which argued that in the 1930s an impoverished Churchill had sold his soul to a shadowy group of Jewish businessmen who together were responsible for plunging Europe into war, vetoing the reasonable peace offers of Hitler and, ultimately, destroying the British Empire.

In 1988 Irving took the final plunge into the ultra-right sewer. He became the champion of a report on Auschwitz—authored by a man whose business was in execution equipment and whose engineering qualifications turned out to be fraudulent—which 'exposed' the 'myth' of the six million dead. Irving now published his own glossy version of the so-called Leuchter report, and threatened that he would send it to every MP and every school in Britain.

Irving had now become a priceless asset for the Holocaust-denial underground. Until Irving's conversion no historian had been associated with this cause. Irving also became the darling of the Austro-German ultra-right. Last year, Australian television showed film of Irving shedding crocodile tears, before an audience of German skinheads, over the British persecution of Hitler's great deputy, Rudolf Hess.

I must admit that I had not realised, until seeing the transcript of a videotape Irving dispatched to Australia recently, how disreputable a scholar or how dreadful a man he had become. Throughout the tape Irving refers to Jews as 'our traditional enemies'. Enemies of whom? Europe? Christianity? Humanity? He refers to the Holocaust as a 'blood lie' against the innocent German people. He treats it as nothing but a conscious big-business swindle by Jewish racketeers to extract vast amounts of money from reparations payments and the entertainment industry.

Of the Jewish eyewitness survivors who passed through Auschwitz, Irving recommends psychiatric investigation. Of the hundreds of Germans of the SS who were tried after the war for their role in the mass extermination, and whose testimony provides thousands of pages of detailed knowledge of every phase of the Nazi genocide, Irving remains silent. Elsewhere he dismisses all this testimony as the tainted fruit of a victor's justice. For Irving, it must be assumed, the vast mountain of evidence concerning the Nazi extermination of the Jews—one of the most exhaustively documented events in history—has all been faked.

Curiously enough, Irving knows little of the Holocaust. He himself has written nothing and conducted no research on the policy of Jewish mass extermination. He boasts, moreover, of his refusal even to read the books of fellow historians—all of whom conclude that between four-and-a-half and upwards of six million Jews were murdered by the Nazis. He nevertheless comes up with a figure, virtually plucked from the air, of 25,000 Jewish murders. In these claims scholarly pretensions have altogether collapsed. Irving defines the 'myth' of the Holocaust thus: 'Adolf Hitler ordered the killing of six million Jews in Auschwitz.'

Even this formula is an Irving invention. No one claims six million Jews died in Auschwitz.

All historians know that the figure of approximately six million Jewish murders refers to the combination of deaths in the labour camps and ghettos of Poland (perhaps 500,000); the shootings in occupied USSR by the SS's *Einsatzgruppen* (perhaps 2.2 million); the gas veins of Chelmno (perhaps 55,000); the death factories of Belzec, Sobibor and Treblinka (perhaps 1.8 million) and the gas chambers of the Auschwitz–Birkenau concentration camp (perhaps 1.5 million).

To argue, as does Irving, that 25,000 Jews were murdered in Auschwitz, and to imply that this constitutes the total of Jewish deaths by murder under Nazism, represents for those who experienced the Holocaust and who survived, and even to those who have reflected upon it, a moral and intellectual scandal almost beyond endurance.

Most people are not in this situation. What has been particularly interesting to me in the controversy thus far is the influence

Irving has been able to exert over a younger generation of Australians, who have picked up at university a half-baked and philosophically confused scepticism regarding the very idea of truth, but who have acquired there virtually no solid historical knowledge.

Take a recent editorial in the *Herald-Sun*: 'The muzzling of David Irving'. This editorial described Irving as a 'controversial' historian who had become 'unpopular' merely because, after thirty years of archival research, he had arrived at the unfashionable view that tens of thousands rather than millions of Jews had been murdered by the Nazis. Such views, the editorialist believed, were offensive to Jews not because they were shockingly false but because of the great postwar Jewish 'article of faith', the Holocaust. Article of faith, indeed!

This editorial is based on profound, but, I suspect, not uncommon historical ignorance. It is also based on breathtaking political naivety. Irving's opinions have nothing whatever to do with genuine historical controversy or archival research. They have everything to do with the attempt by the ultra-right fringe in Europe and America to restore racism and anti-Semitism to respectability.

For the record I must point out that I have become a supporter of a ban on David Irving. An obscure visit is now inconceivable. To lift the ban would present Irving with a heaven-sent opportunity for media-driven mischief and propaganda. The initial ban on Irving was probably, on balance, a mistake. To lift it now would be a far greater one. In politics, circumstances matter.

1993

The Case of Konrad Kalejs

SHORTLY after Konrad Kalejs arrived in Melbourne and Jewish organisations began demanding his deportation, Jeff Kennett reminded the Jews of the Christian virtue of forgiveness. Kennett recalled Christ's last words on the Cross, 'Forgive them for they know not what they do'. Might it not be time, he wondered aloud, for the Jews to show towards Kalejs a little Christian forgiveness? Faced by yet another Jewish fuss concerning the Holocaust, Kennett, no doubt unconsciously, had fallen back on a very old tradition of thought—of the merciful, New Testament Christian and the vengeful, Old Testament Jew.

It is tempting to respond with irony to Jeff Kennett's remarks. For almost two thousand years, until 1945, churches held the Jews responsible, in perpetuity, for the murder of Jesus. The charge of deicide, one of the most potent sources of anti-Semitism in Europe, represented a far from self-evident expression of the Christian virtue of forgiveness on which the Jews were supposed to draw for their moral improvement. Irony, however, is not an answer. Behind the attitudes Kennett revealed in his comments there is something serious to discuss.

There are two main reasons why Australian Jews could not, even if they were so inclined, forgive Konrad Kalejs his crimes. The crimes Kalejs committed are, firstly, not within our capacity to forgive. Kalejs was involved in the murder of Latvian Jewry. What capacity has the Australian Jewish community to forgive him for wrongs done to others? Even more importantly, Kalejs has persistently denied his involvement in the murder of the Jews of Latvia. Forgiveness, in the absence of an acknowledgment of wrongdoing and of a genuine remorse, makes no moral sense.

Perhaps it is not forgiveness Jeff Kennett—and I have no doubt very many non-Jewish Australians—has in mind. Perhaps what he and they are really saying is that it is time for the Jews to put the Holocaust behind them, time to begin to forget. Perhaps I can explain why this is impossible by recounting, briefly, the story of Konrad Kalejs.

The German Army arrived in the Latvian capital, Riga, on 1 July 1941. The mobile killing squads of the SS, the *Einsatzgruppen*, were with them. They carried a Führer-order—for the killing of communists and Jews. Within days of his arrival in Riga the SS leader, General Stahlecker, formed a relationship with a Latvian adventurer, Viktor Arajs. The relationship quickly flourished. Arajs offered Stahlecker assistance in the task of killing. The offer was accepted. In the first days of July 1941 Arajs's men were involved in several outrages against the Jews of Riga, including the incineration of the synagogues.

At its formation the Arajs Commando, as it came to be called, had one purpose only—murder. As the outstanding non-Jewish historian of the Holocaust in Latvia, Andrew Ezergailis, puts it: 'It is an understatement to say that the activities of the Sonderkommando Arajs were gruesome. Plain and simple, the Arajs Commando came into existence for the purpose of killing Jews, communists and Gypsies.' Ezergailis regards every single member of the Arajs Commando who joined before 1942 as a war criminal. Konrad Kalejs, a graduate of the Latvian Military Academy, joined Arajs in late July 1941, as the most eminent historian of the Holocaust, Raul Hillberg, has established. He was no mere member but from the first a leader, a company commander.

As it happened, the mass killings of the Jews of Europe, what we call the Holocaust, began in Latvia. In almost every major anti-Jewish murder operation the Arajs squad was involved. Between July and September 1941 the Arajs Commando escorted thousands of Jewish men from Riga to the pine forest at Bikernieki. These men were led to pits, in groups of ten. Twenty Arajs riflemen awaited them. Each received one bullet in the back and one in the neck. The force of the shots catapulted them into the pits. By September, 5000 Jews had died thus.

In early 1942 the forest operations of the Arajs Commando resumed. This time the victims were those Jews from Germany or Austria who had been transported to Riga. Eight thousand of the Reich Jews, as they were called, were murdered by Arajs's men in the Bikernieki forest. The Arajs Commando did not operate only in the vicinity of Riga. It was also in charge, under German supervision, of the slaughter of those Latvian Jews living in provincial towns. Killing squads of perhaps forty men travelled in blue buses, stocked with sausage, cigarettes and vodka. They wiped out entire populations— men, women, children, babies. Of the 21,000 small-town Jews who perished in Latvia between 1941 and 1944, Ezergailis estimates that 15,000 were murdered by the Arajs Commando.

Despite their efforts, by November 1941, Himmler, the head of the SS, was dissatisfied with the pace of the killings in Latvia. The SS in Ukraine had set a higher standard. He ordered General Jeckeln to Riga. With military precision, over two days— 30 November and 8 December—Jeckeln arranged for the march of the Jews from the ghetto at Riga to the field at Rumbula, ten kilometres away. The Jews were ordered to strip to their underwear, to run a gauntlet towards the pits prepared for them, and to lie in these pits face down, the living upon the dead, before being shot. The shootings at Rumbula were conducted by a dozen Germans, but the entire Arajs Commando of 300 men—obviously including Kalejs—was obliged to assist. The Commando helped clear the ghetto. In the process between 600 and 1000 Jews were killed. One victim was a two-week-old baby, shot through the head. The Commando formed part of the gauntlet at Rumbula which drove the Jews to their graves. It was responsible for trucking the clothes of the dead back to Riga. In two days at Rumbula 24,000 Jews were murdered.

As a senior member of the Arajs Commando—a single-purpose murder squad in 1941—Konrad Kalejs must have been involved in countless unspeakable crimes. According to Ezergailis, the Arajs Commando was responsible for the murder of at least 26,000 Jews. It may have killed as many as 60,000. Throughout the period of the killings, Kalejs was one of its commanders. From 1942, we know, Kalejs was in command of the squads at Latvia's most notorious concentration camp, Saraspils, and of some 'anti-partisan' atrocities on the eastern front. Precisely which anti-Jewish operations he was involved in in the second half of 1941 and how many Jews he and his men then killed may never be known. Even so, the most important fact about Kalejs is clear. Kalejs was a major war criminal. He commanded one of the units of one of Eastern Europe's most vicious murder squads. Undoubtedly, he has thousands of deaths on his conscience.

What, then, can be done about Kalejs? As everyone acknowledges, it is far too late to try him. An acquittal would be far worse than no trial at all. Without enacting retrospective law, it is impossible to deport him. Even with such retrospective law, deportation seems futile. It is far from clear how justice will be served by forcing Kalejs to live out his dotage in Riga rather than Melbourne. What, then, can be done? The truth is stark. Nothing.

1997

Reflections on the Demidenko Affair

HARDLY a day has passed during my adult life when I have not thought, in one way or another, about the Holocaust or was not aware, at the margins of consciousness, of its presence. This strikes me as strange. For the Holocaust touched my life only at one or perhaps even at two removes. Both my parents were able to escape, one from Berlin, one from Vienna, before the Nazis set upon their campaign for the extermination of European Jewry. It was *their* parents who were caught up in the Holocaust. So far as I know, neither of my parents were aware of the circumstances in which their parents had died. I do not even know whether they ever allowed their imaginations to think of their parents on the trains going east; or of their arrival at a death camp, of their being stripped of their clothes, of their heads being shaved, of their being driven by whips into gas chambers. I hope not. In Australia, although the lives of both my parents must have been blighted by the awareness of their parents' and their peoples' fate, so far as I remember neither spoke to me much about Nazism or the

Holocaust. Perhaps they understood what a terrible kind of knowledge it was, what a terrible burden. Perhaps they simply wanted me to be happy.

As it happens, this reticence did not work. As for many Jews of my generation the Holocaust has cast its dark shadow over my life and thought. This is not something of which I am either proud or ashamed. It just happens to be true. And yet, although I have read a good deal about the Holocaust over the years, were it not for a certain event which happened last year I am sure I would never have written at length about it.

Let me remind you, as briefly as I am able, about the event. In the early 1990s a young Queensland girl, of English parents, decided to write a book about the Ukrainian famine of the 1930s and the Jewish Holocaust of the 1940s, and of their supposed connection.* She decided, too, to pretend that she was an Australian-born Irish Ukrainian and that the book she had written told the true story of her own family, on her father's side. She chose for this family the name Demidenko, the name of a Ukrainian guard who had been ordered to shovel the soil over the bodies of the 33,000 Jews who had been slaughtered at Babi Yar. Eventually her publishers convinced her to create a distance between herself and her book's characters by changing their name from Demidenko to Kovalenko. Nonetheless by now she had assumed the identity of the daughter of a Ukrainian who had participated at Babi Yar and of the niece of a Ukrainian who had participated in the gassing of Jews at Treblinka. This imagined uncle was the hero of her book.

The theme of her book was relatively simple. All the members of her Ukrainian family had been persecuted by Jewish Bolsheviks. The Kovalenko father is arrested by Jews during the Ukrainian famine on charges of aiding counter-revolution. As he is led away to his death he curses Jewish Bolshevism and calls upon his people to

---

The Hand That Signed the Paper, Helen Demidenko, Allen & Unwin, 1994.

take revenge upon the Jews when they have the chance. The mother, whose baby is dying, goes to a Jewish woman doctor in her village, to ask for medicine. She is repelled thus: 'I am a physician not a veterinarian.' Later, the doctor's Ukrainian husband warns her. The people will take revenge. She replies, 'Rubbish, Vanya. Comrade Stalin will protect us.' One of their sons is beaten by the village commissar, an ugly Jew, until there are permanent white scars on his back. Their daughter is taken to a communist school, and is beaten half-to-death for her expression of Ukrainian nationalism, by a character known to us only as the Jewess from Leningrad.

When the Germans arrive in the Ukraine, the time for Ukrainian revenge against the Jews has arrived. The Kovalenko daughter becomes the lover and the wife of a German SS man, a leader of one of the *Einsatzgruppen* units, who organises the Jewish slaughter at Babi Yar. She begs him, without success, to be allowed to watch the Jews being murdered. As it happens, one of her brothers participates at Babi Yar. The other goes to Treblinka where he gasses Jews. In general, the Ukrainian guards at Treblinka seem a well-balanced, even joyous group. One, however, is considered mad. He is the sadist, Ivan the Terrible. We learn that he is mad because of an incident in his childhood, where the Jews burned down his family home, with his parents and six brothers and sisters inside.

The famine–Holocaust passages of Helen Demidenko's book are framed within an Australian story. The Kovalenko family have migrated here after the war. Neither brother is even remotely aware of what he has done. Remorse for them, as for the author of their story, is a foreign notion. The Babi Yar brother, a zany, fun-loving character, keeps photographs of the pits filled with Jewish bodies in his bedside table. The Treblinka brother throughout his life wears the gold spectacles of a murdered Jew on his nose.

The Babi Yar character's daughter, Fiona, has discovered that her Treblinka uncle is being persecuted by Australia's Jews and their Zionist agent, Bob Hawke, with the threat of war-crimes trials. The Jews in Australia are, thus, perpetuating the cycle of Ukrainian-Jewish violence which began in the Stalin famine. The Treblinka brother feels renewed hatred for the Jews. His nieces, too, are outraged by Jewish vengefulness. In the end he escapes trial only through natural death. For participating in the murder of thousands, for tossing babies in the air so that his companion can get bayonet practice, we learn that, while he does not feel 'sorry', he is at least, on his deathbed, still trying.

II

I did not read *The Hand that Signed the Paper* until June 1995. By the time I read it it had won the *Australian*/Vogel award as the best novel by an unpublished young writer, the Australian Literature Society's gold medal for outstanding contribution to our literary culture, and the Miles Franklin Award, Australia's most prestigious literary prize. In my judgment the thesis proposed by *The Hand*—that the Holocaust was, in part, a kind of Ukrainian payback for Jewish involvement in the famine—is a malicious falsehood, and the novel's routine identification of Jews with Bolshevism the revival of a doctrine to be found near the heart of Nazi ideology, a doctrine which had been used by the Nazis for what one historian has called its 'warrant for genocide'. In my judgment, too, *The Hand* was written by an author who felt very little indeed about the terrible events she described and whose work seemed to lack altogether the fundamental elements of what one might call a moral grammar. In my judgment, finally, *The Hand* was a work which turned the cultural meaning of the Holocaust on its head; which reminded the Jews that in regard to the catastrophe which was visited upon them they were far from blameless; which suggested a moral equivalence between mass murderers and those who wished to bring these murderers to trial. I thought that Helen Demidenko had only dared to do what she had done because she truly did not know what she was doing or saying.

I was not, of course, surprised that such a book should have been written. There is much strangeness in the world. I was, however, more than surprised that a novel like this should have been warmly praised by virtually all its newspaper critics and regarded as a major achievement by three separate sets of Australian literary judges. As I have expressed it in *The Culture of Forgetting* I experienced the gulf between my reading of *The Hand* and the reading of it by what appeared in June 1995 to be the weight of literary opinion in this country as a kind of cultural destabilisation.* As the rather bitter controversy over *The Hand* passed beyond literary circles, and as it became increasingly clear that at least a part of the intelligentsia regarded harsh criticism of *The Hand* as the product of politically organised, highly censorious and overly sensitive Jews and as an attack on aesthetic licence and free speech, my feeling of cultural destabilisation deepened. I had assumed that most Australian readers regarded the Holocaust as one of the defining moments in our civilisation's self-understanding. I had assumed that they knew it to be an event which mattered not only for Jews but for all human beings. I had also assumed that they would understand why Jews would feel pain about the honouring of a book like *The Hand*. None of these assumptions seemed to be true. I felt compelled to write about Australian culture and the Demidenko affair not because, with regard to the Holocaust, I had something new to say, but for the opposite reason, because I had become convinced that I lived in a culture where ignorance or indifference or forgetfulness seemed to be overtaking what once had been generally known. *The Culture of Forgetting* was an attempt to show how, in honouring *The Hand*, a part of the Australian literary world—through a combination of inattentiveness, literary-critical confusion, historical ignorance and multicultural sentimentality—had mistaken a piece of anti-Semitic juvenilia for a fine work of literature.

In *The Culture of Forgetting* I argued that the honouring of *The Hand* was unconnected with the existence of anti-Semitism in the

---

***The Culture of Forgetting*, Robert Manne, Text Publishing Company, 1996.

literary intelligentsia. As I put it, there is probably in Australia no group more reliably hostile to expressions of racism or anti-Semitism than the literary community. I still believe this to be true. I have, however, come to think that the question of the relationship between the contemporary literary culture and the Holocaust might be more complex than I first imagined; that there might be more involved here—in both the high regard for *The Hand* and the bitterness of the controversy that later surrounded it—than is suggested in the idea of a culture of forgetting.

If one attended closely to Demidenko's book it was not hard to pick up a tone of intense Holocaust irritation. In one sense the whole project of *The Hand* seems to have been driven by a kind of youthful moral revisionism, a deliberate deconstruction and inversion of the Holocaust story, an unmasking of its received cultural meaning. But the irritation I have in mind can also be readily identified in particular passages. In *The Hand* the Kovalenko daughter tells us that her tormentor, the Jewess of Leningrad, would frequently tell her class stories about Cossack pogroms against the Jews in tsarist times. 'It was a sad story, and when she first related it we all felt sorry for her family; but because she had told it so many times, and was such a nasty person, people lost this feeling.' In *The Culture of Forgetting* I commented on this passage, thus: 'What Kateryna feels about the pogroms Helen Demidenko feels about the Holocaust. With interminable stories of Jewish suffering and anti-Semitism she is, like Kateryna "fed up [and] bored".' What I did not say—but what I have come now to think, partly on the basis of a considerable amount of correspondence I have received—is that this kind of Holocaust fed-upness is far more widespread than I had once been willing to allow myself to think. I have received, since publication, many letters which have asked me, in rather aggressive tones, to explain precisely why Jews are so determined to tell their Holocaust story, again and again; and why we are, supposedly, so little interested in the stories of other people's equal or greater suffering; by letters which express, with complete frankness, the anger correspondents feel at the Holocaust story being forced down gentile throats. I have begun to wonder whether at least some of the early admiration for *The Hand* did not reflect the experience of some forbidden pleasure at finding, at last, a literary work which expressed freely a more general Holocaust jadedness.

A less unpleasant theme in the subsequent Demidenko debate—but nonetheless one that interested me and puzzled me somewhat—was the suggestion that *The Hand* had offended Jews chiefly because it challenged a theory of the Holocaust, whose most important theme was the idea that, in human history, the Holocaust was a unique event. This view was founded, in my view, on three misrepresentations. The first was that Jews consider the Holocaust, somehow, their exclusive intellectual property and that they therefore resent non-Jews writing about it in any way. As a matter of fact this view is false. Many of the most respected scholars of the Holocaust are, like Christopher Browning or Hans Mommsen, non-Jews. Nonetheless, it is an interesting misrepresentation. The second was that most serious Jewish studies of the Holocaust are theological rather than historical and rest on faith and doctrine rather than evidence and argument. Once again this is false. The vast bulk of Jewish scholarships on the Holocaust is painstakingly empirical. This body of work is far from uniform in its argument or conclusion. There is simply no settled Jewish view of the Holocaust.

The third misrepresentation is the most revealing of all. While it is true that many Jewish and non-Jewish scholars regard the kind of crime committed in the Holocaust as unique, this does not mean that such scholars regard it as more evil than other politically determined human catastrophes. Even a dictionary will make clear that unique means singular not worse. There can be no doubt that larger numbers of human beings were killed in the Stalin terror or Mao's Great Leap Forward. If the Holocaust is unique, as some believe, its uniqueness rests on the singularity of the ambition of the Nazis—to wipe the entire Jewish people from the face of the earth. To speak of the uniqueness of the Holocaust is to argue that never before in history had a state attempted, remorselessly and systematically, to eliminate, in its entirety and forever, a distinct people. The fact that in the Demidenko debate so many thought that critics of *The Hand* were distressed by her denial of the Holocaust's uniqueness, and that they saw in the idea of the Holocaust's uniqueness nothing but a perverse form of Jewish national egocentricity and self-absorption, seems to me to reveal something rather strange lurking just beneath the surface of the Demidenko debate.

Even more revealing was an idea which was expressed more than once during this debate—the idea that in the persecution of a young author the Jews were demonstrating, yet again, their inability to understand or express one of the most fundamental of the Christian virtues—forgiveness. In a recent edition of *Quadrant* I published a letter which argued against my book thus:

> What Manne does not appreciate, I think, is the moral discomfort aroused in many Australians by the long-term project of retribution which has emerged in the Jewish response to the Holocaust. My guess is that Australians in the Christian tradition are made uneasy by the apparent absence from Jewish discourse of one of the central tenets of Christian morality—the obligation to forgive, to 'love' those who have harmed you. Imperfectly realised though so difficult a precept is bound to be, our society is nevertheless profoundly Christian in its insistence on the eschewing of personal retribution—of giving to Caesar the things that are Caesar's and to God the things that are God's. One has a growing feeling that we are being heavied to take justice out of the courts of Caesar and enshrine it in the courts of the heart… Demidenko perhaps made a case, however imperfect, for forgiveness,

and this may be some part of the reason for her book's deeply disturbing impact on Jews caught up in this latest response.

What interested me about this letter was not so much what appeared to me its moral confusion. How can someone forgive wrongs done to others? How can there be true forgiveness when there is no remorse? What interested me was how easily here one of the oldest ideas of Christian anti-Semitism—found in pure form in *The Merchant of Venice*—where the Christian virtues of forgiveness and mercy are contrasted with the Jewish vice of vengeance, the desire for the pound of flesh—had made its way to the surface. How strange it was, it then seemed to me, how quickly in writing about the Holocaust and Australian culture, I had rediscovered such old and familiar ground.

1996

The Problem of *Schindler's List*

IT is impossible not to be deeply affected by Steven Spielberg's *Schindler's List*. No film I have seen has conveyed the idea of Nazi indifference to life more powerfully. There are sequences within it—the liquidation of the Cracow ghetto or the burning of the exhumed bodies of the Cracow Jews—which are realised with a precision, authenticity and a fiendish intensity I have rarely before experienced in film.

There are, too, single images of extraordinary genius. During the evacuation of the children from the Plaszow labour camp we see a young boy, who has fled, standing to bolt attention in the excrement of the camp latrine. During the liquidation of the Cracow ghetto the camera follows the terrified flight of a very young girl—perhaps she is four or five—who scurries to safety under a sofa. The film is shot in black and white, but at this moment we follow her red coat. Much later in the film—during the incineration of the bodies of the Cracow Jews—the camera fleetingly directs us to a tiny corpse in a red coat. It is a moment of almost unendurable pity.

Yet while there is no denying the force of *Schindler's List* is it, as has generally been claimed, a masterpiece? I think not. There is, firstly, a deep divide between the power of Spielberg's visual imagination and the banality of his moral imagination. In several scenes meaning is undone by cleverness. A young Jewish woman engineer advises the SS commandant at the Plaszow concentration camp, Goeth, that the construction plan for a barracks is faulty. For her insolence she is executed on the spot. Goeth then orders that her advice be adopted. The irony is tricksy and shallow. Or again. There is a scene where Schindler is roused from some pleasant whoring with the news that the man on whom he relies to run his business, the Jew Stern, has been put on a train to Auschwitz. Schindler hurries to the station and approaches a couple of young Nazi soldiers on guard. Can they not get Stern off the train? They assure Schindler they cannot. Orders are orders. Schindler warns them that he is a man of power; if Stern is not released from the Auschwitz cargo they will find themselves before too long on the eastern front. The film cuts to a scene of the soldiers marching along the platform shouting Stern's name. The humour here does not, as some have argued, relieve an unbearable tension. Given the circumstance it is simply cheap.

Such lapses (and there are many) are less important than the deep-seated problem of the film, Spielberg's decision to use the story of Oskar Schindler—the genuinely fascinating tale of the corrupt Nazi businessman who saved more than a thousand Cracow Jews—as his vehicle for the film he genuinely and somewhat audaciously aspired to make, the definitive film of the Holocaust.

Part of the problem is that the Schindler story is wholly atypical. It is fascinating precisely because of its unrepresentative character, because of its capacity to cast a damning light on how the German elite did not behave. A story so unrepresentative is, at the very least, a strange choice for a film which aims to go to the heart of the Holocaust. At best it is irrelevant to Spielberg's deeper ambition.

In fact it is worse than irrelevant; it subverts the film's purpose. The Schindler story—both in reality and in Spielberg's highly sentimentalised version of it—is essentially a story of hope. At the beginning of the film Schindler is a charming, womanising black-marketeer. During the film he is transformed—most critically as he sits on horseback above the ghetto observing the horrors of its liquidation—into a deeply moral man, deploying his money, his not inconsiderable talent for corruption, and his mysterious influence to save his Jews. By the end of the film he has become a saint. Schindler's Jews are saved. He weeps before them. If only he could have saved more.

The film has for some time by now been moving inexorably towards such an ending. Spielberg's cameras have recently taken us to Auschwitz; the train bearing Schindler's Jewish women has gone there by mistake. At Auschwitz all of Schindler's Jews are reprieved. Only the chimneys of the crematoria and the fleeting glimpse of another party of Jews being led down a flight of stairs reminds us that we have arrived in hell and that this is a factory of death. Within the world created by the film the horrors of Cracow and Plaszow have passed. In Spielberg's promised land hell hath no permanent place.

Schindler has gone to Auschwitz to buy the release of his women. The commandant there is not uninterested in the diamonds. For simplicity's sake, however, he offers Schindler, instead of his Jews, another trainload of equivalent number. This offer is rejected contemptuously. There is nothing in the film that suggests that it has even crossed Spielberg's mind that moral questions of a terrible and almost impossible complexity might be involved here. If anything, the film regards it as typical of the Nazis that they should think any old three hundred Jews as worthy as those on Schindler's list! Spielberg here seems altogether unaware of what he is saying.

The same may be true of the film's penultimate scene.

Engraved on the gold ring presented to Schindler are the words from the Talmud: 'Whoever saves a single person saves the world entire.' Once again, there is absolutely nothing in the film which suggests any awareness of the almost pitiful inadequacy of such a thought in the face of what the Nazis did to the millions of Jews; of how profoundly such traditional ways of thinking have been shaken by the radical evils of our age.

My case about *Schindler's List* can be put simply. With visual genius Spielberg has created images of horror concerning the Holocaust as perhaps no other film-maker has or will. But because of a moral thoughtlessness he has undermined these images with a story irrelevant to his larger ambition and, in the end, subversive of it. The contradiction between Spielberg's deeper purpose, to produce a work of art which takes us to the heart of the Holocaust darkness, and the story he has chosen as the vehicle for his purpose, the story of Schindler's salvific mission, have in the end destroyed the integrity of his film. Almost unbelievably a film about the darkest chapter in human history has an uplifting and even, in a curious way, a happy ending.

There were, even in the darkest chapters of the Holocaust, what Primo Levi calls 'moments of reprieve'. There were also within it, stories of human goodness—like the story of Oskar Schindler, which Spielberg has told, or the story of the Jewish doctor in the Warsaw ghetto, Korczak, about whom the great Polish director, Andrzej Wajda, has made a finer, although more modest film. The Holocaust, however, is an historical event from which, in general, no message of hope and no consolation can or should be drawn.

If one wishes to understand even a part of its meaning one must turn, in my view, to those who have studied it 'with pity and with rigour', to authors like Hannah Arendt in *Eichmann in Jerusalem* or Primo Levi in *If This Is a Man*, or film-makers like Claude Lanzmann in *Shoah*.

II

Since these views appeared in the *Age* they have occasioned considerable anger. Isi Leibler pointed out (probably correctly) that 95 per cent of those who had seen the film had been impressed by it. Only smart-alec intellectuals had expressed reservations. He seemed to believe that there existed a kind of political requirement on those who cared about the Holocaust to regard *Schindler's List* as a masterpiece, or, at the very least, to hold their tongues in public. Gerard Henderson agreed. For him Spielberg's film was an invaluable weapon against the historical revisionism of the extreme right. Sure the film might be sentimental, but so what? At least it was not, unlike Claude Lanzmann's *Shoah*, 'too long'.

No one, however, could outdo Bill Rubinstein in this kind of defence of *Schindler's List*:

> By cunningly making Oskar Schindler, an 'Aryan' and, ostensibly, a Nazi, into the hero of the film, Keneally and Spielberg have vastly raised the number of [non-Jewish] viewers who will empathise with him in rescuing Jews. It is genuinely surprising that Dr Baker, and the other local critics of the film, cannot see this obvious fact.

It is not that I cannot see this obvious fact. It is rather that I was educated in a world where voices like those of F. R. Leavis and Lionel Trilling—who thought that the task of criticism was vital to culture—still mattered. This was a time when to call a work of imagination sentimental was not seen as irrelevant to the estimation of its value. This was a time when to speak of a work of art as benign propaganda was not a way of according it the highest praise. I remain attached to this world.

1994

PART SIX

THE WAY WE LIVE NOW

Innocence

OUR six-year-old daughter's current passion is kangaroos. A few weeks ago we came upon a family of them during a late evening stroll. Some of the older kangaroos were grazing or meditating. Two of the younger ones were boxing. A joey hopped confidently towards what it believed was its mother's pouch. She clipped it over the ear and sent it packing to its true mother. Our daughter was hooked.

Shortly thereafter I read her an article in a newspaper about a young man in the bush who had managed to entice kangaroos to come inside his house to feed. From that moment I was nagged mercilessly every evening to join her on taming expeditions. Our main tactic was to lay bread trails leading to the house and to place bread in a nearby tin shed. At the crack of dawn our daughter would run to the shed confident that a tame kangaroo and joey would be waiting for her.

With time this hope has faded. She has opted for a new tactic on the kangaroo front—a letter to Father Christmas. She is an unreconstructed believer in him, and not only in him. Like many children, our daughter is unselfconsciously and idiosyncratically religious. Occasionally she encounters a non-believer among her six-year-old friends. She regards them with a mixture of pity and puzzlement.

She currently believes that certain areas of the local paddocks are enchanted. She believes that not only our family but also all our animals—including a much loved horse who died a few years ago—will be reunited in heaven. She is currently turning over in her mind the possibility that one of our cats is immortal. Above all she believes in a God of justice. Her religion, in so far as I understand it, combines elements of primitive animism, paganism, pantheism, and monotheism.

Like many young children whose lives have been happy, she lives most intensely in the world of her imagination. Of much of the world's evil and suffering she remains innocent. My wife and I have regarded the preservation of this sphere of innocence during her early years as one of our most important parental responsibilities. In the future she will have time to learn of human wickedness and to experience the disenchantment of her world. That time has not yet come. Or so it seems to us.

The price for preserving childhood innocence is, however, as we have discovered, eternal parental vigilance. Consider the case of television and the education system.

In its dramas and news broadcasts, contemporary television conveys into almost every living-room in the land the most vivid filmic images of violence and self-abuse, of mutilation and death. A generation ago the inner censor of the culture forbade even adults from seeing such things. Today, I would think, most adults do not even bother to save their children from the daily passive absorption of these images of horror. What harm we are doing can only be imagined.

Even adults who forbid their children from watching violent fictions or the news cannot, however, rest easy. Some time ago a newsflash interrupted a late-afternoon episode of 'The Muppets'. A Melbourne man had kidnapped his daughter. He had just shot her through the back at close range. Back to 'The Muppets'.

My wife, Anne, tells me that such sensitive programming decisions are far from uncharacteristic—including the ABC.

Even preschools and schools pose threats to those concerned with innocence. Unless they are very wary, parents may one day discover that their young children have been taught a protective behaviour program. Children are meant to learn how to distinguish between physical affection and abuse and, thus, to take action against adults threatening them with sexual harm.

For those children threatened with abuse from a monstrous adult it is highly unlikely that such a program could genuinely help them. For the vast majority who are not threatened it is highly likely that they will experience anxiety and a confusing ambivalence about their physical relations with adult friends and even family.

A society which remembered the value of childhood innocence would not have permitted so ill-conceived and clumsy a program to enter the curriculum uncontested. There are many ways to harm a child. The vilest and most obvious is physical abuse. The most common form for us, however, is the unwitting but unremitting assault on innocence.

1989

Suffer the Feral Children

IN the Australia of the fifties and sixties an unemployment rate of 2 per cent was regarded as a disgrace. We are now slowly becoming reconciled to a world where more than 10 per cent of the workforce is unemployed and where—in many of our provincial towns and old industrial suburbs—50 per cent of our young people cannot find a job. The causes of this change are controversial. The consequences are not. In Australia the social pool of the impoverished, underprivileged and permanently unemployed—that substratum which modern sociologists have come to call the underclass—will deepen during the 1990s.

There is probably no one who understands more intimately what life in the underclass means than John Embling, one of the finest and most remarkable Australians of his generation. In 1975 the young Embling—the son of a very close middle-class family and a somewhat idiosyncratic graduate of Geelong College and the University of Melbourne—joined the staff of a technical college in the working-class western suburbs of Melbourne. His task was to teach remedial English. He instantly encountered wild adolescents with the reading skills of six-year-olds, who lurched in their behaviour between violent destruction and sullen withdrawal. He was astonished to discover children of twelve or thirteen deeply depressed. The education system had, in effect, all but given up on them. Their problems were parcelled out among a bevy of professionals—psychological counsellors, welfare workers, police. Their dismal futures—of violence, alcohol, drugs, fleeting social bonds and promiscuous sex, of asylum or prison or early death—seemed already scripted. Embling could not accept that this should be so.

By chance he came upon a young woman, Heather Pilcher, who had been working with 'street kids' in Williamstown for ten years. Heather was not a middle-class romantic but a hard-headed product of old working-class neighbourhood culture. She treated the young people who were drawn to her with kindness but also with firmness and with what John saw as a kind of spiritual detachment. Other 'street kid' workers he had encountered began with phoney deference and ended with bitter disillusion. Embling tells the story of a typical professional who demonstrated his trust in his young charges by turning over his flat to them for a weekend. He returned to find it ransacked. Heather, he discovered, would never have been so foolish. She was practical and without illusion. Somehow what she was doing worked. John began by turning up at her church-hall annexe on Friday nights. Within six months he had left his teaching post and joined her. 'It was,' as he puts it, 'the triumph of vocation over commonsense.' Their partnership has lasted seventeen years.

The early years together were a considerable financial struggle. Embling had an overnight success with a book which he drew from his experience, *Tom*—but also a couple of years of unemployment. The turning point came when Phillip Adams wrote an article on Embling's work for the *Age*. Real support now flowed in—from the Fraser government (through Senator Chaney), from a number of enlightened businesses and from scores of individuals. A legal foundation was formed; a house in Footscray purchased. In 1985 it was rebuilt to allow eight or ten children to live there comfortably. Half the money needed, some $40,000, came from a retired Castlemaine apple farmer, Ernest Richards. His tweedy photo hangs upstairs now, in what is called the Ernest Richards Wing. The Embling–Pilcher household, which I visited earlier this year, is a miracle of cheerful domesticity, of civilisation (with books and paintings lining the walls) and, above all, of order.

The young who enter this world—the feral children, as Embling calls them—arrive from nightmare worlds beyond middle-class imaginings. Many have suffered violent beatings or sexual abuse, often from the string of men who visit their mothers from time to time. Many who are the victims of violence soon learn how to inflict it on others. These children are often involved, in their early teenage years, in serious and systematic crime. The sexual relations of the feral children are, generally, nasty, brutish and short. Some pick up money by selling sex on the street. Most live on a cocktail diet of alcohol and drugs—generally 'speed' or 'crack', not heroin which is too slow for them. Their street bonds are intense, and fleeting.

Embling has an uncompromising hatred for the drug culture which has long preyed upon these young people. He has attended upwards of thirty-six funerals of children he has known who have died of drugs. Under drugs, he explains, all moral feeling collapses. He tells of a case where a teenager—'not the world's worst kid'—murdered a mate with a knife while under the influence of speed and alcohol.

Invariably these kids come from shattered families. One of Embling's early sociological discoveries about the underclass is the flight of the fathers. Over the years he has become closely involved, as the inevitable extension of his work with children, in the lives of more than two hundred mothers, and three fathers! These absent fathers are not divorced men, who see their children regularly or even occasionally. They have, simply, disappeared altogether.

The lives of the abandoned mothers are routinely chaotic. Most are sunk hopelessly in debt. Many are themselves dependent on alcohol or drugs. Some live pseudo-adolescent lives, out on the town every night; others are so psychologically shattered that they can hardly leave their high-rise Housing Commission flats at all. Most live in utter domestic disorder—with bills unpaid, dishes unwashed, wild children and drunken lovers out of control. In the 1970s Embling often worked with mothers who came out of the old working-class culture. He now, more frequently, deals with second-generation feral children. In the world of these underclass mothers and children, both the extended family and their neighbourhood have simply ceased to exist.

It is John Embling and Heather Pilcher's vocation to try to restore meaning and order to these shattered lives. Their evenings and weekends are, by and large, spent with the children; the days with the mothers. A few children live at the foundation permanently. Others spend part of their week there, and part of it at home. In most cases, however disastrous the circumstances, they need their mothers. In his book *Fragmented Lives* Embling tells the story of the deep protectiveness of one of his lads, Jimmy, towards his drunken, abusive mother. Together one evening while literally lifting her out of the gutter, Jimmy confides, 'She's all I've got, John.'

The young who come to the foundation combine in their character the traits of hardened criminality and child-like vulnerability. At its deepest level it is Embling's aim to draw them back into the human world by allowing them to experience, for the first time in their lives, a real childhood—space, freedom, safety, order, playfulness, love. These are key words in the Embling credo. The dark lure of the street, which Embling certainly does not underestimate, has to be defeated. Children are, he knows, jumping jacks, high-adrenalin animals. At the foundation kids swim, skate, dance or bushwalk in the nearby You Yangs. As at all good schools individual talents are spotted and passions are encouraged.

The motto of the foundation is 'No rights without responsibilities'. Rights are extended gradually, in return for responsibilities assumed. All the children cook and clean. Older ones keep an eye on the well-being of younger children. Bright ones help with school work. Longstanding household members—foundation graduates, as it were—serve as models for the wild newcomers. To their considerable surprise they learn, as Embling puts it, that 'there is subtlety in life, companionship...that there are ways you can relate to others, short of bashing or rape'. Mothers are encouraged to visit.

On the other hand, kids may bring home the order they have experienced at the foundation. Embling tells me of one formerly ultra-violent lad who now makes breakfast for his younger brothers and sisters if his once drug-dependent mother fails to surface. He is the proud owner of an alarm clock. Ultimately, Embling believes, the foundation, in all its complex interactions of single mothers and their children, allows many to experience something they have never before experienced—a real human community.

The recession has hit the Embling–Pilcher household very hard. Although there has been some loss of financial support, this is not what concerns Embling most. The foundation extends its reach from the inner Melbourne suburb of Footscray to the industrial outskirts of Geelong. There is probably no area in Australia more battered by the recession than this.

There are bitter stories here. A number of mothers who had miraculously reconstructed their lives and found good steady jobs have recently been retrenched through no fault of their own. They are shattered. Since the recession hit, the foundation has gone into a new line of business—delivering potatoes (from supporting farmers) and clothing to its families.

Nor, of course, has the recession spared the kids. Once there was ready work to be had, on the docks or in the local meatworks or whatever. Now there is absolutely nothing. Last year, for the first time not one job was forthcoming for even one of these young people. Daily, television bombards them with images of wealth and glamour and with a subliminal moral code differing little from the one once learned on the streets: greed is good, every man for himself. According to Embling many feel bewildered and betrayed by a world that seems now to offer them no future.

1992

Childcare

WHEN I read Penelope Leach's *Children First*, my first thought was, this is very good.* My second thought was, this is trouble. So it has turned out. Over the past fortnight a controversy has been swirling around Penelope Leach's childcare apostasy.

Over the past decade I have taken a keen interest in the question of institutional childcare for infants. There have been, in that time, many arguments for the investment of more public funds to subsidise those who use creches. In recent times there have been counter-arguments for income splitting, to give families a genuine choice about whether they wish to use these creches or look after their young at home. But as to the one really vital issue—whether with institutional daycare there is risk of harm—there has been silence. It has been Penelope Leach's book that has, at long last, broken that taboo.

Leach has angered mainstream feminists. She is no anti-feminist.

**Children First, Penelope Leach, Michael Joseph, 1994.

Her general position is one that my wife Anne (who knows a great deal more about this subject than I do) calls 'child-centred feminism'. No one could read Penelope Leach without realising that she recognises both the inevitability and, even more importantly, the justice of the fundamental ambition of feminism—women's quest for equal treatment and fulfilment in the world beyond the home.

She is, however, also aware of the strains and paradoxes which have attended that quest. Leach points sharply, for example, to the many empirical studies that show the failure of husbands, even in dual-income families, to shoulder anything remotely resembling an equal burden of the dreary labour around the house. For most women, to add a full-time paid workload onto the traditional domestic chores looks more like the road to exhaustion than emancipation.

Even more importantly, Penelope Leach is acutely aware of the terrible tension—which can almost tear a woman apart—between the push towards the fulfilment of her talents in the world and the pull of the love she feels for the children she has brought into it. She does not take lightly women's desire for career but she also acknowledges something which one strand of contemporary feminism seems determined to repress—the extraordinary power of the mother–infant bond.

Her investigation of the mother–baby–father triangle in the earliest days after childbirth is beautifully evocative and precise. She understands that what a woman needs from the father of her child is not exactly shared duties but support for the passionate and highly physical love affair—what she calls the nocturnal 'pas de deux'—she is conducting with her baby.

It is the extension of this kind of phenomenology to the needs of infants that has landed Leach in trouble. She argues that from birth until about their third birthday what babies and toddlers need is as much 'one-on-one' time as possible with familiar adults who love them.

Leach is not, if I might borrow another of my wife's phrases, a gender fundamentalist. After the first few months of the mother–infant affair, she strongly favours the division of tasks between the mother and the father. Where these options are unavailable she favours familial—grandparents or aunts—over non-familial care; and where familial care is unavailable, the placing of infants into reliable other-family homes rather than into creches.

At the conceptual heart of her argument in support of this unfashionable hierarchy of choice is the distinction between the ideas of love and of care. Infants, she argues, can only come to feel at home in the world and to discover who they are in the presence of attentive, loving and more or less permanently present others. Because infants do not have an adult's sense of time or routine they may, she suggests, experience separation from those they are closest to as endless and forever. Protracted daily spells of incomprehension or indifference to an infant's subtle, non-physical needs may be transformed into emotions of bewilderment or anger or withdrawal.

Her rule of thumb for the upbringing of infants is, the more parenting the better. And, where that is impossible, the more quasi-parenting the better. Her understanding of the infant's needs leads her inescapably to an argument that favours the intimacy of the home to the coolness of the creche, and the vocation of the parent or relative to the professionalism of the care-giver.

It is hardly difficult to understand why Penelope Leach's arguments will strike many parents as most unwelcome—as either extremely painful or impossibly foolish. Nevertheless, as the questions she raises are of vital importance to the future of our society, the least that can be expected from those who disagree with her is civility and reason. Thus far, in the debate that has raged around her book, there has been little of either.

Three main lines of argument have been mounted against her. The first suggests that she is some kind of nostalgist yearning for a lost golden age, where dad's in the office, mum's in the kitchen and all's right with the world. When the *Weekend*

Australian published an extract from her book, it was accompanied by two large illustrations in 1950s mode. One showed a mother with a scrubbing brush kneeling by her young son's bathtub. The vision of Leach this iconography suggests could not be further from the truth. The premise of her book is of the inexorable passing of an old world and of the need to regain our balance in the one that is taking its place.

The second line of argument against her is more serious but no less misleading. This is the suggestion that Penelope Leach's views are no more than her personal opinion and that, in the oft-repeated phrase, 'there is no evidence' for institutional daycare for infants bringing with it a risk of harm.

Such a claim is simply untrue. An extensive literature presenting evidence of harm exists. Some of it, written by child-centred feminists like Valerie Suransky, Marian Blum or Selma Fraiberg, is of a theoretical and observational nature. Some of it is the work of empirical psychologists.

In the scientistic age we live in, this may be the only kind of work we regard as hard 'evidence'. If so, an excellent, cautious summary can be found in a recent essay of Jay Belsky's which concludes that in many, although not all studies, the 'evidence seems to support the conclusion that, on average, extensive non-parental care initiated in the first year is a risk factor for developments such as insecure attachment to the mother, non-compliance, aggressiveness, and possibly withdrawn behaviour'. While it is true, as the *Age* editorial pointed out, that the social science 'jury is still out' on the question of daycare, what the editorial did not acknowledge is that on this kind of question it is inconceivable that the jury will ever come in.

The final accusation against Leach takes us to the heart of the matter. She is accused of attempting to instil guilt into mothers and thereby of driving them back into the home.

This is thoroughly unjust. Penelope Leach does not argue that the rearing of the very young is primarily the mother's responsibility, but the parents'. Even more, given that she believes that new parents can make better choices, and given that no one could possibly doubt from the tone of this book that her concern for the well-being of children is genuine, on what basis can she possibly be asked, because of fear of causing pain or giving offence, to hold her tongue?

Not all mothers of infants are members of the upper middle class for whom work means the legal firm or the business office. Some mothers of the very young spend their days on the process line or at a cash register. For these women—and also for those members of the upper middle class who forgo career and social esteem to be a 'mere mother' for a few years—Penelope Leach's book will not instil guilt, but comfort, assurance and hope.

1994

A Case for Censorship

AT regular intervals Australia passes through a minor crisis of conscience over censorship. Two years ago the nation fretted over whether the horrid fantasy *American Psycho*—where the yuppie hero nonchalantly rapes, mutilates, tortures and murders his female victims—could be sold in our bookshops. Eventually the censors decided that it could, although only with a plastic covering. Our conscience was clear. Some months later a well-thumbed copy of *American Psycho* was discovered on the bedside table of the sexually tormented Wade Frankum, when his room was searched after his murderous spree in Sydney.

Recently we fretted over whether or not Pasolini's unbearable politico-sado-sexual nightmare, *Salo*, should be shown in public cinemas. Because Pasolini is a genuine artist, unlike the half-dead author of *American Psycho*, and because in his work the evil is unambiguously condemned, the censorship question raised by *Salo* is genuinely more complex than the one raised by *American Psycho*.

Nevertheless it is now the case that young men are flocking to movie houses across the land to experience the delights of forced buggery, excremental feasting, sexual torture and death. Because the sex in *Salo* is so ugly and unerotic most will probably leave the cinema wishing they had never seen the movie. Some delicate souls will be disturbed. Some twisted souls may be transfixed and tempted by one or another of its images of unspeakable degradation.

Australia's occasional crises of conscience over censorship generally follow a predictable course. The censors and the mainstream intelligentsia who support the release of some new landmark piece of taboo-breaking vileness take their stand on the ground of liberal individualism—the adult's absolute right to choose what he or she can view or read. The liberals assume their own incorruptibility. They are, in general, contemptuous of conservative or religious criticism but slightly nervous of its feminist counterpart.

On occasion prominent members of the libertarian intelligentsia—most famously, in recent times, Richard Neville—break ranks. But they are also nervous. Almost invariably they will preface their argument with the remark that they are 'not in favour of censorship, but...' Only very rarely is the case for the censorship of pornography advanced without ambiguity and embarrassment. It will be here.

The case for censorship must begin with a realistic understanding of the transformation which has occurred in all western societies over the past quarter-century. Up to the mid-1960s, in these societies, sexually explicit materials (both pornography and erotica, to use the contemporary jargon) were severely restricted. This applied to high art and popular entertainment. Pornography, of course, circulated—but only in the underground. Even certain works of great novelists, best known of which is D. H. Lawrence's *Lady Chatterley's Lover*, were banned.

During the 1960s the liberal intelligentsia became outraged by this state of affairs. The war on censorship became one of the fundamental causes of the great anti-puritan cultural revolution which erupted in all western societies, and which changed permanently the way we all lived.

Most liberals believed that pornography was a product of puritanism. They believed that when censorship was lifted and the forbidden pornographic fruit was tasted, its attractions would soon fade for all but a small band of maladjusted males. For this pathetic and diminishing raincoat brigade pornography might continue to provide a cathartic substitute-sexuality. For the rest of us, the puritanical *ancien régime*—of which censorship and pornography were a vital expression—would be transcended by a bright new world of sexual liberation and celebration. In our arts and entertainment, they believed, the erotic would flower and the pornographic wither.

How wrong they all were. A mere quarter-century after the censorship regime was dismantled the dreams of the cultural revolutionaries have been dispelled; the worst nightmares of the counter-revolutionaries realised.

Pornography once existed on the margins of society. It is now a huge mainstream business. In 1985 *Harper's* magazine estimated that it was larger than the film and record industries combined, grossing some eight billion dollars in the USA annually. Pornography can now be consumed in a bewildering variety of forms—in books and magazines, on film and video, through cable and satellite television, via telephone dial-a-porn services, and on the internet.

As the outlets for pornography have expanded with the communications revolution, its content has become nastier and nastier. A number of detailed analyses have been made in the US, Britain and Canada. In a recent study, for example, of thirteen 'adult' stores in four major American cities, one quarter of the more than 5000 books, magazines and films that were sampled involved one or other form of sexual violence: sado-masochism, whipping or 'fisting'; 10 per cent involved 'pseudo-child' pornography, with young women dressed as children or with pubic hair shaved. So far as I am aware we do not know in detail what kind of material is legally and illegally available in Australia.

The overseas studies have shown the pornographic market is now highly specialised, catering for every possible fantasy or fetish—be it gang rape, group sex, mutilation, buggery, bestiality, defecation, necrophilia or whatever. For those unsatisfied with the legal market there are both overseas and in Australia, I have been told by a senior prosecutor, flourishing black markets (frequently poorly policed) in child pornography and even in so-called snuff movies, where male sexual climax comes with the actual (non-simulated) murder and mutilation of a woman. No worst, there is none.

As feminists have rightly and repeatedly pointed out, a great deal of the produce of the pornographic industry centres on the theme of misogyny—hatred of women. At its most 'innocent', women are treated by the pornographer as a sexual meal prepared for the appetite of the male predator. Very commonly women are physically immobilised and abused: bound, trussed, gagged, penetrated by metallic objects, mutilated or worse. Very commonly they are shown to be enjoying their subjection. The classic narrative of mainstream pornography is, according to a number of those who have conducted content analysis, brutal rape leading to multiple female orgasm, nymphomania or adoration of the rapist.

Polly Toynbee was a member of Professor Bernard Williams' commission into pornography, conducted in Britain in 1979. This was how she described what she witnessed: 'Cannibalism, flaying, the crushing of breasts in vices, exploding vaginas packed with hand grenades, eyes gouged out, beatings, dismemberings, burnings, multiple rape and every other horror that could befall the human body.' After viewing such material she concluded, along with the other committee members, that pornography did no harm!

The hardcore pornographic industry is not, of course,

quarantined from the mainstream culture; its influence resonates throughout the entertainment industry. As Michael Medved has shown in his recent book, *Hollywood v America*, one of the most vicious sources of pornography is the pop music industry. Here are two lines from a Guns 'n Roses album, which sold twelve million copies in the US:

> Panties round your knees, with your ass in debris
> Tied up, tied down, up against the wall

Sado-masochistic clubs, or clubs for the practice of group sex, now exist in Australia. The content of mainstream 'slasher' films or sexual thrillers, like *Texas Chainsaw Massacre* or *Basic Instinct*, would have been the subject of instant legal action two decades ago. As the sociologist Diane Russell puts it: 'What is considered hard-core in the past has become soft-core in the present. Where will this end? Will we as a culture forever refuse to read the writing on the wall?'

At present it seems as if we will. Confronted by the nastiness of the pornographic culture and its remorseless advance, bemused anti-censorship liberals are not yet silent. It might be true, they will concede, that the desire for pornography has not declined with the end of censorship. It might also be true, they will agree, that contemporary pornography is puerile, distasteful and, yes, even vile. But where, they will ask as good Millian liberals, is the evidence that pornography actually does harm?

It is actually difficult, at the deepest level, to take such a question seriously. If we allowed commonsense to be our guide on the question of pornography the answer to the liberal question would be obvious on the basis of the kind of evidence presented already. An adolescent whose concept of sexuality is shaped while gazing at pornographic videos has already experienced a form of corruption. An adult who finds pleasure in the depiction of a woman being raped or bound or beaten has, regardless of any other consequences, suffered significant moral and spiritual harm. All this should be obvious. In our society for some reason it is not. To be drawn into the world of pornography is to be drawn into a world of affectionless, loveless and solipsistic carnality. As D. H. Lawrence, the novelist of the erotic, once put it: pornography does dirt on life. Harm is not extrinsic to the consumption of pornography. The consumption of pornography is itself a form of harm.

Many anti-censorship liberals will, I am sure, be quite unconvinced by this line of reasoning. They will demand more substantial, more 'scientific', evidence of the damage wrought by pornography.

As it happens such evidence exists, in abundance. For the past twenty years a number of psychologists—Zillmann, Bryant, Malamuth, Donnerstein are the most prominent—have conducted hundreds of laboratory experiments into the effects of pornography. The overwhelming result of this research is that a diet of either violent or non-violent but degrading pornography has a profound and negative impact on socio-sexual attitudes.

Time and again it has been shown that male university students who are exposed to such kinds of pornography become desensitised to sexual brutality, more aggressive and callous towards women, more willing to believe that women are responsible for their own rapes, more tolerant of rapists or of the rape fantasies and temptations in themselves, more dissatisfied with the appearance and the sexual performance of their female partners, and so on.

In a recent work, *Pornography*, edited by Catherine Itzin, a psychologist, James Weaver, summarises these research findings thus: 'The fact that exposure to contemporary pornography can activate sexually callous perceptions of women and promote manipulative and, in some instances, aggressive behaviour is highlighted consistently in the research evidence.' In the same book Diane Russell elaborated on its broader cultural meaning: 'I believe we are seeing on a massive scale some of the very effects so brilliantly and carefully documented in some of the experiments by Malamuth, Donnerstein, Bryant, Zillmann and their colleagues.'

But, the anti-censorship liberal may now object, these are only laboratory experiments. Where is the evidence that pornography causes crime?

Again there exists abundant evidence here, although it comes in a variety of forms. One form is the experience of many sexual therapists. The American, Victor Cline, told the US attorney-general's Commission on Pornography in 1985 that he had uncovered a consistent pattern in the 225 males he had treated over sixteen years, whose lives had been seriously distorted by pornography. This pattern involved a movement from addiction to escalation (the desire for stronger and stronger stuff) to desensitisation (the obliteration of disgust and taboo) to the desire to act out the fantasies. Or again, the British therapist, Ray Wyre, has written time and again of the role pornography has played in each step taken (by those he has treated) along the road to sexual crime. A summary of his views can be found in the Itzin volume. Does the anti-censorship liberal believe he or she knows more of these matters than do those who work at the coalface?

In case they do, there also exist many statistical indicators of the linkage between the consumption of pornography and the commission of sexual crime. According to one study of thirty-six serial killers in the USA, conducted by the FBI, 'twenty-nine were attracted to pornography and incorporated it into their sexual activity which included serial rape-murder'. According to another study, conducted by the Chicago police, pornography was incorporated, in one way or another, in almost 100 per cent of the paedophilia cases they dealt with.

There is, finally, abundant 'anecdotal' evidence in the police files of the linkage between pornography and sexual crime. I have read details of scores of these cases where the link is direct and unambiguous. Let three cases suffice. In Australia, Ian Melrose Patterson was an addict of bondage magazines, prior to his frenzied sexual attack in 1981 on a young woman. Interestingly, after he had inflicted more than two hundred wounds on his victim, he left her to find a love nest where the couple might live together happily ever after. Such is the power of the mad fantasy—women's desire for brute subjection—that lurks at the heart of standard pornography.

In the USA, the multiple rapist and one-time murderer, Thomas Schiro, obsessively took pornography with him to the scenes of all his crimes, including the final one that involved murder and necrophiliac rape. Or again, on the day before his execution, perhaps the most infamous of all sexual-serial murderers, Ted Bundy, spoke thus of his pornography addiction:

> It happened in stages, gradually it didn't necessarily… happen overnight…Once you become addicted to it [you] keep looking for more potent, more explicit, more graphic kinds of material…You reach a point where pornography only goes so far. You reach that jumping-off point where you begin to wonder if maybe actually doing it would give you that which is beyond just reading it or looking at it.

Such evidence may not be conclusive, but it is surely of some interest.

Given the laboratory, clinical, statistical and anecdotal evidence concerning the linkage of pornography and sexual crime, the anti-censorship liberal has only one remaining argument in reserve. How, they will protest, can it be proved that pornography was the sole cause of any particular crime?

The answer here is straightforward. It cannot be proved. No one, for example, could say that Wade Frankum's killings were caused by his reading of *American Psycho*. Complex human actions are never explicable according to a simple cause-effect model. Pornography will of course act on different individuals in different ways for reasons we will never fully understand. From a variety of angles, however, what can be demonstrated is that pornography is implicated—through corruption, addiction, stimulation, even imitation—in the commission of sexual crime. No one can claim it is the sole cause. If, however, the logic of the anti-censorship liberal were to be applied to the question of smoking, no health warnings could legitimately be carried on cigarette packets.

We arrive now at our central problem. Why, despite all the evidence, is the western liberal so vehemently opposed to the censorship of pornography?

This is a genuine puzzle, in part, because it rests on a principle so nonsensical that even a moment's reflection can refute it. Who among our liberals supports the legal distribution of films showing young children being sexually used and abused by men? Who among them would support the legal distribution of snuff movies? Despite the fact that anti-censorship liberals believe they are opposed to censorship 'on principle', their opposition to the distribution of such materials shows their belief to be false.

In the *Age* the literary critic Peter Craven tried to deny the force of this argument by suggesting that he opposed the legal distribution of snuff movies and child pornography only 'because their production involves the actual abuse of children and the actual mutilation and death of real women'. 'The criminal law,' he assured us, 'is quite capable of dealing with these matters without invoking the principles of censorship.' A second moment's reflection could have convinced Peter Craven of the simple falsity of this piece of special pleading. Let us imagine a snuff movie made in Brazil thirty years ago where all the participants in the production (not only the main actress) are known to be dead. Unless the principle of censorship is invoked such a film would not be of the slightest interest to the criminal law. Craven's evasion is typical of the anti-censorship liberal. Despite such evasions it is clear that even anti-censorship liberals do favour a certain form of censorship. They differ from those, like myself, who will admit that they are in favour of censorship, only on the practical question of where they wish the censorship line to be drawn.

Not only this. The main supporting arguments of the anti-censorship liberals are as false as is their claim to oppose censorship on principle. Liberals argue that censorship of pornography is some kind of authoritarian 'thin edge of the wedge', which poses a threat to our civil liberties and our democracy.

In part the confusion here is linguistic. *Censorship* is a bogey word. Even anti-pornography feminists—who generally belong to the left—distance themselves from the word while they desire its results. Unhappily in English the same word is used for two quite different actions—the restriction of pornography and of political free speech.

There is, in fact, no contradiction between the maintenance of civil liberties and the restriction of pornography. The liberal and democratic culture of modernity developed in Britain, the United States, Scandinavia and Australia at a time when they all severely restricted explicit sexual material. Indeed there are good reasons for believing that unrestricted access to pornography narrows rather than enlarges the sphere of individual liberty. For males in its grip, pornography acts as a form of imprisonment rather than liberation. For many women it expands the realm not of freedom but of its enemy, fear.

Liberals, finally, oppose censorship because they see in it an enemy of artistic freedom. Once this was a genuine issue. Indeed many liberals entered the censorship battle after World War II precisely because there was, at this moment, real conflict between the artist and the censor. During the 1960s, however, this battle was resolved decisively in favour of the artist. Since that time, with rare exceptions (*Salo* being one of them) the politically serious questions of censorship have been concerned not with questions of art but with low-grade cultural garbage. Anti-censorship liberals are like retired generals, continually re-enacting the campaigns of the last war. They think they are still fighting the battle of *Lady Chatterley's Lover*. They seem not to have noticed that they are, in fact, defending the ground for those who make their fortunes from *Deep Throat*.

This points to something deep. Opposition to censorship is a species of ideological inertia, 1960s nostalgia. The war against censorship was part of a greater cultural revolution, fought in the name of sexual liberation. To admit that even one aspect of that revolution has failed, that we have travelled here recklessly, too far and too fast, requires from the liberal an admission of serious error. It requires, that is to say, humility, sobriety and courage.

1993

The First Stone

IT is said that Helen Garner's book on the Ormond College affair, *The First Stone*, sold 30,000 copies in its first fortnight.* Clearly there is something in this eminently middle-class story of sexual politics which touches some contemporary nerve.

The story itself is relatively simple. On 16 October 1991, the Master of Ormond College, Dr Alan Gregory, socialised with students at the college after the valedictory dinner. There are differing accounts of what transpired. According to two of the female students—whom Garner calls Nicole and Elizabeth—Gregory behaved improperly. Nicole claimed that on the dance floor he twice squeezed her breast; Elizabeth that, in chatting with her that evening in his office, he expressed lascivious thoughts and fondled her. While Dr Gregory acknowledges that he had indeed danced with Nicole and chatted in his office with Elizabeth, he has consistently denied altogether behaving improperly.

The First Stone, Helen Garner, Picador, 1995.

It is not open to outsiders to be certain about who is telling the truth here. For this reason neither the college nor the courts in the end found Dr Gregory guilty of anything. Yet, as Garner's book makes clear, it is not the question of whether or not Gregory in fact behaved improperly which has created the interest in his case. In Garner's version, the key question of the Ormond College affair is this. Even assuming that Dr Gregory did what he is charged with having done, did he deserve the fate which befell him?

What was this fate? On the day following the valedictory dinner an emissary from one of the young women went to the college vice-master with a complaint. Because he had agreed to treat the complaint as confidential, the vice-master felt in no position to approach Dr Gregory. Gregory only learnt even of the existence of a complaint after the same emissary took to the chairman of the college, the High Court judge, Sir Daryl Dawson, unsigned statements from the young women. Shortly after, the emissary phoned Dawson and asked him to tear up the statements. Instead, Dawson now issued Gregory with a friendly warning about the dangers to which the enthusiasm of his post-valedictory socialising had exposed him.

Fully five months after the dinner, charges were laid against the master. A committee of three was established to formalise the complaints. By now the atmosphere in the college was electric. Pro- and anti-Gregory camps had formed. At the end of March 1992—for reasons Garner does not make particularly clear—the college council while not doubting the bona fides of Nicole or Elizabeth failed to find against Dr Gregory. The young women went directly to the police. By April the Master of Ormond was the subject of a criminal investigation. By August he was in court. The charges concerning his approaches to Elizabeth in his office were dismissed. Those concerning Nicole on the dance floor were at first upheld, and then overturned on appeal. The complainants went straight to the Equal Opportunity Commission. At its suggestion, the college apologised to them for the way it had handled their complaints. It had by now in fact withdrawn its support for the master. In May 1993—still protesting his innocence—the now notorious Dr Gregory resigned as Master of Ormond.

So far two interpretations of the meaning of the affair have been offered. The first took the form of an interview in the literary journal *RePublica* with one of the young women's college supporters, Dr Jenna Mead. It amounted to a kind of pre-emptive strike against the upcoming Garner book. Dr Mead's analysis is essentially political. The Master of Ormond is for her a representative of white, Protestant, male power. His post-valedictory behaviour was not the expression of folly or drink but of patriarchy—of an aggressively masculinist sexual politics. Bravely, in the Mead account, the young women decided to take the political fight to Dr Gregory. Not unexpectedly, the Ormond establishment resisted by closing ranks around the Master. What was unexpected was that one of the girls had, as a father, a civilised 'tycoon' with the money to transfer the case from the college to the courts and the commission. It was here eventually in the text of the college apology that a landmark victory, within what Dr Mead calls the discourse on sexual harassment, was won.

For Dr Mead, Helen Garner's book represents a 'backlash' against the political gains of contemporary feminism. For her the success of the Garner book is an expression of the 'moral panic' such victories have inspired within the 'establishment'. Unlike Garner, she refuses to rank Dr Gregory's suffering higher than the young women's. It simply does not weigh with her that the young women's suffering amounted to having their breasts squeezed, and Dr Gregory's to having his life destroyed.

It is, precisely, sympathy for Dr Gregory's suffering, and an astonishment at the disproportion between his actions and their consequence, that drew Helen Garner to this subject. Hers is essentially a non-political interpretation. While Dr Mead sees Dr

Gregory's behaviour of 16 October as a sinister expression of the political power of the Master, Garner sees it as, at worst, nothing more than a 'nerdish pass', of a middle-class and middle-aged academic whose life was otherwise one of faithful, gentle, dull and slightly dorkish convention. What the novelist in Garner intuits is that there is far *less* to Dr Gregory than is dreamt of in the philosophising of Dr Mead.

As it happens, the question that haunts Helen Garner's interpretation does not concern Dr Gregory but the young women. What was it, she asks, that led them to the police? For these young women, whom she is never to meet, Garner feels contradictory emotions. She is attracted to their self-possession, their courage, their erotic power, even their stubborn intransigence with regard to her. But she is also dismayed by their self-conception as victims of gender politics. At one brilliant moment in her narrative she wonders by what falsity Elizabeth, the self-willed and sensuous and impudent goddess, had been able to claim that, at the very moment she supposedly had the Master on his knees before her, she felt herself to be a 'worthless sexual object'. From where did these splendid young women's self-pity, and their pitilessness towards Dr Gregory, spring?

Precisely because her account of the affair is so non-political, answers to these questions are unnecessarily obscure. When Helen Garner interviewed Dr Gregory he claimed to her that he was a victim of an orchestrated political campaign. Unfortunately she does not pursue this theme. Yet from her book we learn that, at the critical moment of the affair, a vicious leaflet was circulated throughout the college. In part it read: 'If attacked by Gregory, please—do not panic—call the police. There is no guarantee his next crime will not be rape or battery.' We learn also that when Dr Gregory was negotiating for a post at Monash University, phone calls to the university were made on a number of occasions, threatening reprisals if he should be employed. It is clear that no understanding of the fate which befell Dr Gregory is possible without a psycho-political analysis of the radical forces at Ormond which worked together to bring him down. Yet of these forces Garner offers only glimpses. Because politics does not take a grip on her imagination, an essential dimension of the Ormond affair is missing from her account.

This is not its only weakness. We live at a time of sexual transition, where unprecedented freedom and disabling uncertainty about codes of behaviour coexist uneasily. At such a time the responsibilities of those in the position of the Master of Ormond, and the dangers or temptations to which they are exposed, are great. If Dr Gregory did nothing on 16 October he has been the victim of a terrible injustice. If he did 'merely' what Nicole and Elizabeth allege, then it was, surely, as Helen Garner believes, both pitiless and disproportionate that, as a consequence, his life was ruined. Yet if the Master of Ormond, charged as he was with the duty of care over a new generation of undergraduates, did 'as much' as Nicole and Elizabeth allege, it amounted, surely, to much more than a mere 'nerdish pass'. Dr Gregory is, of course, not alone in being caught in the paradoxes between two sexual eras or in the crossfire of a ferocious sexual-political warfare. It is perhaps for these reasons that his case interests so many of us so deeply.

1995

The Second Stone

DURING the course of the Ormond College Affair it became known that the key adviser to the two students who complained about Dr Gregory was a tutor at the college, Jenna Mead. Recently she compiled and edited a collection of essays on the affair, *bodyjamming*.* As a rather battle-scarred cultural warrior it takes quite a lot these days to shock me. By the time I had completed *bodyjamming* I was, however, genuinely shocked. For its central purpose is not so much to throw new light on the Ormond affair as to destroy the reputation of Helen Garner once and for all.

The tone is set by Jenna Mead. The 'inflammatory language' Garner has supposedly deployed to 'tear strips off the young women'—an absurd parody of the complex of feelings Garner shows towards the two students in *The First Stone*—is, in Mead's interpretation, a 'code' that teaches women to accept submission

---

***bodyjamming: sexual harassment, feminism and public life*, ed. Jenna Mead, Random House Australia, 1997.

and men that 'women will do the dirty work, even against other women'. Ann Curthoys agrees. Garner will lead us, she argues, into the blind alley of 'envy, vengefulness and punitive violence' towards young women. According to Professor Rosi Braidotti, the only people needing a book like Garner's are 'dying white males whose crisis is terminal'. None of this is self-parody. All is written in deadly earnest.

For Mead's contributors Helen Garner is the voice of patriarchy at its moment of crisis. Time and again Mead speaks of the 'moral panic' that has now gripped the patriarchy. Mead uses the idea of moral panic in much the way her opponents on the right use the idea of political correctness—as a thought-evading mental tic.

Mead tells us that all her contributors have written 'in a spirit of commitment to public debate, without rancour'. Is it then in such a spirit that Foong Ling Kong writes of Helen Garner as the mercenary of gender treachery? 'Her feminist credentials have been imbibed, mined and cashed in for cold, hard dollars.' Is it in such a spirit that Professor Braidotti has managed to discover in Helen Garner something few had previously spotted: the voice of 'white Australian women born and raised on the "white Australia policy" '?

There are many strange essays in *bodyjamming* but none quite so strange as Braidotti's. As it happened, Rosi Braidotti was a fifth-form student at Fitzroy High in the early 1970s, when Helen Garner was very publicly dismissed from the school after an explicit discussion of sex with her class. Braidotti provides a bizarre cultural interpretation of this affair. In essence, she argues that Garner—because of her opportunism, her narcissism, her ethnocentrism—more or less deliberately sabotaged the work of the worthy teachers at her school who were trying to help migrant kids like herself by improving the public image of Fitzroy High. The timing of the Garner scandal was no accident. Everyone decent at the school was only too pleased to see the back of her.

Braidotti's essay strikes me as genuinely cruel. She refers to Garner thus: 'Mediocre artists are vampires who bleed their victims over prolonged periods of time.' There is, she writes, something truly pathetic about the sight of a feminist ageing badly. Yet there is also in it an inexplicable streak of self-pity. For her, she says, the Garner scandal was one of 'most painful periods' of her life where she, despite winning the 3UZ 'nicest listener award', had been 'massively silenced'.

How can Jenna Mead mistake all this for rancour-free public debate? I believe there is something in her introductory essay which provides a clue. Mead begins this essay with the description of a meeting of the Politics Society at La Trobe University in which both she and I participated. According to her account the meeting had a secret agenda. Students from the politics department, who had been well drilled by their teachers in the lessons of *The First Stone*, had come along, with closed minds and fixed expressions, to see Jenna Mead being 'nailed' by me. They had not been, according to Mead, disappointed. After the talks, she claims I turned upon her and accused her of conducting a 'feminist conspiracy' that had 'ruined the Master of Ormond's career'. My colleague, Judith Brett, she claims, chimed in by arguing that Dr Gregory 'had been denied natural justice'. Only Mead's revelation, at evening's end, that Helen Garner had divided her into six or seven characters in *The First Stone* to avoid legal action, slightly spoiled our planned pleasures.

Jenna Mead's account of this meeting bears a highly peculiar relationship to reality. The kind of secret agenda she imagines is pure fantasy. The meeting was organised on the suggestion of one of her strongest supporters at La Trobe, the Dean of Humanities, Dr Graeme Duncan, who also chaired the meeting. He and the two other speakers were, on balance, far more sympathetic to Mead than to me. The discussion from the floor was more or less evenly divided between those who sympathised with Jenna Mead and those who sympathised with Helen Garner. At no stage of the meeting did I accuse Jenna Mead of leading a feminist conspiracy. At no stage did Judith Brett argue that Alan Gregory had been denied natural justice. Her intervention concerned an unrelated question, the intrusion of law into private life. I spoke not of the ruin of his career but the wreckage of his life. There was not the slightest feeling that anyone had come to see Jenna Mead nailed. Discussion was interesting and calm. At its end, Professor Duncan, without sarcasm, thanked us all.

The difference between my account of this meeting and Mead's does not rest on a conflict of memory. A tape recording of the meeting was made by the Politics Society. After reading Mead's book I listened to it carefully. In both content and spirit it reveals an utterly different meeting from the one Jenna Mead, no doubt sincerely, remembers having attended.

Jenna Mead was a central player in the Gregory affair. In the light of this affair and the smouldering anti-Garner hostility which animates *bodyjamming* throughout, Mead's interpretation of what occurred during our one and only encounter strikes me at least as unintentionally illuminating.

1997

The President and Paula Jones

IN recent months sex scandals seem to have become an increasingly common feature of the political life of the two countries of greatest interest to the Australian public and from which, in general, we take our cultural bearings—Great Britain and the United States.

In early May the political career of the Tory whip, Michael Brown, was at least temporarily ruined after a newspaper reported that he had holidayed with a young man. In his disgrace Mr Brown joined the ranks of fellow British 'back to basics' victims: the environment minister, Tim Yeo; the parliamentary private secretary, Hartley Booth; and the chief of the defence forces, Sir Peter Harding.

At much the same time as the fall of the Tory whip, and far more importantly, the President of the United States had come to be preoccupied not only with the tragedy of Bosnia or the conundrum of American public health, but also with the momentous question of whether or not, in 1991, he met an attractive young woman in a hotel in Little Rock and whether or not, while there, he harassed her sexually. The future of American politics now hinges on Paula Jones' legal suit, and in particular on whether or not she will be able to identify to the satisfaction of a grand jury the peculiarities of the President's genitalia. It does not require political genius to sense that there is something deeply disordered in all this.

In reflecting on the fates which had befallen Messrs Yeo, Booth, Harding, Brown and Clinton I found myself, at first, brooding gloomily on the strange hypocrisy of an age which allows its popular culture to be dominated by the morality of the libertine and its political culture by the unforgiving and prudish ethic of the puritan. My gloom, however, soon lifted. It occurred to me, as a pleasant surprise, that in all the time I have been observing Australian politics nothing even remotely resembling the recent minor tragedy of the Tory whip, let alone the major political crisis which has overtaken the American president, had ever come to pass. There was an interesting question to be answered here. Why has the Australian democracy managed so much more successfully than its British or American counterparts to safeguard the moral and sexual privacy of its public figures?

I discounted instantly one possible line of explanation. It should be obvious to even the most casual political observer that, sexually speaking, the behaviour of Australian politicians is no more spotless than their British or American alternatives. Perhaps, if anything, the reverse. The explanation for the absence of sexual scandal in Australia clearly, then, lies elsewhere. But where?

I suspect in the very different temper of public life in Britain, America and Australia. In Britain the two vital ingredients of political sex scandal are a corrupt press and the cultural sediments of class politics. Here the fiercely competitive tabloid press is involved in a constant search for salacious material to satisfy the appetite of its mass readership. It would appear that nothing feeds this appetite more satisfactorily than a steady diet of sexual scandals involving and compromising the political representatives of the upper class. Labour Party sexual scandals in Britain are virtually unknown.

It is not only Tory scandal but also Tory hypocrisy on the sexual front which is particularly welcome. The decision of the Major government to moralise to the nation about good old-fashioned 'back to basics' virtues was, for the amoralists of Fleet Street, a godsend. In the shadow of such rhetoric, disingenuous high-minded defences concerning the public duty to expose Tory hypocrisy became all too easy. The escalation of the sex scandal in recent British politics was the predictable result.

The sources of similar scandals in the contemporary United States appear to be rather different. Here the key ingredients are not a debased press and the embers of old class hostility but personal greed and ideological bitterness.

It is reported by no less an authority than Paula Jones' own sister that, following her one and only alleged sexual encounter with Governor Clinton in 1991, Ms Jones emerged from the Little Rock hotel room not with stars but with dollar signs in her eyes. Ms Jones claims to have been traumatised by Governor Clinton's sexual suggestions. This, however, did not in any way inhibit her decision to act upon one of the great unacknowledged laws of American social life: my misfortune can be my fortune. So already it has, most likely, turned out.

It is interesting, however, to notice that this is not at all because of an over-eagerness on the part of the American media to exploit her story. At first she was ignored. The crucial support she received came not from the media but from the sworn enemies of President Clinton and American liberalism, namely from the intellectual right. In January 1994, one of its key organs, the *American Spectator*, published a long and unintentionally humorous exposé of the secret sexual adventures of Bill Clinton—which chiefly focused on the furtive attempts of the future president to escape the surveillance of Hillary's steely gaze—based upon the testimony of certain disaffected Arkansas troopers.

This article was conservative America's revenge for the unscrupulous attack which had been levelled by liberals and feminists against the black Republican nominee to the Supreme Court, Clarence Thomas. The critical troopers article was written by none other than the author of *The Real Anita Hill*, the key conservative polemic of this controversy.

At first the American liberal press refused to investigate the anti-Clinton charges. The conservatives in April 1994 mounted a fierce campaign, pointing to the Thomas case and accusing the liberal press, not implausibly, of double standards. Ms Jones, the dollar signs still in her eyes, seized her opportunity to sue her president. As the liberal press could no longer turn its back on the issue, the question of the president's morals had finally become the central question of American public life. The conservatives at last had their revenge. The consequence would be the future absorption of the president and the great American press and public in the mother of all soap operas; the cost the even deeper debasement of the American public sphere.

Compared with the venomous tabloids in Britain, Australia's popular press is both responsible and restrained. Compared with Britain, our social ethos is far more egalitarian, far less influenced by the old resentments of class. Unlike the Americans, we have not, or at least not yet, mastered the art of transforming adversity into wealth. Unlike them, the ideological divisions of the left and the right run far less deep.

There may, however, be other, more indigenous, reasons for the failure of political sex scandal to reach our shores. Perhaps as a nation rooted in the convict experience we have learned not to inquire too deeply into each other's pasts or private business. Perhaps we are simply altogether too relaxed as a people or, as D. H. Lawrence would have it, altogether too indifferent to each other's affairs, to become too excited about the private lives of our public figures. Perhaps because our politicians and journalists have lived for so long so closely together in the relative isolation of

Canberra they have developed a strong common interest in the defence of the line which demarcates the public from the private sphere of life.

I cannot pretend to know precisely what mixture of good judgment and good luck has allowed us to maintain the powerful traditional taboo which protects the privacy of our public figures. I am, moreover, not at all sure whether this taboo will survive the new atmosphere created by the current wave of sexual harassment hysteria. Of one thing only I am quite convinced. To allow the private lives of our politicians to make a belated entrance upon our public stage will in the end achieve nothing except to make our country a less pleasant and civilised place in which to live. If ever we are so tempted, we can do no better than to think hard on the case of the president and Paula Jones.

1994

Life and Death on the Slippery Slope

IN 1995 the parliament of the Northern Territory passed the world's first voluntary euthanasia law. Perhaps for the only time since World War I, the eyes of progressive humanity will now be focused on Australia or, even more improbably, on Darwin.

What matters with this legislation is not the strangeness of the cultural alliance behind its passage—between those of the New Right like Marshall Perron and radical utilitarians like Peter Singer—nor even the motives of its advocates. What matters is its likely consequence for us all, in the short and longer term.

One of the illusions of those who support voluntary euthanasia legislation is that individuals who are in the final stages of a terminal illness will be able to make their decisions about whether or not to ask a doctor to kill them in a kind of social vacuum, freed from pressures of family or society. In my view this will not always be the case.

In discussions of voluntary euthanasia it is generally assumed that families of the terminally ill can be relied upon to be compassionate, altruistic and sensitive to the needs not of themselves but of their 'loved ones'. Yet even the most elementary knowledge of human nature will tell us that while some families will treat older parents afflicted by terrible illness with love and respect, others will find the pain of their elderly parents merely ugly and their obligation of endless hospital visits over weeks or months distinctly tiresome.

In such circumstances is it not at least possible that in the family discussions concerning the future, pressure will be applied which will suggest to someone who is terminally ill that no good can come from their purposeless clinging to life, that they have become a mere burden, and that they owe it to their suffering family to request an officially sanctioned death? Will it not be the case that even among those of the afflicted who are genuinely loved that some, in the depths of depression and fear, will imagine falsely that it is their death that their families most desire? And is it not precisely because of the recognition that, in a situation of legalised euthanasia, we cannot protect all of the terminally ill from insidious pressure of this kind that thus far no legislature in the world—other than that of the Northern Territory—has passed such a law?

Nor is it merely from family pressure that abuse may occur. We live, notoriously, at a time where the population is ageing, where our health systems are under great financial pressure, and where an economic rationalist view of the world is emerging triumphant in one sphere after another. In such circumstances, once the cultural bridge leading to officially sanctioned killing has been crossed, is there anyone who can seriously doubt that, in the long term, social pressures will build for cutting costs by rationalising the process of death in the case of the terminally ill?

Discussions of voluntary euthanasia almost all proceed on the basis of a second assumption: namely that laws concerning voluntary euthanasia, which permit doctors under certain clearly specified conditions to kill patients on request, are single, isolated legal acts which do not of necessity lead us down a slippery slope into new and unexpected moral territory. In my view such an assumption can be shown, with near certainty, to be false.

The idea of the slippery slope invoked here is relatively simple. It is founded on an understanding that our society has been built around certain traditional prohibitions and taboos; that in the past thirty years or so we have passed through a vast cultural revolution, where many of these taboos have been breached at their most vulnerable points; and that, once breached, we have been drawn inexorably down a path which few citizens, at the point of the initial breach, either anticipated or desired, and which many now, in whole or part, regret.

I am already old enough to have witnessed a number of such passages down such slippery slopes. Pornography is the most obvious instance. Thirty years ago liberals were arguing the case for the publication of *Lady Chatterly's Lover*. Today they are defending the distribution of misogynist vileness. Thirty years ago they predicted that the taste for pornography would die off after the forbidden fruit was tasted. Today the pornography industry is immense and growing. A conservative who thirty years ago warned of any of this would have been laughed to scorn.

Or take the morally more complex case of abortion, which is more directly relevant to the current debate over euthanasia. Thirty years ago my generation of students debated the question of whether or not abortion was justified where pregnancy threatened health or was a consequence of rape. Today's students are more likely to be debating where the limits to infanticide lie. Once again, a conservative who predicted such a moral trajectory thirty years ago would have been regarded as a bigot or a fool.

These moral journeys had certain features in common. At each way station liberals claimed that the next step forward would be the last. Even more importantly, during the course of these journeys most citizens gradually lost the sense of what they had once believed or why. As Peter Singer has rightly pointed out, the fundamental direction of the moral journey we have undertaken during the past generation is from a society founded upon the idea of the 'sanctity of human life' to one founded, instead, upon the idea of 'quality of life'. In this journey voluntary euthanasia is merely the most recent proposal of the liberals.

Yet if we are to learn from our own recent history and from the experience of the Dutch—the only country in the world where voluntary euthanasia is legally practised—it should be quite clear that voluntary euthanasia will not be for us a final destination but merely another way station. Where will it lead? Firstly and most obviously to non-voluntary euthanasia.

According to the Northern Territory legislation only patients who request their deaths can be killed. Yet why pretend that the distinction between voluntary and non-voluntary euthanasia will hold? If we permit doctors to kill on request a patient who is terminally ill, for how long do we imagine we will be willing to prevent, that is to say prosecute, doctors who, without request, take the life of a terminally ill patient, whose mind has gone or whose descent into coma seems irreversible and who, to put it crudely, is costing the taxpayer a great deal of money to keep alive?

Perhaps, those who currently support voluntary euthanasia also, like Peter Singer, support non-voluntary euthanasia. If so they should say. If they do not, and if they think there will be no movement over time, both in law and in practice, to non-voluntary euthanasia, they are, in my opinion, very naive.

If we are to judge by Dutch experience, the road from voluntary euthanasia leads not only to non-voluntary euthanasia for the terminally ill. It also leads to voluntary euthanasia for the non-terminally ill. It is estimated that as many as one quarter of AIDS sufferers in Holland request and are granted euthanasia. Many are not yet in the final stages of the disease. For anyone who understands social processes the expansion of the circle of those who can be killed will come as no surprise. For once we agree to the principle of doctors performing voluntary euthanasia, by what effort of societal will, on what rock of ethical principle, can we resist its extension to ever new categories of sufferers? There is no such will; no such fixed and reliable principle.

The slippery slope, here as elsewhere, amounts to more than progressive, logically connected changes in social practice. It also involves, as Raimond Gaita has shown us time and again in his column in *Quadrant*, a slow and subtle transformation of ethical sensibility. Over time we become blind to how we once thought and what we once valued. We become accustomed or attracted to thoughts we would once have found unthinkable.

To demonstrate the strangeness to which we have already become accustomed in our journey towards the conceptual world of 'quality of life' let me give a brief paraphrase of some central ideas of our most influential and highly regarded practical ethicist. For Peter Singer it is a form of speciesism to draw any ethical distinction between human beings and animals. For him the central ethical distinction is, rather, between persons and non-persons. Persons are creatures endowed with autonomy, self-consciousness, reason. Some animals (e.g. pigs) are persons. Some human beings (e.g. babies) are not. Intrinsically it is wrong only to kill persons. Non-persons, like babies, may under certain conditions be killed.

Although nature, according to Singer, has played a kind of Darwinian trick on us by making babies 'cute', and although Christianity has left us with some residual superstitions about the sanctity of human life, the fact is that a baby has less right to life than a pig and no more than a fish. If, therefore, parents wish to kill a severely disabled baby, with (say) spina bifida, nothing can stand in their way. Nor should anything stand in their way if they wish to kill a Down syndrome baby (whose life prospect may even be joyful) or a haemophiliac baby (whose life prospect is excellent) and replace it with a healthier specimen. Only after twenty-eight days (a figure taken from the hat, which makes no sense given Singer's definition of personhood) should babies be invested with personhood and legal protection against being killed.

According to Singer there is no slippery slope. According to my way of thinking the fact that we now listen earnestly to arguments like these is a sign of how far down this particular slippery slope we have already travelled.

1995

The University Question

OVER the past few weeks I have followed, with considerable interest and not a little dismay, the debate about the future of universities in Australia. Concerning funding levels and methods there have been bitter disagreements. Concerning fundamentals a self-serving consensus has reigned. Both the education minister, Senator Vanstone, and her critics seem to take it for granted that the university sector in Australia is in fundamentally sound shape. As one who has been at the university chalk-face for the past twenty years, during the period of the explosion of mass higher education in Australia, I am afraid that I am unable to agree.

Inescapably my doubts are coloured by personal experience and observation as a teacher at La Trobe University, a newish university in the outer, northern suburbs of Melbourne. In general, the quality of my academic colleagues is excellent, the quality of a large part of the undergraduates we take in each year decidedly, in some ways alarmingly, poor.

Every year, without fail, I encounter a group of first-year students, a sizeable minority, who know why they have arrived at a university. They are intellectually curious. They enjoy reading. They relish discussion and rarely miss a tutorial. Frequently they engage in discussions after lectures and tutorials. Many, eventually, often from less privileged backgrounds, complete outstanding degrees.

The remaining first-year students fall into two broad types. One group soon drop out of their studies. They usually attend one or two tutorials and lectures and then begin to drift away. Sometimes they withdraw after failing to complete the first piece of written work required of them. Only rarely do they discuss their problems with a teacher or explain their decision to drop out. Between one-third and one-half of our first-year students withdraw in this way from one or all of their subjects.

Another group of students pursue their subjects to the end. They are not really curious about what they are studying. Sometimes they appear to have chosen their courses almost at random. Some of these students at best experience momentary interest in a lecture or tutorial. Few take pleasure in independent reading. Many of these students are very nervous when asked to write an essay. Not without reason. The essays they do submit are often extremely poor. It is not merely, or even mainly, that they involve endless misspellings, bizarre punctuation, idiosyncratic syntax. It is far more that their work is deeply disorganised and conceptually confused. Their essays are genuinely distressing to read. As a university teacher I am always puzzled about what has happened to these students during their twelve long years at school. Clearly the near-complete absence of basic writing and analytical skills has been no impediment to steady progress through the grades. Manifestly it has not barred the way to selection for university study.

Many of the students who drop out or who persist doggedly, but without real interest or joy, are fine young men and women.

They have been deceived by a world which has led them to believe that university study is appropriate to them. Many would dearly love to be learning a skill or a trade which might lead them eventually to a job. Many, oddly enough, have decided to study at a traditional university—which is of necessity committed to initiating the young into the most abstract and difficult of disciplines, the sciences and mathematics, history and philosophy—only because their secondary school scores were too low to gain them entry to a course in hotel management or physiotherapy. They are compelled to study Plato because they failed to qualify for podiatry. Such compulsion involves an unintended but nevertheless cruel betrayal of our young.

Nor does the absurdity end there. In the humanities, students at the modern university are taught by methods we adapted from the Oxbridge–Edinburgh model of the nineteenth century. In the subjects they take the students are generally asked to attend two one-hour lectures and one one-hour tutorial per week. In effect the students are on their own. The Oxbridge–Edinburgh model assumes a highly educated and self-directed undergraduate. Even for a reasonably promising student at a contemporary Australian university this level of teaching is inadequate. For a typical student it is laughable.

If we are to continue with the experiment in mass university education three things seem to me important. The universities themselves must, firstly, find some method of their own for the selection of students. They must acknowledge in their practice the obvious truth that a certain level of proven intellectual capacity is the *sine qua non* for initiation into the serious study of a genuine university discipline in either the sciences or the humanities. They must acknowledge in their rhetoric that in this area a certain kind of woolly-minded idealism is destructive both to their students and to the university tradition it is their duty to sustain.

Secondly, for the students who meet the more rigorous standards of entry and embark upon university studies, teachers on the humanities side must abandon the Australian adaptation of the Oxbridge–Edinburgh system. We must be willing to spend several hours each week teaching fewer students, as many scientific disciplines now do.

Finally we must abandon the pursuit of university expansion come what may. We must acknowledge that a large number of students who accidentally enter our doors would be far better off, humanly speaking, if they could find a place at a tertiary vocational college or as an apprentice to a trade. Universities must avoid the temptation of pretending they are vocational colleges. In our own long-term interest we should support the growth of a diverse range of non-university vocational training opportunities for the young.

The present fight for the fiscal status quo is justified. The last thing we could afford now is less teaching. But it is not enough. Unless academics acknowledge openly the problems they face, the noble experiment in mass university education is in danger of turning sour.

1996

Gang Warfare

IF public intellectual life is to have meaning one must argue with one's critics. I am one of the main targets of Mark Davis's highly publicised new book on the cultural politics of generationalism, *gangland*.* I feel I owe him some response.

The first theme of Davis's book is how a younger generation has been prevented from making their mark in the world by an earlier 1960s generation, who still monopolise the Australian cultural stage. As it happens, I have considerable sympathy with this part of his book. I am sure it is true an older generation does dominate cultural discussion in Australia. I also think it true that the sensibility of this generation is importantly different from the sensibility of a younger generation. Davis begins his book with reference to the cultural meaning of the suicide of Kurt Cobain. At the time of his death it seemed to me emblematic of something

---

*gangland: cultural elites and the new generationalism, Mark Davis, Allen & Unwin, 1997.

I knew I did not understand. It also seemed to me that to turn one's back on questions of this kind was to turn one's back on the world. If Mark Davis's book alerts editors to the need to hear more from the voices of talented younger writers it will have done us all a lot of good.

Nor do I entirely disagree with the more overtly political dimension of his analysis. Davis is highly critical of the way the idea of political correctness is now used on the right, as a means of stifling argument. So am I. In *The Culture of Forgetting* I advocated the abandonment of the idea of political correctness on similar grounds. The suggestion was not, to put it mildly, taken up. I have, however, another suggestion to make. Throughout *gangland* Mark Davis deploys the left's conceptual equivalent to political correctness, namely 'moral panic'. At one point Davis dismisses a diverse range of writings of the sixties generation merely by referring to 'a logic of "moral panic", as if the ethical stuff of society is in danger of being fatally destabilised'. Just as the right now deploys the idea of political correctness as a way of avoiding the need for serious discussion of questions concerning race or female emancipation or the environment, so does the left use the idea of moral panic as a means of avoiding discussion of contemporary sexual barbarism or family or neighbourhood breakdown or drug abuse or youth suicide. If it is time for intelligent cultural critics of the right to abandon political correctness it is also time for those on the left to jettison moral panic.

In *gangland* Davis pays particular attention to three works he sees as emerging from the new cultural establishment—Robert Hughes' *The Culture of Complaint*, David Williamson's *Dead White Males* and Helen Garner's *The First Stone*. What Davis sees in all these works are cases where members of a generation of writers, who once played a culturally liberating role, have sourly turned against the progressive ideas of a new generation which has outgrown them. Behind Hughes' analysis of the cult of the victim within the new politics of identity, Williamson's celebration of literature and life over the greyness of literary theory and Garner's anxiety about the primness and punitiveness of the theory and practice of contemporary feminism, Davis can see nothing more than cases of former liberators turning towards a new cultural conservatism. He cannot even see the shadow of what is true in anything they say. In his key instances his analysis seems to me polemical, rigid, imperceptive, ungenerous.

Concerning his fourth main target—my book *The Culture of Forgetting*—his analysis strikes me at least as genuinely bizarre. Davis acknowledges, without ambiguity, that Helen Demidenko's *The Hand that Signed the Paper* is an anti-Semitic book. He knows that it is a novel about the Holocaust. Nevertheless he thinks the real scandal of the Demidenko affair is not that *The Hand* was the most celebrated Australian novel of 1995, but rather that its opponents—whom he describes as totalitarians and bullyboys—argued with passion against the enthusiasm of its reception. I am not sure what kind of response he thinks appropriate to the honouring of an anti-Semitic novel about the murder of five to six million Jews.

Davis sees in the gangland mafiosi not only the new cultural establishment. Even more seriously he sees in them the sworn enemy of the new waves of thought—critical theory, deconstructionism, postmodernism—which have transformed the humanities faculties at Australian universities over the past twenty years.

In the course of his defence of critical theory Davis lands some telling punches. As he argues, some of the criticism of postmodernism is based on near-complete ignorance. Far from being the Mickey Mouse subjects of conservative imagination, those courses that are anchored in critical theory are, in fact, extraordinarily demanding. Sometimes, more plausibly, postmodernists are criticised for the opposite reason: for the hyper-difficulty of their enterprise. Yet phrased in a certain way this criticism, too, seems to me unfair. Critical theorists deal with some of the most difficult problems of philosophy. It is hardly surprising that the language in which these discussions are embedded is opaque.

Some criticisms of the postmodernist enterprise are, then, unjust. Some, however, are not. The key figures in critical theory, like Jacques Derrida or Jean Baudrillard, come at the end of a long continental European tradition of philosophy—Hegel, Nietzsche, Heidegger—which is both very complex and also quite distinct from the tradition of philosophy pursued in the English-speaking world. Within this world, critical theory has spread rapidly not in the schools of philosophy but of literature, history, visual arts. It is far from obvious to me that those who work in these fields are equipped intellectually for what they do.

When Mark Davis tells us in *gangland* that all that is required for a university student to begin to participate in the tradition that stretches from Hegel to Derrida is a willingness to learn a handful of new terms, he is deluding either his readers or himself. I suspect it is not merely his readers he is deluding. Davis discusses *The Culture of Forgetting* at length. Much of this discussion is so loosely phrased as to be close to meaningless. Let one example suffice. Davis informs us that 'the orthodoxy was that *The Hand that Signed the Paper*...was universally anti-Semitic and universally bad, not just for its critics, but for everyone'. What conceptual work is 'universally' doing here? In what ways does the judgment being made here go beyond the most primitive form of relativism, that any opinion is as good as any other?

Nor does legitimate criticism of the postmodernist academic project end here. In many contemporary university faculties critical theorists seem now to be assuming dominant positions. What this means is that the plainer tasks of empirical scholarship are being gradually devalued, either pushed to the margins or made to seem second-rate. At the heart of critical theory is the impulse to what Mark Davis calls 'self-reflexivity', or, as I would put it, the impulse not merely to think about one's subject but to think about thinking.

What critical theorists will not admit is that, if this kind of self-reflexivity becomes the dominant field of work in the humanities, other indispensable kinds of work will no longer be pursued by our best minds. If this should come to pass certain traditional kinds of scholarship would be in danger of dying out. Let me try to illustrate this point with a concrete example. When Konrad Kalejs arrived in Melbourne, I began to search for a reliable history of the Holocaust in Latvia. Eventually I found precisely what I needed. It was a work of rigorous, old-fashioned scholarship. If it had been written by a Derrida scholar I would have felt dismay.

Davis is not wrong to see in some of the old gang's criticism of the postmodern project complacency or ignorance. What he does not see, however, is that if the new critical theory gang he has joined ever manages to corner the study of humanities in Australia something very old and very valuable will have been lost.

1997

Short Cuts

I watched last month, for a second time, a film with which I am greatly taken, Robert Altman's *Short Cuts*. For me at least, *Short Cuts* is a masterpiece which seems to take us—in a way no other Hollywood film I have ever seen even remotely manages to do—to the heart of the contemporary condition.

It is set in the city of all our futures, Los Angeles, and is based, very loosely, on certain themes drawn from the bleak and marvellously spare short stories of Raymond Carver. Unlike Carver, Altman draws these stories together into a single, loosely connected narrative and, unlike Carver, he fashions from them a compelling portrait of an age. Perhaps something of the power of this portrait may be conveyed by retelling, as simply as I am able, some of these tales.

One story concerns three men on a weekend fishing trip. At a chosen stretch of river, after a long trek into the wilderness, the men discover, under the water, the dead body of a young woman. What are they to do? They have hiked for several hours to get to this fishing point. Are they now to abandon their weekend to alert the police? Without too much effort they talk each other around to the collective decision to continue their fishing. What use would it be to the young woman to break off now? They fish, with some success, in the proximity of the body. Whatever remains of some dimly recollected duty of piety to the dead has quickly evaporated. Something else takes its place. The men attach the leg to rocks to prevent the body floating away. Under the influence of liquor, it now becomes—especially for one of them—a site of voyeuristic curiosity. He photographs it; he is stirred by necrophiliac imaginings.

We follow one of the men—the one who was at first most uneasy about what had been done and left undone—to his Los Angeles home. He is aroused, and makes passionate love to his wife. Afterwards, perhaps obscurely aware of the meaning of what has happened, he tells her of the experience with the young woman's dead body. When the content of his words gradually sink in, she withdraws from the bed in sheerest horror.

The next morning she finds the details of the rape-murder of the young woman in the daily paper. Without a word of explanation for her husband, she attends the funeral service for this stranger. In her the ancient human duty to the dead has, somehow, survived. Later at a drunken orgiastic party with a couple they barely know, she reminds her husband of what he has done, with a taunting nursery rhyme.

A second story in *Short Cuts* is set in the genteel, conservative suburban upper middle class. The father of the house, we learn, is a famous television personality, who delivers moralising editorials on the network news. He is married to a loving, protective, protected, rather helpless wife. Their story begins on an ordinary morning. She offers her only and much doted-upon young son a lift to school. He prefers to walk. On his way, when crossing the street, he is knocked down by a car. The working-class woman driver is distraught. Is he all right? Can she drive him home? The little boy has been taught not to accept lifts with strangers. Dutifully, he shuffles home on foot. It is one of the simplest and most affecting sequences I have ever seen on film.

His mother returns home. She has been on an errand at the local baker's, ordering a cake for her son's birthday. She finds him half-asleep on the couch. In panic, she tries to get the story from him. She doesn't know what to do. Eventually she telephones her husband. At once he takes the situation in hand.

The little boy is in hospital, in the best of hands. They are assured that he will be all right. But he will not wake up. The parents take shifts at the bedside. When the father goes home the phone rings. It is the baker. Why has the cake not been collected? The father, who does not want to be troubled by such trivialities, hangs up without explanation. The baker rings—again and again. The father, the television moraliser, now explodes in obscene rage. The mother has been pressed to get some sleep at home. She arrives to incessant, threatening, obscure phone calls. She flees back to the hospital. During the vigil her son's eyes flicker open, unseeing. The parents rush to him. A few moments later he is dead.

At home, sleepless in her grief, the mother suddenly realises who has been making the phone calls. Together she and her husband go at once to the baker's and demand entrance. They confront him with their knowledge, and tell him of the death of their son. 'Shame on you.' In the context of the film these words have an extraordinary power. The baker sees what he has done, and what he has become. In their common misery, and in their recognition of the tragic nature of things, and in their turning to each other for consolation the three are, at this moment, as close as human beings can be. They eat together.

A third story takes us even more directly to the heart of Altman's meditation on the modern condition. This story, which once again concerns a married couple, is set in the world of the lower middle class. The husband here is a swimming pool cleaner, a simple and rather baffled man. Big Bear, his pretty, shallow wife calls him. It is the nature of her work which baffles him. She is employed at home in the telephone pornography business. As she feeds the baby, or changes its nappies, or merely picks her toenails, her job is to bring strangers at the other end of the phone to sexual climax. She is obviously competent at her job and obviously bored by it. When her clients have done, she records the details listlessly in her book of accounts. But there is nothing to suggest she finds the work particularly distasteful. As she explains to her husband when he complains, he should be pleased that she is able to work from home and look after the kids.

Big Bear, however, cannot make any sense of these calls. In part he is excited by the sluttish talk. In part he is jealous and does not understand why she cannot talk to him like this. Most deeply, perhaps, he simply cannot fathom a world where the intimacy and sacredness of the domestic and the familial is thus invaded and profaned, with such indifference to meaning. In him there grows an inarticulate primal horror with the moral disturbance of the world.

The couple go with their kids and another couple to a picnic. Two teenage girls pass by their picnic spot on bike. Big Bear's friend convinces him to pursue the girls. They meet near the attraction of the picnic ground—a bat-infested cave. The girls are willing. The friend leads his choice towards the cave. Big Bear's girl spills some beer on her shirt and begins, matter of factly, to strip. The friend hears a scream and looks back. He sees Big Bear's arm raised, ready to strike, in the gesture of a murderer and of an avenging god. The bloodied girl falls to the ground, dead. The earth rumbles. The screeching bats fly from the cave into the sunlight. Los Angeles television tells us that there has been an earthquake—although not the long-awaited, the long-dreaded big one.

Short Cuts is an extraordinarily dark and daring film. If I am not mistaken what Altman has given us here is a terrifying portrait of a world in which the bonds of community and marriage have disintegrated; where moral palates are jaded; where pleasure, above all things, is joylessly pursued; and where savagery and fecklessness threaten to drain both sexuality and death of their meaning.

The signals of our age are uncommonly difficult to read. Never have the young been freer or more privileged than they are now; never have the levels of nihilism, drug dependency, depression and, at its extreme, youth suicide, been higher. No age has felt so uncomfortable with corporal punishment or capital punishment or death in battle as ours; yet no age has embraced more enthusiastically the drift towards abortion, infanticide and euthanasia. No other age has condemned all forms of violence more fiercely than we do; yet in our age the crimes of spree killing or serial murder have been (or almost been) invented. No age has been more relaxed about sex than ours. No age has been more obsessed by sexual crime.

In the end I do not know whether or, rather, to what extent Altman's understanding of the modern condition is right. To get a true measure of one's own age when one is abandoned, as it were, in the middle of things, is almost impossibly difficult. What I do know, however, is that I watched this remarkable film in fear and trembling.

1994

Raimond, My Friend

I encountered Raimond Gaita thirty years ago. My memory tells me that it was at a forum at the University of Melbourne on existentialism. One of the speakers was a senior member of the Department of Philosophy. One was a rather flamboyant student personality. The third was Rai Gaita. His talk made the speech of the philosopher seem superficial and the speech of the famous undergraduate unbearably frivolous. I was drawn to something in his manner—a seriousness, a kind of genuine openness to experience, a purity of spirit.

We became friends, and gradually close friends. From those days I remember most of all our conversations, which would often go on until four or five in the morning. We frequently discussed questions concerned with the idea of justice. It was the time of the Vietnam War. There was, as I remember it, an argument we had many times—about whether in pursuit of a good end, it was possible, permissible, to commit acts which were evil. Rai believed as passionately then as he does now that it was not.

I cannot recall how much I knew at this time about Raimond Gaita's childhood and teenage years. I know that his mother had died and that before her death she had been greatly troubled and that he had grown up largely without her. I knew that he had a protector in Melbourne, a friend of his father, whom he called simply Hora and always spoke of with the greatest warmth. Above all I knew that his deepest connection was with his father—a man whom I knew of chiefly at the time through the 100 per cent proof plum brandy Rai would bring back proudly after visits to Maryborough.

Since reading Rai's book *Romulus, My Father* I have thought back on these days. I am struck now by how high-spirited Rai was, how alive to the world, and how free from self-pity, despite having passed through experiences, many of which I learnt about for the first time in this book, which would have numbed or embittered many others.* I am certain that these are the qualities—the radical absence of self-pity, the aliveness to the world—which will first strike many readers of *Romulus, My Father*.

Some things about it are less self-evident. It cannot be emphasised too strongly that this is a book of filial love and tribute, not a work of philosophy. But because it is written by Raimond Gaita, and because he is who he is, it is also marked by the conceptual clarity and moral depth that so distinguishes his philosophical writing. Rai has no intention other than to tell the story of his father's life. But in its truthful telling, the nature of friendship, the terrors of madness, the relationship between work and the moral order, the poverty of a prudentialist ethic that would tell us to be honest because it pays, above all what the love between man and woman and between father and son might mean, are revealed as lucidly as in any book I have read. Many passages show the luminous quality of the writing and the supple

---

*Romulus, My Father, Raimond Gaita, Text Publishing Company, 1998.

movement in it between memory and reflection, the particular and the universal. Here is one:

> My father's behaviour to his animals struck some people as sentimental. Some said he treated his dogs as though they were human beings. They were quite wrong, for his practice always expressed a wisely judged sense of the radical difference in kind between human beings and animals, even though he sometimes blurred that distinction in conversation. When his dogs died, he was heartbroken and cried. He told me that sometimes the pain in his chest lasted for weeks and tears would catch him without warning. Even so, he merely buried them in a hole in the backyard and would have thought it absurd to observe any of the rituals we think appropriate when human beings die. Sometimes, to explain his generous treatment of his dogs, he would say that if dogs go to heaven, and he met them there, he hoped that they would say he treated them well. I always thought that to be a beautiful sentiment, beautifully expressed.

Before reading *Romulus, My Father* I had not understood so clearly how firmly what is central to Raimond Gaita's ethical writing is rooted in the experiences of his childhood and his reflections upon them. No one could read his account of the Lithuanian, Vacek—which records in equal measure, with fondness and amusement, and without the slightest hint of condescension or sentimentality, his idiosyncrasies (cooking his food in his own urine), his gentleness, his estrangement from the world, the rather terrifying effect of his strangeness on others—without understanding what Rai means when he places a sense of the preciousness of each individual at the centre of his ethics. No one could follow the moral narrative of Romulus's life with attention and then fail to understand why it is that Rai has given his philosophic life to the elucidation of Socrates' thought—better to suffer evil than to do it—or why it was that he chose these words for the epitaph on his father's grave.

Our age is haunted by the threat of a collapse into meaninglessness and by what the novelist Kundera calls the unbearable lightness of being. There is no lightness of being in *Romulus, My Father*.

As the central story at its heart unfolds—of Romulus and Christine, of Hora and Mitru—even though this story shaped the life of a dear friend and even though it is told with a transparent desire for a plain truthfulness to the facts, it has for me the simplicity of myth and the force of tragedy. Within this story everything has weight. In it words and acts have meanings, often terrible ones, which resonate through the years. *Romulus, My Father* tells of a world very far indeed from the one Kundera understands and fears. Its moral landscape may, for this reason, seem to some readers strange and unfamiliar.

When Rai told me he was writing a book about his father I knew that it would reflect his moral understanding and philosophical lucidity. I was not, however, quite prepared for the fact that his memory would be so fresh and vivid or that he would be able to tell his story with such spareness and humour and with such an unerring eye for detail. There are dozens of examples one could use to illustrate this point. I will make do with two. Because Romulus Gaita established his first wrought-iron workshop at the nearby farm of Tom Lillie, young Raimond got to know Tom, his wife and her sister, Miss Collard. The sisters had what Rai calls 'character', but there was in Miss Collard something livelier, something which leads Rai to call her 'a character'. Tom and his wife and her sister were, when Rai knew them, all rather old. Nonetheless one day, he tells us, he caught a glimpse of Miss Collard on Tom Lillie's knee. A tiny snatch of memory illuminates a world. Or again: as a young boy, during times he spent with his mother in Melbourne, Rai asked railway officials, policemen, even an air-force officer, if he might wear one of their peaked caps. He recalls perhaps fifty refusals. When the 1950s are sentimentalised, he tells us, he remembers this detail.

The story Rai tells is in very large part, a tragic one—concerning suffering beyond measure, madness and its terrors, suicide and despair. And yet—and this is one of the aspects that makes it so remarkable—*Romulus* is ultimately a book written out of a deep sense of gratitude for what he has been given. Rai has recalled the many acts of kindness that came his way, like that of the primary-school teacher, Mottek, who saw in him an intelligence that should be encouraged, or of his school friend, the loner, John Dunstan, who came to Frogmore one Christmas to help Rai deliver his father's iron furniture at a time when his father had succumbed to madness. The fact that Rai has found such small acts of kindness worth remembering deepens for me at least that larger sense of gratitude Rai is able to express in this book. At its heart it is a gratitude for having been blessed in having Hora as his support and his father's friend, and for having so deeply fine a man as Romulus as his father. In one of the most striking passages in his book Rai puts it thus:

> The philosopher Plato said that those who love and seek wisdom are clinging in recollection to things they once saw. On many occasions in my life I have had the need to say, and thankfully have been able to say: I know what a good workman is; I know what an honest man is; I know what friendship is; I know because I remember these things in the person of my father, in the person of his friend Hora, and in the example of their friendship.

In the end Rai Gaita's great achievement in this book is, in my view, to have been able to tell with such plainness and truthfulness a story so terrible as this and yet, in the telling of it, to have suffused it, so naturally and rightly and unselfconsciously, with so deep a sense of gratitude for what he has been given. I know of no other book where the story of the love between father and son has been so beautifully expressed.

1998

Why I Have Resigned

I was appointed to the editorship of *Quadrant* on the very day that the Berlin Wall was breached. In November 1997, almost exactly eight years later, I resigned. I am writing this article to explain with as much objectivity as I can muster the reasons for that resignation.

Quadrant was founded in the summer of 1956–57. Contrary to received opinion it was not founded as a right-wing magazine but as a magazine devoted to the struggle against the totalitarian politics of both the fascist right and communist left. In its early days the *Quadrant* community was volatile, lively, argumentative, diverse—united only by a common anti-totalitarianism. In its pages Catholic traditionalists, rationalistic liberals, sceptical Andersonians, anticommunist social democrats, all rubbed shoulders.

Magazines inevitably change with their editors and with their times. In the 1980s a new kind of spirit emerged at *Quadrant*. While much superb writing could still be found in its pages, what was most valuable was, in my view, frequently undermined by too many articles of thoughtless anti-leftism, often written in a bitter and sneering tone. Some readers, even loyal ones, were repelled by this new style. Others found it very attractive. For such readers *Quadrant* provided a kind of monthly ideological fix. They became addicted to its harsh polemical style and were convinced by the illusion it fostered, that the new issues generated by the cultural revolution of the 1960s and 1970s—feminism, environmentalism, multiculturalism, indigenous rights, anti-racism, sexual liberation, postmodernism —were as simple as the communist issue and could be disposed of, once and for all, by a few sharply delivered knock-out blows.

The 1980s *Quadrant* appealed to a narrower circle than it once had. But it appealed to this circle deeply. As I have discovered, such people had no wish to allow their kind of *Quadrant* to fade quietly away.

It would be dishonest of me to pretend that I knew in advance the direction I would try to take *Quadrant* when I assumed the editorship. Only two things were reasonably clear. One was that if *Quadrant* was to survive in the post-communist world it would have to move on from its anticommunist past. The other was that if it was to attract new writers and readers it had to shrug off its embattled mood; to open its pages to a wider variety of styles and opinions; to jettison forever that idea that on every issue under the sun there existed a *Quadrant* party line; and to resist fiercely the old polemical temptation.

Over time I came to think that this last challenge was the most important of all, that the creation of a forum where complex, open-ended conversation could take place was of far greater cultural significance than any attempt I might have made to mobilise the resources of *Quadrant* for some new all-embracing post-Cold War political campaign.

I would like to think that to some extent at least I succeeded in what I was trying to do. During my editorship *Quadrant* doubled its circulation. More importantly, it won the respect and interest of a far more diverse spectrum of opinion in this country than had previously been the case.

Not everyone, to put it mildly, was pleased with the direction of the new *Quadrant*. One group of the old guard had hoped that I would turn *Quadrant* into an Australian Thatcherite magazine, socially conservative and economically dry. Such a direction was not open to me. In economic matters my views have always been more social democratic than neo-liberal. When I opened the pages of *Quadrant* to a discussion of 'economic rationalism' in the early 1990s—in a period before such discussions had become fashionable—this group was seriously displeased. A first set of determined enemies of my editorship of *Quadrant* formed.

More recently other issues of division have emerged. By far the most important concern the new politics of race—the meaning of Hansonism, *Mabo* and *Wik*, the question of how the Australian government and people should respond to the report into the separation of Aboriginal babies and children from their parents. My editorials and the columns of one of *Quadrant*'s writers, Raimond Gaita, have been preoccupied with exploring the terrible issues raised in the stolen children report, including the most difficult and sensitive issue of all, the question of genocide.

Some readers have responded warmly to these discussions; others, interestingly enough, with visceral anger. I have never before received so much hate mail from *Quadrant* readers as I have received this year, narrowly over the question of *Quadrant* and Aboriginal issues, more generally over the claim that under my editorship *Quadrant* has somehow caved in to the left.

I suppose it was inevitable, given the bitterness of this divide, that things would eventually come to a head. Late in 1996 *Quadrant*'s literary editor, Les Murray, for reasons I did not fully understand, began prosecuting what he described as a 'feud' with me. This feud turned to open warfare after I wrote to Murray explaining why I had rejected an article written by a member of the *Quadrant* old guard which, preposterously enough, claimed that Manning Clark was an anti-Semite. Murray now attacked me in unrestrained language over my role in the Demidenko affair and for what he called my opportunistic capitulation to the left on Aboriginal matters. After Murray's letter I concluded, in my view not unreasonably, that relations between us were at an end.

On 21 July this year I wrote to the chair of *Quadrant*'s small Committee of Management, Dame Leonie Kramer, outlining the breakdown of my relations with Les Murray and asking for the support of the committee in my decision to appoint a new literary editor. The details of what transpired over the next four months are too complex to outline here. The simple truth, however, is that what I had taken to be the clear decisions of the committee in regard to Les Murray were not carried out and that, in the end, I received the support of only half of *Quadrant*'s committee in my request for the appointment of a new literary editor.

A meeting of the *Quadrant* Committee of Management was held in Sydney in November. At the beginning of the meeting I announced my resignation as editor. Despite this, after a vote of thanks had been passed, the next hour or so was devoted to criticism of my editorship. Under me *Quadrant*, I was informed, had become 'politically correct'. It had lost its good old boots-and-all, polemical edge. It had become far too obsessed with questions of Aboriginal justice. I was wrong not to publish a particular article which argued the case for root-and-branch assimilation of a people called the 'Antipodeans'. *Quadrant* had become a voice for postmodernism and moral relativism. It had not lent support to the cause of an Australian native monarchy. It was even, God forbid, the kind of magazine that academics in the humanities faculties of contemporary Australian universities might read with interest or pleasure. None of this criticism revealed the slightest interest in the kind of magazine I had been trying in the past eight years to create. I listened to all this, as did my three supporters on the committee—Martin Krygier, Tom Gregory and Terry Tobin—with feelings of genuine dismay. Had the past eight years been, then, a complete waste of time?

I believe not. During the past eight years *Quadrant* has provided a place where some of the most important Australian essayists have come to feel at home and from where the voices of many new writers have flourished and come for the first time to be heard. Even more, *Quadrant* has, I believe, created a kind of reflective space, beyond the old ideological divides, where writers and readers have met and conversed in a manner not all that common in Australia—seriously, courteously, passionately.

These writers and readers have come over the years to form what I think of as *Quadrant*'s invisible community. Very many would have liked that community to continue to exist. I am sorry that it cannot be. To them, all I can offer are my thanks and my regrets.

1997